NORWEGIAN RESISTANCE 1940-1945

Parade of German troops in front of the Royal Palace, Oslo.

NORWEGIAN RESISTANCE

1940-1945

BY

TORE GJELSVIK

TRANSLATED FROM THE NORWEGIAN BY

THOMAS KINGSTON DERRY

MONTREAL

McGILL-QUEEN'S UNIVERSITY PRESS

First published in the United Kingdom
by C. Hurst & Co. (Publishers) Ltd.,
1-2 Henrietta Street, London WC2E 8PS

Published in Canada
by McGill-Queen's University Press
1020 Pine Avenue West, Montreal H3A 1A2

Norwegian edition *Hjemmefronten: den sivile motstand under okkupasjonen 1940-1945*

Translated from the Norwegian by Thomas Kingston Derry

ISBN 0-7735-0507-5

Legal deposit 2nd quarter 1979
Bibliothèque Nationale du Québec

Printed in Great Britain

CONTENTS

PLATES

DIAGRAM

MAP

PREFACE

This is an account of the way in which civil resistance was organised and conducted from the Norwegian capital during the German occupation in 1940-5, and of the considerations which determined the choice of methods. It is not intended to give a broad, comprehensive picture of the resistance in Norway, which would require many volumes and could hardly be undertaken by one person. Many of those who took part will inevitably feel that their sphere of action gets too little coverage, but the framework and objective which the author has chosen make a close concentration essential. Moreover, certain important aspects of the resistance, such as the action of the Supreme Court, the Church and the schools, receive fewer pages than they intrinsically deserve; but they have already been described in a number of books, so they are included only to the extent that is required for a balanced picture. Organisational details are likewise excluded, as is the military side (*Milorg*) — except in connection with the choosing of lines of action and in a single section which touches upon little-known aspects of the early stages in its development.

It has not been my ambition to write as a historian, but to the best of my ability I have tried to follow scientific methods of presentation. In particular, it has been my object to base the deliberations and decisions to which I refer upon what we knew at the time, weeding out the information which has come to light since. It needs to be borne in mind that the resistance campaign took place under quite exceptional circumstances, in a country where the normal means of communication with other lands were shut down and all the regular sources of information were censored or controlled by the occupation authorities or their Norwegian henchmen. Decisions could only be founded upon a slender basis of firm knowledge, and they often had to rest upon a subjective interpretation of enemy intentions.

Internally, too, there were serious problems of communication. The work had to be kept as secret as possible, with no one knowing more than was absolutely necessary about the way in which it was organised and with a general cover of anonymity. One must beware of supposing that in the first years of the war there were the same clear forms of organisation and the same pattern of cooperation as obtained within the Home Front during its latter half. Much of the co-ordination was haphazard, deriving from personal or local connections and formed without any long-term outlook. It came into existence fumblingly, in obscurity and secrecy, in the absence of proper communications, not only between Norway and Britain but between one district and another. Written agreements and reports were banned, and much was done very hastily. It is part of the picture that even we who were participants had over-simplified and incomplete notions of how the whole thing was organised. *Milorg* and *Sivorg* — 'the military organisation' and 'the civil organisation' — and similar names were not such clear and unambiguous terms as we imagined in wartime, while to map out their inter-relationships in retrospect is a hard task. The archives contain very few reports from the early period, and all too many of the pioneers did not survive.

The present account is based on personal experience of the five years, but what is written more than thirty years after the event can of course be founded only to a small extent upon memory, whether one's own or other people's. As far as time has allowed, I have been through the available archives in the Home Front Museum, the Storting and the Foreign Ministry as well as books, so that in most cases I feel that I am on firm ground as regards the timing of actions and general instructions. The documentation is weakest for the first two years, with few documents in the archives and those few in many cases undated. The best material is presumably to be found in reports delivered in Stockholm and London, but the latter in particular are seldom to be discovered among Norwegian records and I have had no opportunity to go through those in Britain. Reports made after the war have also been perused, but where they disagree with those of the war period, I have normally taken the latter as my basis. Finally, during the progress of the work I have been in contact with members of leading organs in the Home Front who played important parts in various periods and phases of the struggle; thirteen of them have read the draft in its entirety or in part. Their criticisms and observations have been taken into account, but the responsibility for the text rests with me.

Some readers may wonder why this account comes so long after the events. When the war was over, I needed to earn my living at the earliest possible moment. But in the late 1960s and early 1970s work in connection with the exhibits for the Home Front Museum required me to make a detailed study of the archives from the war period. This showed me how difficult it must be for researchers to find their way among them, and to grasp the background and inter-relationship of the scattered documents. It was therefore in the hope that this work might be of use to later generations that I continued it in the leisure available from other duties, with a summary presentation as my final aim.

A foreign public may like to be reminded of the physical setting for the events described in my book — a land one-third larger than the United Kingdom with a population (in 1940) of only 3 millions. Though so sparsely inhabited, Norway had to import more than half the food supply for man and beast: no more than 3 per cent of the total area was arable and less than 25 per cent forested, the major part being a wilderness of barren mountains. Only the rolling flatlands of the south-east were at all densely settled; elsewhere habitation was confined largely to the heavily indented coastline and narrow valleys debouching into the fiords. Oslo, with nearly 300,000 citizens, and Bergen, with more than 100,000, were the only towns of considerable size, the others being mainly small ports with some industrial basis, dependent upon communications by sea more than by rail or road.

Once Norway had been successfully invaded, secret activity against the occupying power (including preparations for guerrilla warfare) would have been most practicable in the large, wooded valleys of the south-east. Any action here, however, was doubly handicapped: Quisling's followers among the rural population were more numerous here than anywhere else, which meant grave risks of discovery, and the area was remote from Allied seaborne support of any kind. The west coast had relatively easy contacts with Britain, but the smallness of the local communities (already mentioned) meant that secret activities came quickly to the knowledge of any potential informer. Moreover, the hinterland in the west and north did not encourage patriots to 'take to the heather', since the subarctic environment of the mountain area made it impossible to exist for any length of time above the tree-line without adequate shelter and an imported food supply.

The occupying power, on the other hand, took systematic advantage of the physical conditions. Having seized all the main centres of communications and administration by a single hazardous stroke at the outset of their two months campaign in Norway, they had little difficulty subsequently in fanning out over the entire country, from the Arctic coast to the Naze, from the Atlantic to the Swedish border. After the British coastal raids of 1941 the Germans further consolidated their position by building fortifications, naval bases and airfields at every point of strategic importance, so that Norway bristled with defences along the entire coastline. Since this *Festung Norwegen* was destined in the end to fall without a blow being struck in its defence, its construction is often lightly dismissed as one of Hitler's follies. This may be so, but in reading the present account of civil resistance in Norway it is important to bear in mind the dark shadow cast by an enemy garrison varying between 300,000 and 400,000 men, more than one-tenth the size of the entire Norwegian population.

The translation embodies a few minor corrections and omits some passages and references to persons and places which are only of interest to Norwegians. A more important omission is that of more than 500 references to sources; however, nearly all the books and documentary material in question are accessible only to readers of our language. Such of the reference notes as contain significant additional information have been incorporated in the text by the translator, who has also furnished it with some explanatory footnotes.

Oslo, June 1978 *T.G.*

1

'WE WERE ON THE VERGE OF SURRENDER...'

The German *Blitzkrieg* against Norway on the night of 9 April 1940 came as a shock to all of us. A paralysing, almost unreal nightmare; in the course of a few hours our capital and the principal towns of the country were taken, together with every important airfield, coastal fortification, and supply of weapons. Opposition was improvised in South Norway, but defeat was inescapable, a long series of retreats being interrupted only by 'delaying actions' where natural conditions offered an opportunity. However, individual achievements and deeds of self-sacrifice during the uneven struggle — such as the sinking of the cruiser *Blücher* at Oscarsborg, the actions in Valdres, at Midtskogen and Vinjesvingen, and the Hegra Fort which refused to surrender* — gave the nation a dawning self-respect, and the hope of effective help from the Allies kept our courage up. Even the capitulation in South Norway in May did not completely destroy our morale, for the fight went on in the north — and went on well: Narvik was recaptured. But suddenly the Allied forces withdrew, and on 7 June King Haakon went on board the British cruiser *Devonshire* to journey to London with his Government. His message broadcast from Tromsö informed the people that the operations were at an end; the 6th Division had to capitulate; and the Chief of Defence, General Otto Ruge, was taken prisoner. All our hopes collapsed, and the people felt that they had been abandoned and deserted by their leaders and their allies.

King Haakon's unyielding attitude during the invasion and the campaign had won him the respect and admiration of his fellow-countrymen, but criticism of the Nygaardsvold Government was strong in all classes of the population, increasing each

*An appraisal by a military expert, which stresses the Norwegian achievements, is Major-General J.L. Moulton's *Norwegian Campaign of 1940* (London 1966).

Reichskommissar Terboven, with Quisling on his left, speaking in Akershus Castle, Oslo, 1 February 1942.

time a defeat was reported. Resentment over the lost possibilities of defence — the chaos in connection with mobilisation, the failure to lay out the minefields, the absence of defence preparations — all this and much else created bitterness among the people, especially among the untrained soldiers who had to face German tanks and aircraft with obsolete field-guns and small arms. Many hard words were said during the unequal struggle, and still harder ones in the campaign districts and the prisoner-of-war camps when the defeat sank into people's consciousness.

Politically, the invasion had created a kind of vacuum. When the Germans occupied Oslo on 9 April the native Nazi adventurer, Vidkun Quisling, had proclaimed himself prime minister and initially received Hitler's firm support. But the general detestation for his 'Government' of traitors hampered practical dealings between the Germans and the population of the regions which had already fallen under their power. Accordingly, after six days the Supreme Court was allowed to nominate an Administrative Council composed of prominent officials, and the quislings temporarily disappeared from view. On 24

April, however, Hitler appointed Josef Terboven as Reichskommissar, directly responsible to him for all except military matters — a responsibility which he retained for the rest of the war. In the hope that this was only an interim arrangement, a despondent and bewildered population looked to the Administrative Council for guidance.

Within a few days of the capitulation in North Norway, the front in France also collapsed. More and more people lost confidence in the Western Powers. There was much talk about how badly the British troops in Norway had fought, and criticism of the political leadership and of our democratic system in general grew stronger. The mood was so unstable that, given more sagacity and restraint, the Germans could have created a dangerous political situation in that fateful early summer. There were those who allowed themselves to be impressed by the energy and capacity for political organisation of the winning side, and one heard it said more and more often that 'the Nazis had at any rate put an end to unemployment in Germany' — to quote one of the many pro-German arguments which began to find their way into people's conversation.

We were afraid for the future, knowing that the country was far from self-sufficient, and that it was cut off from supplies of bread-corn and other foodstuffs from the traditional markets. Much had been destroyed by the war: many towns had been bombed and set on fire, stocks had been lost, bridges, roads, harbours and railways put out of action. In some places economic life had come to a standstill for want of raw materials and money, and there was a big rise in unemployment. In all classes of the population there was a vociferous demand 'to get the wheels turning again', and managements felt a heavy responsibility for employees and their families. Most people were naturally enough anxious about themselves and those near to them, so that they could not face more than the problems of each day, although they clung to the hope that the fortune of war would turn before it was too late. The most anxious of all were the parents of the young men who at the end of the campaign had been made prisoners-of-war by the Germans.

Shameful things happened in building and construction activities. Even while fighting was in progress nearby, Norwegian entrepreneurs, labourers and skilled artisans took part in the improvement of captured airfields and harbour-works in South Norway; some of them were admittedly put under heavy pressure and consented only on the advice of local authorities which feared reprisals against the population.

Very many were anxious about what was happening to the economy. Thus on 15 May *Aftenposten* reported a meeting of *fylkesmenn** in occupied South Norway, at which it was said: 'For us the main thing has really been the questions of food and work, questions of money... Furthermore, communications and how we might co-operate with the German authorities to establish connections between the various districts and Oslo... We have tried to follow the line of trying to keep work going to the greatest possible extent ...'

Others were ready to go further in matters of politics. On the same day as *Aftenposten's* report, the Communist Party secretariat urged the Administrative Council to act as follows: '1. to re-establish peace in the country and prevent any further shedding of Norwegian blood on either side of the Great Power conflict; 2. to take every measure to maintain economic activity; 3. to maintain the standard of living and make sure of supplies.' One way of achieving the last objective was to be 'an increased exchange of goods with Germany ...'

The principal Communist Party paper, *Arbeideren*, had from the first days of the campaign opposed the participation of Norwegian forces in a war caused by 'criminal provocation from the British imperialists'; it had called the Western Powers the main enemy of the neutral states, urged that Norwegian forces should give up the fight, and warned against 'all forms of sabotage and acts of destruction'. This Party and its press became more and more outspoken advocates of peace and cooperation with Germany, a line which they pursued consistently during the Council of State negotiations of that summer (referred to below), when they agitated for the removal from office of the King and Government and the formation of a new government based on workers, farmers, and fishermen, which would make peace with Germany.

After the whole country had fallen into the hands of the enemy and fighting had stopped, it was still more difficult to steer a national course in economic affairs. On 14 June the Federation of Norwegian Industries sent out a statement from the legal officer of the Cabinet, which included the following:

*For *fylkesmenn* see footnote, p.28. *Aftenposten*, the newspaper with the largest circulation in Norway, was widely representative of business interests.

'The consequence is that any Norwegian citizen — or any Norwegian company — is legally entitled to make contracts with the occupying power for any work or service whatever within the confines of the realm.' The floodgates were open; this 'right' was more and more widely used. Circles in business and cultural life, which were well disposed towards Germany (though not necessarily towards Nazism), began to talk of a 'sensible' arrangement with the occupying power. The occupation did not only call forth self-sacrifice and patriotism; it was also fertile soil for egotism and greed for gain.

Unemployment was the scourge which drove some of those who sought 'work for the Germans', especially at the outset, but there were also other reasons for the gathering of a body of men the numbers of which rose by degrees to 150,000-200,000. The fear of unemployment blinded many eyes: the Administrative Council's prisoner-of-war committee even urged employers to give released soldiers the first chance of employment on German construction sites! The economic uncertainty caused such an important social factor as the central trade union organisation (LO) to be a weak link from a national point of view in that early period. Since the LO constituted the first line of defence for the economic position of the workers, its influence had to be safeguarded; all the more so as strong forces in the leadership of its natural counterpart, the Federation of Norwegian Industries, counted on a German victory and appeared to be making its arrangements accordingly. But the LO contained an aggressive, loud-voiced faction, the Trade Union Opposition, made up partly of Communists and 'fellow-travellers' and partly of adherents or defectors to the NS,* which strongly supported a peace settlement with the Germans. Individuals belonging to this faction had close links with the Gestapo and the Reichskommissariat, which could use them to keep track of the trade union leaders. Furthermore, the end of the campaign had been immediately followed by a clash between the old trade union leadership under Nordahl and Evensen, who had left the capital to join the public authorities and the fighting forces, and those who had stayed behind the German lines and taken over the posts thus left vacant and the responsibilities that went with them. The latter — those who 'had remained at their posts' — were unwilling to give way to

**Nasjonal Samling*, Quisling's Party: see footnote, p.14.

the elected leaders on their return to Oslo after the capitulation in June. The Germans and the NS knew how to exploit this confused situation: the trade union secretariat accepted a German ban on the return of the old leaders to their duties, which meant that an important sector of the front was beginning to give way.

Immediately after the capitulation in North Norway, when the British evacuation from Dunkirk had already foreshadowed the total collapse of the Allied campaign on the Western Front, the German occupation authorities put forward new political demands. The Storting was to be assembled in order to remove the King and the Nygaardsvold Government from office* and nominate a new 'constitutional' Government, in return for which the Reichskommissar would be withdrawn. With the mood then prevalent in large sections of the people, and the turn which the war had taken down in Europe, the Administrative Council and the remaining state authorities did not dare refuse to negotiate. A delegation consisting of the Chief Justice of the Supreme Court Paal Berg,† Bishop Eivind Berggrav the Primate, and a district magistrate, was nominated to negotiate on the condition that the King was not to be deposed; but they considered that their function was at an end when it appeared that the condition was unacceptable. Thereupon the Presidential Board of the Storting had to take over the negotiations. At the end of June this group agreed under heavy pressure to a proposal for calling upon the King to abdicate, and summoning the Storting, which was to cancel the plenary powers which had been granted at Elverum, withdraw the recognition of the

*Since 9 April, King Haakon VII's resolute attitude to the invasion and to Quisling's *coup* had made him the symbol of national independence, but the Nygaardsvold Government, which had been in office since 1935, was thoroughly discredited by the bankruptcy of its defence policy. This remained true, although the Storting in its meeting at Elverum on the evening of the 9th had authorised the Labour Cabinet to govern if necessary from abroad, and it had been to some extent reinforced from other parties. Hence the involvement of the Presidential Board (i.e. the president and deputy president of the Storting and its two subdivisions) and the party groups in the negotiations of June-September 1940. The historical background is outlined in T.K. Derry, *A History of Modern Norway 1814-1972* (Oxford 1973).

†Paal Berg (1873-1968) was a Cabinet minister twice before his appointment as Chief Justice in 1929; as the formal head of the resistance movement he was nominated as Premier in 1945, but declined office on account of some party opposition. For Berggrav, see footnote, p.34.

Nygaardsvold Government, remove the constitutional rights of the Royal House, and nominate a 'Council of State' to take control of the country until a new election could be held after peace had been made.

Bewilderment, despondency, and pessimism prevailed at that juncture within large sections of the Norwegian people; belief in an Allied victory had suffered a severe blow, and there was mounting criticism of the Government and of the Western powers. Influential circles in political life, in professional and business organisations, and in society at large supported negotiation. The acting-leader of the trade unions threatened at the decisive meeting on 17 June that, 'if the Presidential body would not bring the negotiations to a successful conclusion, the LO would take the matter into its own hands.' On the same day the main Communist paper wrote: 'The Government and the King who are sitting in London have left Norway in the lurch.' On the 20th it continued: 'Norway needs a new governmental authority, a Cabinet prepared to make peace with Germany and to lead the people out of the present war among the Great Powers. The workers must throw their weight onto the scales on the side of peace between Norway and Germany ...' More influential newspapers were not far behind.

Resistance revives

Few of our political leaders withstood the darkest day of all — 17 June, when France surrendered. Among those who had influence on the negotiations in Oslo, Gunnar Jahn* was indeed the only one who still spoke clearly against the removal from office of the King and Government. But when the news of the Presidential Board's application to the King for his abdication became known throughout the country, together with his firm and well-founded 'No', there was great bitterness. That the King's courageous and unselfish efforts should be rewarded by the Storting with an application for his retirement appeared so unjust and unreasonable that the will to action sprang up again in people's hearts: our hope of recovering freedom and national independence was embodied in the King. Some rose

*Gunnar Jahn (1883-1971), a former Minister of Finance, had been for many years Director of the Statistical Office; he was the first post-war finance minister and in 1946-54 the Governor of the Bank of Norway.

spontaneously to resist, and soon there was an embryo organisation. The King's reply was stencilled and circulated, as was General Ruge's appeal to the soldiers to be steadfast after the capitulation in North Norway; a poem which the former republican Överland addressed 'To the King' was likewise stencilled and reached many people; and there were still more who read the courageous articles of Johan Scharffenberg in *Arbeiderbladet*.*

The press was gagged, and had long been forbidden to write anything in favour of the Royal House, so an action was started for writing letters of protest to the Presidential Board. They came in both from groups and from individuals, including one who wrote as follows:

> The Germans are in power in our country today. They can do what they like. That is no disgrace for us. The thing that is dangerous and fateful is the fact that Norwegians in posts of the highest national responsibility contribute to what is impending. In the first place the King has been treated dishonourably. In the second place the treatment is likely to have the gravest consequences in future for our people's morale and self-respect, its will and capacity to keep itself upright and one day rise again. Outside forces do not break a people, but treachery can poison it...

At that juncture there was little chance of influencing the negotiations, but the affair of the protest sowed the first tiny seeds of an organised resistance movement. A list of protesters from Trondheim in July 1940 contains the names of most of those who in subsequent years organised the civil and military resistance movements in the Trondheim region.

The Storting was no sheet-anchor in the hour of danger, neither were the political parties. The men from whom the resistance people could seek advice were first and foremost Chief Justice Berg, Bishop Berggrav and the economist Gunnar Jahn, who had been the strong man of the Administrative Council.

It soon became an unwritten law that party politics and agitation were taboo. This attitude resulted in the agreement

*The support now given to the monarchy by Dr. Scharffenberg (1869-1965) was particularly significant since he had led the agitation for a republic at the time of Norway's separation from the Swedish Crown in 1905. As the Norwegian counterpart to Bertrand Russell, Scharffenberg was a frequent contributor of radical articles to *Arbeiderbladet*, the principal Labour newspaper.

for co-operation made among the four main parties in August, providing for a party truce and cooperation in the principal tasks for the nation as long as Norway remained under occupation.

When the negotiations were resumed in September and the members of the Storting voted in their party groups over the matter of the King and the proposal for a Council of State, the weakness of our political defences was exposed in earnest, as the negotiators let themselves be driven back from one position after another. But the opposition group was increasing in weight and numbers, and was reinforced by people — some of them politicians — who now woke up properly and realised that they must throw themsleves into the struggle. Eventually, after the Presidential Board had accepted one replacement after another of patriotic candidates for the Council of State by NS people, the party groups refused to accept a NS man as Minister of Justice, whereupon the Germans broke off the negotiations.

On 25 September Reichskommissar Terboven made a speech, in which he ridiculed and abused those with whom he had been negotiating and the political system which they represented, removed the Administrative Council from office, and installed a commissary government.* Political parties other than the NS were banned, so the Norwegian people might know that there was 'only one way to freedom and independence, namely through NS'.

The wind blows more freshly in the west

The description of the situation in the summer of 1940, as given above, needs some addition, because it is chiefly applicable to Oslo and East Norway, where the enemy was most active in political matters and where the population felt itself to be most closely hemmed in and cut off from the outside world. In the coastal districts of the west and south the feeling was rather different. The first boats which penetrated the German air and sea blockade left the west coast early in May, and by then small

*Composed of *kommissariske statsråder*, who were for the most part NS members or sympathisers; they ran government departments under direct German supervision, and waited a year before receiving formal German recognition as 'ministers'. Quisling continued as Leader of his Party, but Terboven was able to keep him out of office until 1 February 1942, when Hitler authorised his appointment as 'Minister-President' with a Cabinet of his own supporters.

Norwegian intelligence groups had already been formed, which got hold of radio transmitters and tried to make contact with England. These groups consisted to a great extent of soliders who had fought together in April, could not reconcile themselves to defeat, and wanted to start preparing for a new effort. Inspired by an indomitable fighting spirit and glad to believe that the British would soon be returning, they took upon themselves varied assignments without having any experience of secret work or a strong sense of how to protect themselves. In small towns it was not easy, even for those who later had more experience, to work clandestinely under cover of anonymity. The groups were very quickly drawn into a hectic 'traffic with England' carried on by fishing boats and other small vessels; these conveyed officers and young men to the forces in Great Britain, returning with weapons, radio transmitters and instructors for the groups.

The first such group, organised and led by a journalist, was in existence in Haugesund by the middle of May and had ramifications down to Stavanger, where another group was set up immediately afterwards under the leadership of a lawyer who was a reserve captain in the army. Bergen had several smaller groups and two larger organisations with military intelligence and the traffic with England as their main objects. One of these was led by officers, but contained a strong element of people from business circles in the town, shipping and the learned professions. The other, which took up newspaper work as well as military tasks, was under the leadership of Kristian Stein, a postal official on the express coastal steamers; it included people from every class, with links extending from Stavanger in the south to Kristiansund in the north.

In Ålesund the police headquarters was the nerve centre of the traffic with England. Its first group, led by a solicitor, Harald Torsvik, quickly made contact with resistance groups in Oslo, while others sprang up successively which depended on the enterprise and seamanship of this fishing district. In lower Telemark and round Arendal an organisation, formed originally to support the fighting in that area in the spring, continued as a resistance group for such purposes as illegal newspaper work and the traffic with England; it included many people from the Labour movement, while a Conservative member of the Storting, Carl P. Wright, was one of its most vigorous leaders. In Trondheim an intelligence group was started in September

1940 by a student of the Technical High School who came over secretly from England; but the organisation was brought under the leadership of Leif Tronstad, a gifted scientist and professor at the High School. Among its functions was industrial espionage — and among the objects of its attention the heavy-water production at Norsk Hydro. Tronstad, who had a remarkable ability to rouse the will and the capacity for resistance among young people, ranks high in the Norwegian resistance movement alike for his pioneer work at home and, later, for his leadership of Norwegian fighting units in Great Britain.*

During the summer of 1940 Norwegian naval officers established intelligence groups with radio transmitters in the larger towns around the coast, which soon came into contact with those which had been organised by local enterprise, as described above.

The resistance groups in Haugesund and the coastal district from Arendal northwards had been started first, and they were likewise the first to suffer; in both cases disclosure began in August 1940. About 100 of the group in the Arendal area were arrested, five being condemned to death but reprieved, and many others sent to concentration camps in Germany. The occupying power struck more heavily against the group centred on Haugesund, since intelligence activities were what they feared most, and as many as ten young men were sentenced to death in February 1941. As these were the first death sentences for acts undertaken since the ending of military operations in June 1940, they made a deep impression. Later they were commuted to imprisonment for life, after four of the condemned had undertaken to remove and dismantle unexploded bombs. In both cases the Gestapo had the help of Norwegian informers in destroying the resistance groups.

As 1941 brought a big increase in the traffic with England, the Gestapo concentrated upon its destruction, which was gradually achieved, again with the help of native informers. As early as Easter of that year, Torsvik's pioneer organisation in Ålesund was smashed. The telegraphist in an intelligence group with which it co-operated in Oslo was caught red-handed, which enabled three of the Oslo leaders to be taken at once. An

*Leif Tronstad (1903-45) largely planned the operations against the heavy water plant at Rjukan, was parachuted into that area in November 1944, and was killed in a fight with informers in the following March. For the Linge Company, with which he was closely associated, see footnote, p.75.

informer and *agent provocateur* was then thrown, with simulated wounds, into the cell where one of them had been placed at Oslo Police Headquarters, and succeeded in winning his confidence because his own father was a friend of the resistance leader in question. In this way the Gestapo got hold of a thread which brought them to Torsvik, who was arrested along with his closest associates. After a trial, from which came reports of his steadfastness and strength of mind, Torsvik was sentenced to death and executed together with four others, including a brother of the resistance leader in Stavanger, who went on unflinchingly with his activity in their home town.

Three Norwegian soldiers had returned from England in the autumn of 1940 to organise intelligence work, and contacted one of the bigger groups in Bergen. But the Germans got wind of their arrival in a fishing-boat, arrested its crew, and tracked down the soldiers, all three of whom were sentenced to death and shot. These executions, the first in the resistance movement, were followed by numerous arrests in Bergen; Tronstad's organisation in Trondheim, too, was not immune. After the Gestapo had surprised a wireless group, a number of students were taken, which cost some of them their lives; others, including Tronstad himself, luckily got away and continued their war effort outside Norway.

In the West Norway towns, many smaller intelligence groups had been set up by degrees, directed specially to espionage against German shipping; some of these kept going for a long time, while others collapsed quite soon. A group in Stavanger under the leadership of a doctor fell victim to an *agent provocateur* in the summer of 1941; about twenty were arrested, including the leaders, of whom eleven were sentenced to death and did not survive the year. In Bergen one espionage group was brought to light early in 1941; of the thirty-seven arrested members, as many as seventeen were later executed and seven died in prison camps. In the course of 1941 most of the intelligence groups in the city were smashed, particularly heavy losses being suffered by the Stein organisation, where the Gestapo got hold of a list with the names of several hundred participants. Stein himself and eleven others were sentenced to death and executed; about fifty died in prison; and fifteen lost their lives at sea.

The Resistance takes new forms

It was from West Norway, too, that the Reichskommissar's speech of 25 September 1940 received the sharpest reply: 'No Norwegian for sale', wrote the Stavanger Labour paper, *First of May*. In spite of Terboven's bombastic words about the way to Norway's freedom lying through the NS, the real meaning of his action was that the Party was too weak to be entrusted with power, which was to remain in his own hands. But the Party had been granted a period of grace for acquiring substantially more popular support and control over the life of the community, so that it might become a usable political partner for the occupying authority. It was Quisling's clearly stated goal to form a national government, make peace with Germany and take part in the European New Order. The events of 25 September 1940 brought back to life national energies which, since 9 April, had been as it were paralysed in most of us. Thus the first feeling of resentment, grief and bitterness over the dishonourable negotiations gave place to a liberating sense of relief. We breathed purer air because the situation had at last been clarified: resistance was the only way to go, however long and difficult the way might be.

In the weeks and months which followed, the NS made every effort to reach its goal as quickly as possible in a community where political activity was forbidden to its opponents, the free press was muzzled, and every open means of influencing the politics of the people was controlled by the advocates of 'the new era'. The war outlook was gloomy, now that all military resistance to the Axis powers on the continent had been crushed and a solitary, almost unarmed Britain was exposed to violent bombardment from the air ('the Blitz'), while the threat of a German invasion of the island kingdom was the subject of daily conversation in our streets and lanes. In Norway, as in the other oppressed countries, one hoped for a miraculous turn in the fortunes of war, but a realistic calculation forced the admission that liberation would be delayed for a long time.

Quisling's treasonable action on 9 April had created a gulf between the NS and the people of Norway which might appear to be unbridgeable, but the NS did not require to have a majority behind it — only a sufficient number of members to be able to convince its German masters that it was a party which could be 'the pillar of the state'. The pressure from within and without was so great that sections of the people which lacked political leadership were in danger of slipping. As there were still many unemployed, one of the Nazi arguments which was listened to in 1940 was that Hitler had got rid of unemployment in Germany. At such times there are also business speculators, opportunists and malcontents of different kinds ready to exploit the situation. Last but by no means least, there were the people in public service, whose livelihood depended upon the will of the authorities and whom the NS showered with both threats and promises. The autumn was to witness a large increase in the membership of the Party.*

However, Terboven's speech had also roused many people to awareness of the danger: *If Quisling were to achieve his political goal, he would be able to make peace with Germany and send the youth of the country to war on the enemy's side. To prevent this was the principal object of resistance, the red thread in every phase of the struggle almost to the last day of the war.*

The struggle was not started by any central command: people in every class and district tried to withstand the pressure individually and collectively, so that it became a struggle on various lines and with many fronts. First, there was *open resistance* in big organisations and institutions, opposing the NS infiltration and control. Secondly, there was the *illegal establishment* of a free press to break the monopoly of public information, which the NS tried to achieve through censorship of the press and broadcasting and the setting up of a Department for Propaganda. Thirdly, secret *maintenance funds* were built up to help the dependants of persons who were arrested or had to flee, likewise for exposed groups such as the police and other public servants — support which was of quite decisive importance for keeping the front line intact. Fourthly, there was the strengthening of the *morale* at all levels by hindering fraternisation with the enemy and isolating him and his Norwegian henchmen — the wearing of 'H7' (the King's monogram) and

*At the last pre-war election in 1936, Quisling's Party of 'National Unity' had polled only 26,576 votes (1.84 per cent) — rather less than in 1933, the year of it foundation, and by 1939 it was disintegrating for want of unity and money. But Quisling retained a nucleus of hard-headed supporters, more ruthless and less hampered by cloudy political ideas than their leader. In 1940-2 adult membership of the NS rose from 7,000 to 37,000, and in 1943 it reached a peak of 43,000. Its policies aped those of its German masters, but for the sake of clarity have been labelled 'NS' rather than 'Nazi', except where the German Nazis appear to be directly involved. An objective study is that of P.M. Hayes, *Quisling* (Newton Abbot 1971).

other emblems, the cold-shouldering of Nazis on the trams and in the street, and strikes at theatres, cinemas and sports events.*

No clear distinction can be drawn between the open and the illegal struggle:† both played a large part in the development of the Home Front in 1940-1, and each affected the other. In that phase the same individuals might perform openly in one situation and illegally in another.

A series of small, stencilled newspapers saw the light of day (or rather of night) shortly after 25 September, both in Oslo and in other major towns. The first civil resistance groups were organised, and the many military groups in readiness, which had been formed locally, were also collected into larger units. Thus an organised resistance movement began to take shape, often through local and 'private' ventures, but to some extent through the inspiration emanating from the resistance centres in Oslo and other major towns aforesaid. Moreover, resistance — particularly in the form of the illicit press and the 'export' organisation for escaping abroad — also required money if it was to function effectively. The business expanded in all directions. At the outset work was conducted through contributions from members; later on, money was collected from private sources and was obtained to a growing extent from the Government via the Norwegian Legation in Stockholm. Aage Biering and Tor Skjönsberg, both of whom were later to be central figures in many resistance activities, took on at an early stage the difficult and important task of obtaining money and channelling it in a satisfactory way to the continually increasing number of resistance groups and organisations for their economic support in Oslo and throughout the country.

The 'Norwegian Front' and the R-group

We had lost our capacity for further military resistance, which could only be reconstructed on a long-term basis and in relation to an Allied invasion. But the struggle against the political pressure and against a subversion of the mind had to be taken

*See pp.25, 33 and 38.

†The author's frequent use of 'illegal', where 'underground' might seem more natural, may be explained by a quotation from one of his wartime colleagues. 'After 125 years of peace and freedom we had no traditions of illegality to build upon, such as were possessed for example by the Finns, Poles, Czechs, Belgians and French ... The whole technique of illegality had to be learnt from the beginning while the struggle was going on.' (C.A.R. Christensen, *Vårt Folks Historie*, Oslo, IX, 244).

up at once, or else the basis for other forms of resistance at a later period would crumble away. The moulding of the press by the Germans and the NS was felt more and more as a choking of the spirit, to which an answer had to be found.

Immediately after Terboven's speech of 25 September a number of officers, journalists, trade unionists and people from the academic and business worlds, who had been brought into contact with each other as opponents of the negotiations for a Council of State, joined together in a 'Norwegian Front'. The object was to create a broad and nation-wide resistance front under central leadership, and they arranged themselves in groups, such as one for organisation under John Rognes and one for information and propaganda services under C.A.R. Christensen.* On the initiative of Einar Gerhardsen the latter group produced from November onwards a nameless fortnightly bulletin of information, later known as *The Bulletin*, to which *Fri Fagbevegelse* ('Free Trade Unionism') was added at the turn of the year as the main organ for the trade unionists, conducted by some of the resistance elements in the Labour movement. *The Bulletin* was intended both as an internal organ of communication for the leaders of illegal resistance and as a source of information for the illicit press, with reviews of the situation at home and abroad as well as appeals and instructions for keeping up the struggle. Other groups looked after contact with other organisations of a professional, mercantile and sporting nature or saw to the finances. The leaders formed a kind of 'main committee', and advice and information were sought from leading personages such as Berg, Jahn, Berggrav and Scharffenberg, without their being formally associated with the 'R-group', as the central organisation came to be called.

The group established a connection with the underground military organisation then being constructed. This comprised military preparations, especially the formation of local fighting units and military intelligence groups. No clear division of labour was practised, either between the two main branches or individually, some of the principal figures in the group working in the civil and military sectors alike.

The R-group did not see it as its task to direct resistance, but rather to get hold of key men inside the various organisations, partly as links in a chain of contact and partly as central points

*B.1906; a leading journalist, who in 1947-9 became a member of the UN sub-committee on the freedom of the press.

for the formation of opinion and the will to resist. If necessary, they might also take the initiative for counter-measures in precarious situations. The group therefore refrained from establishing any secretariat to support the leadership of the organisation.

The R-group played an active part during the autumn of 1940 and in 1941, particularly in connection with the pressure on those in public service and during the most acute phases of the sports strike. In the first crises at the University it took the initiative in the formation of a secret committee of action. It did most important work on the information front through the two principal organs of the illicit press, which were started by it, and the information group also gave financial support to a number of illegal papers in different parts of the country. In the autumn of 1941 a little 'press bureau' was set up, which supplied the same papers with news from home and abroad. All that the R-group accomplished in gathering the resistance forces transcending party groupings and old class barriers had lasting significance for the struggle.

Its subordinate detachments made a considerable effort in 1940-1 both to start and to support resistance activities, and a man in the publishing business was sent on a comprehensive tour of South Norway to contact resistance people who were willing to organise their districts and act as a link with the central organisation. Contacts were made through various channels with individuals as far north as Hammerfest, but no extensive district organisations were in fact established.

A communications group, consisting of a Reader in Anatomy named Jan Jansen,* a fellow-student of mine, and myself, started a system of connections in October 1940 to link the R-group with its district contacts, partly through reliable railwaymen, bus drivers and crewmen on the coastal steamers, and partly through people who travelled frequently and were suitable as couriers. We distributed information material, in the first place the *Bulletin* and *Fri Fagbevegelse*. But the manager and editor of the latter — two tireless and devoted partners — soon fell victims to the Gestapo's counter-measures. More generally, it was not long before leaders in the R-group were in

*J.B. Jansen (b.1898), a neurologist of international reputation; as Warden of the Hall of Residence, he had unusually close contacts with university students in Oslo.

danger; as early as February-March 1941 three were arrested, and several others had to flee the country.

Our district contacts, too, disappeared one after another without being replaced, and except for the newspapers, the material we were to pass on became thinner and more sporadic. After a while we were given a further assignment, to distribute the information material to the central leadership and its contacts in Oslo. But in 1941-2 most of them were arrested or had to disappear, and there were seldom any replacements. Jansen, who as the head of our little communications section maintained relations with those above us, was a prudent law-breaker who never disclosed any more, as regards either names or the set-up of the organisation, than our work at any moment required. Nevertheless, he found it increasingly difficult to explain to his younger fellow-workers why there was so little material to forward and why the network of contacts about the country was not repaired. But we kept the thing going by sending both papers to a steadily dwindling number of 'old' customers in town and country and filling out with new ones at our discretion.

Early in 1942, when the editorial and printing arrangements and some of the intermediary stages for both papers were discovered, the ground was hot under our feet for a time. We lost all contact with *Fri Fagbevegelse*, and in the course of the summer the new arrangements for editing and printing the *Bulletin* also broke down. But Jansen then performed the astonishing feat of producing the *Bulletin* for the next two years quite alone and getting it stencilled, without even we, his closest associates, having any idea that he was the editor.

In connection with the arrests in February 1941 one of the R-group leaders had been obliged to travel to Sweden, where he informed Frihagen, a member of the Norwegian Cabinet in London, of its establishment and activities; this put them in touch with the Government for such purposes as financial support.* But in the course of 1942 the R-group ceased to

*The long land frontier made escape to Sweden (and re-entry into Norway) possible at all times, though often hazardous. In western Sweden most people sympathised deeply with their Norwegian neighbours, while contributions to humanitarian aid came from all parts of the country. The Swedish Government, however, had two wartime aims, which commanded general support: to remain neutral, and to safeguard the country's future by making concessions to the winning side. Thus it was not until 1943 that it encouraged the Norwegian resistance movement by such measures as the training of the police troops (see footnote, p.117).

function as a centre of civil resistance, so we in the communications section gradually took on other jobs.

I for my part was increasingly engaged in military intelligence work, as several of my fellow-students had leading positions in XU, the largest organisation of that kind. Jansen had come into contact early on with the key figures in the Co-ordination Committee and the Circle, the two groups which gradually took over the leadership of the civil resistance. With the help of Alf Sanengen, who joined us in the spring of 1942, we conducted a rather many-sided illegal activity with my small apartment in Oslo as a base.

Some of the waverers

In the autumn of 1940, the NS went forward on a wide front with a view to winning a sufficient political foothold in the Norwegian community. Promises of good jobs and economic privileges drew a good many thousand malcontents, opportunists and other feeble spirits who now saw their chance. But that was not enough. To recruit further membership, occupational groups of various sizes, especially those in public service, were put under pressure; control over the central administration, the police, and the judiciary was considered particularly important. The police were the first victims, as a department which for many reasons it was important to bring under control. Its strong man was Welhaven, the Oslo Chief of Police, who was dismissed immediately after 25 September; and in the course of the autumn and winter the NS 'Minister of Police', Jonas Lie, succeeded in frightening more than 60 per cent of all police officials and 40 per cent of the rank and file into joining the Party — and that without direct threats of dismissal. It was a sorry downfall, due to weak leadership of the police organisation and the absence of counter-measures. The rural police chiefs (*lensmenn*) were beginning to go the same way, but in their case a collapse was prevented by a counter-action, which the chairman of their association set up in collaboration with Judge Ferdinand Schjelderup.*

Many of the people in the police who joined the Party

*T.F. Schjelderup (1886-1955), a judge of the Supreme Court from 1928; he published three volumes on the history of the occupation down to his escape to Sweden in 1944.

certainly believed that they were doing so in the interests of the rest of the population, because they were thus preventing the police service from being taken over by dangerous NS-men. It should also be put on record that many of them later ran great risks to give help to their compatriots under arrest and to illicit organisations. But a resistance front cannot be established on such a premise, a lesson which was learnt by other classes of public officials.

The NS tried at the same time to obtain control over the principal business organisations, starting with the weakest among them, the Farmers' Union (*Norges Bondelag*). By a stroke of chance I was enabled to follow what happened in this case at close range and take my test as an illegal worker in its closing phase. My father was the head of *Ny Jord* (an association for bringing new land under cultivation), and had his office in the building in Oslo in which was the headquarters of the Farmers' Union. The latter had as its chairman an ex-Cabinet minister, Johan E. Mellbye, who was also chairman of *Ny Jord*, and another of my father's friends was the general secretary of the Union, who lived in my home town of Ski, not far from Oslo. Within a few days of Terboven's speech in September 1940, it came to my ears that the many NS sympathisers in the top level of the Farmers' Union had proposed that the organisation should go in for the 'new era' and merge with the NS Guild of Farmers. This was a step in Quisling's plans for establishing a Nazi 'corporative state' in Norway, and the matter would be brought up at a meeting of the national council of the Union later in the autumn.

It was quite natural that the NS should direct its first effort towards this organisation, which had provided Quisling with considerable support from the time when he had been a Cabinet minister in the Agrarian Government of the 1930s. A good deal of vague national romanticism prevailed in the organisation, and many large farmers and forest-owners still felt bitter towards the forest-workers on account of the labour struggles of the inter-war period, old wounds having been re-opened by a long strike of land-workers in the spring of 1940, which was only called off on the day of the invasion, 9 April. There was likewise widespread discontent among the farmers over their poor economic circumstances, due partly to the drastic increase in their liabilities when the authorities revalued the currency in 1928, and partly to the low prices for their produce during the depression of the 1930s. Under prevailing conditions, these sentiments might provide a fertile soil for Nazi sympathies; what was worse was the presence of several active NS members in key positions, including the chairman of the women's organisation (*Norges Bondekvinnelag*) and several of the secretaries in the central office.

The Farmers' Union came under pressure at an early stage, when people had little experience of the clandestine methods required for political resistance in face of enemy bayonets. At the decisive national committee meeting in November, an effort was made openly from within and from outside to prevent the organisation from being ensnared by the NS; but for a long time it looked as though Quisling's supporters would win, and a trial vote yielded a slight majority in favour of collaboration. Following advice from several quarters, Mellbye then found it necessary to make it clear that he would resign if the proposal for collaboration was adopted. A postponement was proposed and adopted by a large majority, which meant in effect a break in the negotiations.

In the months which followed, the intrigues which the NS fomented and the pressures it exerted — both vice-chairmen, for example, were induced to retire — secured its supporters a majority in the executive committee of the Union. The chairman was powerless to stop this development, so he tried to dissolve the organisation by legal means — which the executive prevented. In early March 1941, when it became evident that Mellbye would not let himself be manipulated, both he and the general secretary were removed from office by the commissary minister in the Department of Agriculture, acting with people from the Reichskommissariat and the Gestapo. Mellbye was interned on his farm up-country.

My conversations with the general secretary on the train between Ski and Oslo had kept me abreast of these developments, and with my father's help I had formed a picture of relationships inside the executive and the office of the Union. As it was impossible to find an energetic opposition group within the organisation, I had to attempt something on my own. A reliable woman assistant in the office gave me a list of representatives in their nationwide groups. Mellbye having been dismissed and interned, I immediately drew up an unsigned circular to the representatives, giving detailed information of the action against the chairman and what had led to it. The conclusion was a high-flown appeal:

The Union of Norwegian Farmers has ceased to be a free organisation for the protection of the farmer's needs; it has become the instrument of Quisling's interests. *Every farmer in Norway must see to it that this instrument is knocked out of the tyrant's hands*. There is only one way of doing this: *By resigning from what was formerly the Union of Norwegian Farmers*... Rally round your old chief, the former Cabinet Minister Mellbye. He and his life-work are in danger, but you and you alone can save both him and it by lining up firmly *with* him *against* those who imperil the Norwegian cause. You now possess the power in the land, nobody can govern today against the farmers' will! Let Minister Mellbye's urgent appeal to the district chairmen find a response in every honest farmer in Norway. Let us hold together, let us show strength!

I stencilled the circular and posted it to every single representative in the association; I also forwarded it through illicit channels to the BBC, and with pleasure — and a touch of self-satisfaction — heard it broadcast in its entirety.

There was great commotion within the nest of NS people in the office of the Union, and the Gestapo was called in. But they did not find the offender, whom the documents of the investigation certified as 'having an extremely good knowledge of the domestic concerns of the Farmers' Union and practice in writing for its members'.

It was impossible to ascertain how many followed the recommendation to resign, the office being completely under NS control. The main importance of the circular was probably the knowledge which the nation-wide branches received of the intrigue and unfair actions directed agtainst the chairman, who was immensely popular with the farmers. What had been done presumably contributed to the fact that the Nazified Union became a paper organisation supported exclusively by NS farmers.

The shipowners stand firm

Few professional groups in wartime Norway were exposed to such continuous pressure and persecution as the shipowners, who were also affected by economic penalties and ruthless taxation.

The first demand came from the occupation authorities in the summer of 1940: the owners were to broadcast orders, individually and in a personal way, for captains of ships sailing in Allied service to return to Norway. The shipowners unanimously refused. In October the same year, the president and administrative director of the Shipowners' Association were arrested; they were released for short periods during the winter, but in the autumn of 1941 they were sent to Germany, where a military tribunal sentenced both of them to four years imprisonment. After the president's arrest the Germans tried to get a moderate NS shipowner elected to the presidency. This man was known to be able and upright, having shown solidarity with his fellows when they were exposed to criticism and pressure from the German side earlier in the summer; he could thus be expected to help his colleagues considerably in dealings with the occupation authorities. Nevertheless, the shipowners refused to elect him, thereby rejecting the solution which appeared least risky and most appropriate from the standpoint of convenience and narrow professional interests. By choosing a line of resistance on principle, which at the same time strengthened the resistance front in the nation as a whole, the shipowners set an example for others to emulate, even in those first years of the war. Their refusal came immediately before the vote on co-operation in the Farmers' Union, where it helped to strengthen the opposition.

Olaf Helset and his sportsmen

One of the major objectives of the NS was to secure control over the youth of the nation and its upbringing. A separate Department for Labour Service and Sport was set up on 25 September 1940, with Axel Stang as commissary minister. He was unknown in sporting circles, but he believed that a promise of increased financial support would induce the crowds of young people who belonged to the sports movement to back up the 'new era'. This proved to be one of the biggest miscalculations which Quisling and his men made during the whole of the war.

In the inter-war period Norwegian sport had been split between two main organisations: the National Association for Sport, which was much the larger, and the Workers' Sports Association, which had a party basis. Immediately before the war negotiations had been started for a merger between them, thanks in particular to the National Association's chairman, Major Olaf Helset,* who enjoyed wide popularity and respect; a

*B.1897; he commanded the Norwegian Police Troops in Sweden in 1944-45, and for two years after the war was C.-in-C. of the Norwegian Army.

meeting on the subject on the night of 8-9 April was broken off by the German invasion. After the end of the campaign in the spring there came a German request for the resumption of sporting connections between Norway and Germany, but this was turned down. These circumstances stimulated the resumption of the merger negotiations, which were speeded up and completed just before the key date of 25 September. Helset and his opposite number in the rival association managed to reach full agreement on uniting in a new nationwide, non-political sports organisation, *Norges Idrettsforbund*, with Helset as chairman of its provisional board. The re-organisation of the separate associations and branches was going on and would be handled at sports assemblies, the first of which was arranged for 10 November. But the Department for Labour Service and Sport forbade these meetings, and decided that national and international sports events would be held under its own auspices and not under the associations, as was usual. The provisional board counter-attacked at once by refusing to accept the decisions, and in the dramatic negotiations which followed in October, Helset and his two fellow-negotiators stood as firm as a rock upon the two basic principles of the new Association — no interference with freedom and self-determination in the affairs of sport, and no introduction of party politics into such matters.

Accounts of the meetings and correspondence with the authorities in the final phase during the second half of October were circulated inside the Association and printed in large issues of the illicit press. It was indeed a relief, in a time of so much weakness and hesitation among leading people, to read of the forthright rejection of party intervention in sport and Helset's pithy rejoinder to the Minister, when the latter bemoaned the Government's difficulties: 'The Government was after all the nominee of the occupying power, so it was of course extremely difficult for it to reach decisions which paid sufficient regard to the national interests ...'

As the Department got nowhere with the provisional board, it tried to create a split by calling in the chairmen of the component associations, but Stang met with the same stonewall tactics there. The board protested sharply in a letter of 9 November, threatening to abandon its functions if interference by the Department in the affairs of the sports organisations continued. On the 22nd Stang proceeded to dismiss the provisional board and appoint a 'sports leader' to reorganise

Norwegian sport on the Nazi German model. This made the situation for the NS party worse than ever. The dispute continued during the winter at association, district and team level all over the country, but everywhere the elected managements refused to recognise the new sports leadership and resigned. Sporting activities were paralysed, and the few NS people who were set up as team leaders received virtually no backing.

There was a parallel development on the field of play, which had revived to some extent after the end of the campaign. With few exceptions German demands to take part in club activities or sports meetings were rejected, and when the attempt to establish a New Order in sport became known, a total sports strike was started. Every local, national or international match which the new leadership tried to arrange was boycotted both by participants and spectators. Well-known sportsmen, especially skiers and skaters, were put under great pressure, some of them even being arrested — which made the opposition still more acute. The struggle went on all through the winter and by the summer it had reached the individual athletics clubs. But the news that our skiing champions and star skaters were being disqualified or arrested strengthened not only the sports front but the resistance struggle as a whole. Thus Bishop Berggrav tells of Professor Hallesby* exclaiming at a meeting of the Joint Christian Council at that time: 'Do you know what I should like to do? Go up the Palace Hill, wave my hat, and shout "Hurrah for our young sportsmen!"'

Quisling achieved the opposite of what he intended. Some 300,000 young athletes stood up against the NS, resistance to which gained a nation-wide coverage through the sports strike. There was hardly a hamlet anywhere in the country without a team, so many places which had been spared any direct inroads on the part of the NS became aware of the danger. Local athletic leaders came to play a big role in various aspects of the Home Front, the athletes being particularly important in the building up of the secret fighting-groups which were then under formation. In many places, groups of friends from the sports teams provided the nucleus. Nor did the sports strike mean that physical training for sport was brought to an end; the woods and mountains were often brought into use, so as to keep in

*See footnote, p.34.

condition for a contribution to the liberation of Norway when the time came.

The Supreme Court maintains that the state is based on law

The Supreme Court — the third element in our form of government — was the only one which remained in the occupied capital in the days of April. In the chaos which followed the invasion, the Court, with Chief Justice Paal Berg at its head, played an important part in getting Quisling removed from office and the Administrative Council established. Paal Berg was again a central figure in the first phase of the negotiations over a Council of State, but he withdrew from them when it proved not to be feasible to settle the question of the King without a breach of the constitution.

In the middle of November 1940 the NS Minister of Justice (Riisnæs) assumed the right — regardless of the rules prescribed for the courts by law — to appoint and dismiss assessors, and so set aside the principle of judicial independence. The Supreme Court protested sharply. The NS's next steps in undermining legal security in the country came at the beginning of December, when the Minister of Justice lowered the age limit for public officials from seventy to sixty-five years with immediate effect. The obvious intention of this was to open the way for unwanted judges to be replaced by henchmen of the Party. A few days later the Reichskommissar sent a letter to the Supreme Court, forbidding it to test the validity of ordinances in his name, which meant that *he alone* would decide what was lawful and right. On 12 December the Supreme Court addressed a letter to the Department of Justice, which included the following passage:

> We wish to maintain that under Norwegian constitutional law it is the duty of the courts to test the validity of statutes and administrative ordinances. During a military occupation the courts in our opinion must in the same way ... be able to take a stand on the validity under international law of ordinances issued by organs of the occupying power. We cannot endorse the view of the courts' authority which is expressed in the Reichskommissar's letter without acting contrary to our duties as judges of the Norwegian Supreme Court.
>
> We therefore find ourselves unable to continue in our offices.

The Supreme Court asked in the same letter for a conference with the Department on the time for their withdrawal. When the answer was delayed, the Court ascertained privately that the

NS authorities intended to dismiss all Supreme Court judges over the age of sixty-five with immediate effect and appoint NS judges in their place, thus securing the Party a majority in the Court. A full meeting was called in all haste in order to forestall the NS, and a new letter was sent with the information that the judges would all leave office on 21 December. Later the same day, eight judges, including the Chief Justice, were informed of their dismissal under the new age regulations, the others being instructed to continue until further notice. It was too late; the members of the Court had withdrawn one and all.

The news of the Supreme Court's resignation and what had led to it became known immediately, the correspondence being printed in the illicit newspapers, spread by handbills, and reported on the BBC's Norwegian Service. It was an eye-opener for the nation as a whole and gave incalculable encouragement to the incipient resistance movement; now that the Supreme Court had actually ranged itself on its side, the movement knew that it had a basis in law. The 'illicit' opposition had been legalised. Chief Justice Paal Berg had led the Court quickly and steadily through the critical period, thus laying the foundation for the key position which he was later to hold in the Home Front. Other Supreme Court judges came to play important parts in the struggle at a later stage.

The breakdown in local self-government

The newly established commissarial Department for Home Affairs, which was headed by the 'strong man' of the Party, A.V. Hagelin,* issued several ordinances during the autumn with a view to securing centralised control over local administration. On the very day when the Supreme Court ceased to function, there came an ordinance for changing local government law, and the *Führerprinzip* (leader-principle) was introduced into county and district administration: district representatives were no longer to be elected, and chairmen and vice-chairmen were to be nominated by the Department. At their

*He had been for many years in business in Germany, where he provided an important early link between Quisling and the Nazi Party. Apart from Skancke (p.34), Hagelin was the only minister who shared their leader's fate of execution for high treason. Jones Lie (p.69) committed suicide and Riisnæs (p.131) was found to be insane.

side they were to have a council of 'foremen', nominated by the *fylkesmann** in each county in consultation with the county leader of the NS and the nominee to the chairmanship. The matter was very urgent, as the new system was to be brought into force on 1 January. To be able to manage this, the Department sent the *fylkesmenn* a confidential circular on 10 December, outlining the new system, and giving them one week's notice to propose candidates for the posts of chairman and vice-chairman; in this time they were to consult the NS leaders in their respective counties. Although they felt doubts, and some advanced cautious criticisms of the ordinance, they all sent in proposals for chairmen within the time limit; in most cases they proposed the chairmen previously elected, but also some new candidates, including NS members. The *fylkesmenn* have claimed that they were under pressure from leading politicians and other influential people in the districts, and considered that it was best for the population that they should retain their positions in the new situation. In due course, however, having rendered this service to the Party, they were dismissed.

This demand to the *fylkesmenn* had materialised so suddenly that there was no time for conferring and counter-action. But in the next phase — when the question was whether previous chairmen or other experienced local politicians who were not NS supporters should accept the task — energetic attempts were made from various quarters to induce them to refuse. One *fylkesmann*, J. Cappelen, who had just been dismissed from his post in the county of South Tröndelag, saw at once how dangerous would be the consequence of falling in line. In the short run, the effect would be to give added political strength to the position of the NS in the eyes of the population and of the Germans, while in the long run it would give it the time it needed to train its own people and then turn out the old politicians. Finally, Cappelen saw the danger which co-operation between the earlier chairmen and the NS authorities signified in the way of obscuring the clear line which it was necessary to maintain against the NS and all its ways. Cappelen travelled to Oslo, where he contacted Judge Schjelderup and other friends.

*An official with considerable executive powers, appointed by the central government to represent its interests in each county. The *fylkesmann* for the Oslo area was chairman of the Administrative Council.

Schjelderup was already on the point of organising a counter-action on the same lines, so he arranged for the copying and sending out of two letters, one from Cappelen and the other from himself, to every chairman in the country. At the same time he sent a letter to the *fylkesmenn* to induce them to change their attitude, while opposition was also raised from other circles, including the R-group.

But to organise an opposition which could reach every district in our extensive and thinly populated country was impossible at that time. In many places it was not by any means easy for an isolated district chairman when the *fylkesmann* of his county, whom he regarded as a loyal Norwegian citizen, urged him to stay in office in order to safeguard national interests. Particularly in places where there were few NS party members, the old local politicians likewise believed that they would be able to retain control. On the whole, these exertions produced little result. A few sporadic instances of fearless outright refusal merely bring out the general rule — that in most places the old local politicians agreed to be nominated, thus helping to break down local self-government and to burden the resistance with one of the biggest defeats of the war. It was not long before the old chairmen were replaced by NS members or sympathisers, except in cases where they themselves changed party.

The archives of the post-war official enquiry indicate that in April 1944, 82 per cent of district chairmen were members of the NS and that at the liberation of Norway every one was a member or a fellow-traveller. In some counties in East Norway one in five of the old chairmen either was or later became a member of the NS. Thus at local level too, few of the old political leaders served as a sheet-anchor in the emergency. In seamen's language, most of them were mere sea-anchors in the great political storms to which the German occupation had exposed the Norwegian community.

2
THE RISING OF THE PEOPLE AGAINST THE NS

During the autumn of 1940, the political struggle acquired much greater scope and intensity. The NS combined siren tones for attracting members with a shaking of the fist at their opponents, who became numerous all over the country with the dawning realisation of the values that were at stake. The struggle was to be most comprehensive in Oslo which, besides being the seat of government and therefore of the central administration, was the centre of important educational institutions and the economic activities of the country, and where most of the national professional and trade organisations likewise had their head offices. Here too the resistance movement had its centres, for the struggle against the NS and the occupation authorities had to be conducted from the capital. But this did not prevent important initiatives from being taken elsewhere; open resistance by the general public could indeed be more violent in the smaller towns.

After it had 'come into power', the NS demanded declarations of loyalty from public servants, who were already under threat from the Reichskommissar's ordinance of 4 October: 'Public servants whose political attitude offers no guarantee that they will co-operate with all their force in the political New Order may be dismissed from the service.' Doctors and teachers were the first to come into the line of fire. A NS professor had proposed that the Norwegian Medical Association should join the NS Guild for Health and Hygiene, and that its national committee should give a declaration of loyalty to the new body. This was refused at the beginning of November by a vote of 35:2 in the committee, which shortly afterwards protested sharply to the Department of Home Affairs when four doctors in the Directorate of Medicine were dismissed on political grounds.

The teachers had already had some outpost skirmishing in October, in cases where local NS leaders had threatened teachers with dismissal if they did not join the Party. In that connection the teachers' organisations had sent out a joint circular to their members, referring to their right to reject such pressure on the basis of the Hague Convention. In mid-November the R-group's organisation leader secured a proof copy of a circular which was to be sent out on the 20th to all teachers. This contained a demand that teachers should give positive and active support to the new authorities and educate their pupils in the spirit of the new era. Finally, the Reichskommissar's ordinance of 4 October concerning this dismissal of unco-operative officials was used as a threat, and a declaration of loyalty was demanded of the teachers, on pain of immediate dismissal.

A professor who supported educational independence was alerted; he at once contacted Bishop Berggrav, who drafted a counter-declaration — the first nationwide directive (*parole*)* in the 'Standfast' struggle. It was discussed with a group of teachers' leaders and with Judge Schjelderup, and then sent out through the teachers' organisations in the following form: 'With reference to the enquiry received, I hereby declare that I will remain true to my teaching vocation and my conscience, and that on that basis I shall, in the future as in the past, carry out the decisions relating to my work which are lawfully given by my superiors.' The NS declaration was sent out in some districts, but when the Department was merely confronted with the counter-declaration, the pressure stopped. The action brought the central and local leaders of the teachers' organisations into close contact, and a strong solidarity developed among the members. Moreover, the counter-declaration provided a pattern for other groups of public officials from whom declarations of loyalty were demanded.

The *parole* was a weapon which proved, both on this occasion and later, to be an effective and distinctive instrument of warfare in the Norwegian resistance to nazification. It was an instruction for a definite common attitude in a concrete operational situation. Magnus Jensen, who came to write more such directives than anyone else during the occupation, has described their significance as follows: 'Inside the separate organisations

*In the early period, when civil resistance was largely concerned with morale (the 'Standfast struggle'), the *parole* had more the character of a slogan or watchword, but it gradually assumed the status of a directive.

they created at a quite early stage the feeling of solidarity which was a necessity for the civil struggle. They broke down the isolation of the individual, the dread of standing all alone which was the most important weapon of the Nazi terror.'

The departure of the Supreme Court was a shock to the legal profession, and in the following months the boards of both the Association of Lawyers and the Association of Magistrates conducted an acrimonious correspondence with the Minister of Justice about the independence of the courts, though the former Association decided that a refusal to conduct cases before the new Supreme Court would be too prejudicial to the interest of their clients. There were several dangerous indications that legal security was being undermined. In December an ordinance widened the duty of individuals to act as witnesses, and removed the obligation of clergy, doctors and lawyers to respect confidences. Just before this, a 'People's Court' was set up, which could deal with criminal cases at the request of the authorities in 'special circumstances'. We were soon to learn what this meant. The Labour Party group in the executive committee of the Oslo City Council was denounced and imprisoned because it had proposed at a meeting a resolution protesting in unmistakable terms against a document from the Department of Home Affairs, which demanded that the *fylkesmenn* should strictly require local government authorities 'throughout their activities to follow the NS and the principles of the New Era'. Their committal to prison was annulled by the assize court for East Norway, but the Gestapo intervened and prevented their release, against which the judge and the prison director protested sharply but without success. At the end of February 1941 the group were sentenced by the new 'People's Court' to imprisonment for at least one year — a very clear demonstration that justice had given way to lawlessness. The executive committee of the Lawyers' Association pointed out the following month in an earnest letter to the Departments of Justice and Police that the setting up of the People's Court and the new ordinances conflicted with the basic principles of Norwegian jurisprudence: 'Unquiet times are precisely those in which it can be fatal to give people the feeling that they have lost their legal rights.' There was no answer.

After 25 September the NS had organised a series of meetings, at which Quisling and other 'top brass' tried to enlist supporters; Goebbels himself was invited to come up to help. Despite this, fiasco followed fiasco, and on 2 December the *Bulletin* published this description:

> The new meetings held by the NS have mostly turned out as before, with small attendances inside the room but in many cases with big demonstrations against the NS outside. At Larvik Acting-Minister Lunde tried to address the crowd from the balcony, as there were no people inside the meeting room. As if at a signal the crowd left the place, first singing the national anthem — and then *God Save the King*. After the meeting the *Hird** was chased home by the crowd ... At Moss, Sarpsborg and Askim it came to demonstrations against Quisling. At Askim the fire-alarm on the factory started just as Quisling was about to begin speaking — and the result was that all the people, both those in the meeting and those assembled outside, left the premises and went off to the factory. Quisling was left with an empty room.

There was a lot of trouble in the streets and the schools, the pupils and other youngsters being in a state of ferment. They took every opportunity of displaying their national feeling and their detestation of the Germans and the NS with woollen caps, paper clips,† 'H7' signs, and similar symbols of their sympathies, which made life bitter for NS supporters. Arrests of individuals made the atmosphere still more explosive. The young men in the *Hird* on their side were aggressive and brutal: at some schools both teachers and pupils were badly molested, and the *Hird* also made havoc in the streets, usually without any intervention by the police, who had been ordered to give them their active support. It was a time of brute force and mob rule in Norway. In January 1941 Himmler, the dreaded leader of the Gestapo, came on an 'official' visit, which was a warning of still harder times yet to come.

Next month the unrest among pupils in the Oslo schools reached new heights, in connection with a demand from the authorities that they should visit a Hitler Youth exhibition; demonstration marches and protest meetings were arranged. At the same time, there was a school strike in Bergen on account of the *Hird* disorders. The strong opposition and fighting spirit

*Set up by Quisling in the 1930s as a bodyguard to preserve order at his open-air meetings, and modelled on Hitler's SA; the name was properly that of the retainers in the service of the medieval Norwegian kings.

†As with 'H7' (for Haakon VII), the wearing of a red woollen cap or the sporting of a paper clip in the coat lapel was an accepted sign of loyalty to the King.

of their pupils influenced the attitude of the school heads and teachers, a majority of whom had at first voted to attend the exhibition under protest, and there was a final agreement to answer with a clear 'No'. The NS authorities had to retreat, and their advance on the school front was interrupted. The struggle against the Hitler Youth exhibition occasioned the formation of the 'Oslo ring' — the first illicit leadership for the secondary schools — consisting of one or two representatives of each institution. It was the Oslo ring which discussed and finalised each important directive for that branch of education.

The mob-rule of the *Hird* and the pressure exerted by the NS on public officials in the autumn and winter months of 1940-1 produced a feeling of lawlessness and irregularity, which many people found less easy to endure than the more systematic terror of the later war years. The Norwegian Church could no longer hold its peace. It possessed an energetic and fearless leader in the Bishop of Oslo, Eivind Berggrav, who was inspired by the attitude of the Supreme Court and aroused by the conduct of the *Hird* to take the initiative in a letter of protest from all the bishops to the head of the Department for Church and Education, Acting-Minister Skancke. This letter of 15 January 1941 pointed to the growing disquiet and anxiety among the people over the disintegration of law and justice and the resort to violence by the *Hird*, and to the conflict of conscience with which school people were confronted by the demand that they should pledge themselves to a positive and active support for the new government of the country. Finally, the bishops protested in strong terms against the ordinance removing the duty of silence from priests in their calling, and demanded that the Minister should state his position.

Some months before this, all the main divisions in the Norwegian Church had come together in a Joint Christian Council, in which the leading members were Bishop Berggrav, Professor Hallesby of the Low Church Theological College, and the lay preacher Ludvig Hope.* As was to be expected, this did

*The stand taken by Eivind Berggrav (1884-1959), Bishop of Oslo and therefore Primate since 1937, became more widely known through his book, *With God in the Darkness*, published in London in 1943. O.K. Hallesby (1879-1961) was a fundamentalist divine, who had held a Chair since 1909 in the institution (founded under lay auspices) where more than half the Norwegian clergy received their training, and L. Hope (1871-1954) a lay preacher with a large following in West Norway.

not take place without trouble from minor ecclesiastics, especially in West Norway. But Hope travelled with Berggrav to meet them in Bergen and stopped every sign of division. This union of all the forces within the Norwegian Church, which in pre-war times bitterly opposed each other, was to prove of inestimable importance for the resistance movement. After discussion with Hallesby and Hope, Berggrav and two of the other bishops delivered a letter from all the bishops at a meeting with the Acting-Minister in late January. This time the points were made still more firmly:

> When those in authority in the community tolerate violence and injustice and oppress the souls of men, then the Church is the guardian of men's consciences.... On that account the bishops of the Church have laid before the Minister some of the facts and official announcements concerning the administration of the community... which the church finds to be in conflict with the law of God....

The episcopal letter quickly found its way to London and was broadcast from there, and it was likewise duplicated and distributed, tens of thousands of copies reaching every part of the country. In February the bishops had the letters repeated in a *pastoral letter*, which was read from the pulpit on Sunday the 9th. In March, Berggrav also lectured at clergy meetings in different parts of the country, in order to rid them of any 'exaggerated Lutheran attitude of submission to the powers that be'. NS tried to counter the bishops by police actions in and outside the churches, and in many places the pastoral letter was confiscated. Bishop Berggrav was summoned to meet Reichskommissar Terboven and Himmler to answer for his doings, which only emphasised the serious defeat inflicted on the Party.

The leaders of the other denominations and Church organisations supported the bishops in their applications to the Church Department. The pastoral letter — and in particular the many dramatic episodes when NS police tried to prevent it from being read out — aroused new groups to understand the seriousness of the situation. It was a powerful stimulus for the resistance movement that it now had the blessing of the Church added to that of the Supreme Court.

Neither the appeals nor the threats which were aimed at public functionaries to induce them to become Party members or to work actively for 'the new era' had produced adequate results in the course of the first two months after the September *coup*. So in mid-December Hagelin, as Acting-Minister for Home Affairs, found that it was time to give a further turn to the screw by sending out a circular in which he demanded that public servants should give a declaration of positive and active support for the NS and the new authorities. 'Failure in any degree will be treated as action against the State', to be visited with 'drastic penalties'. The resistance front was clear over the danger in this demand for loyalty, and counter-actions were set to work in mounting numbers and with increasing strength. What was most urgently required was a way to give the individual who was under pressure an assurance that he and his family would not be left helpless and completely alone if he should be dismissed. Funds to provide aid were set up by subscription from every member in some threatened branches of service, and other support came from private companies and, surreptitiously, from the Norwegian Legation in Stockholm.

The R-group sent out a directive to functionaries to hold together and not to yield. What was more important, however, was the open resistance to the demand for loyalty which arose inside the organisations, usually under the leadership of their elected representatives. Thus the chairman of the Union of Local Government Officials, a Bergen man, co-operated with the management of the Association of Local Authorities in a nation-wide counter-action. This took the form of individual declarations from the members to the effect that the injunction from the Department was an infringement of their service obligations; and the protest was widely supported.

Unrest and bitterness spread steadily into new sections of the population. The chairman of the Commercial Association and its business manager had contacted other large economic organisations as early as November about a joint application to the Reichskommissar in connection with the misuse of power by the NS, the assaults by the *Hird*, and the growth of lawlessness. Then in January 1941 representatives of a number of professional bodies considered how the NS's pressure for membership should be faced, but no resolution was adopted at their meeting. Shortly afterwards, the chairman of the Association of Lawyers discussed with the Commercial Association's manager the possibility of a joint protest from their two Associations, and immediately after that he was approached by two leading professors at Oslo University, who had been working towards a similar result in academic circles and had produced a draft protest. However at this first attempt nothing came of the discussions, which involved most of the professional and trade organisations of the country.

On 15 February the NS took a new step by announcing the establishment of an office for supervision, the NS Personnel Office for the Public Service, to give its prior approval to all appointments. New efforts were then made to arrange a protest on the widest possible basis, but this was not put into action because of opposition from the Rector of the University, D.A. Seip, and other individuals who considered that it would give the authorities an excuse for drastic action against the organisations. He himself would not sign because he did not want the University to be closed. The consequence was that on 3 April twenty-two associations which were directly affected by the institution of the new NS Office made a sharp protest to the Reichskommissar against party membership being placed before professional qualifications in appointments to public offices and against the role which had been assigned to the new NS organ. The Reichskommissar ignored the application, and the NS went steadily on its way. An attempt was made to remove several well-known civil servants with the help of the provisional regulation for earlier retirement, and there was also an episode at an Oslo municipal hospital which attracted much attention. A trivial matter of order was exploited by a subordinate functionary, who was the local NS 'leader', to have the superintendent doctor removed and arrested. But when all the other doctors under the municipality and the senior doctors at the other Norwegian hospitals threatened to walk out, and were backed by the main town hall officials and other important functionaries, the NS was forced to retreat and free the senior doctor. The case helped to arouse the medical profession, so that a strikingly large number of doctors were later to be found in prominent positions in both the civil and the military resistance movement. It also led to the formation of a self-constituted secret committee of action in the Medical Association.

Discussions about a common protest were resumed in early May, this time with success, a letter to Terboven being signed on the 15th by the chairmen of forty-three national organisations representing labour, business, cultural, legal, church and educational activities. The signatories pointed in unmistakable terms to the abuse of power by the NS, to the tyrannies of the

Hird, to ordinances and decisions that were in conflict with international law and Norwegian statutes, to the breaking-down of the judicial system, to the pressure exerted upon public functionaries and the disregard for professional qualifications. The application was a vigorous and fearless document of protest, without any exact parallel in the other countries occupied by the Germans in the Second World War. The letter took the offensive, calling the Reichskommissar to account and ending thus:

> Accompanied by threats or other forms of pressure, a demand to join the [NS] Party or to work actively for the advance of the Party represents for the overwhelming majority of Norwegians a deliberate attempt to induce them to compromise with their consciences and depart from what they consider right and proper.
>
> It is plainly evident that among our people everywhere this has led to a growth of disquiet, which greatly impedes ordinary daily work and so damages the country. The disquiet and irritation have lately approximated to a state of embitterment.
>
> We venture to request the Reichskommissar urgently for a reply, to be given at the earliest possible moment, to the letter of 3 April as well as to the present application.

The answer came quite soon, but in the meantime there were dramatic events on the cultural front. The acting profession had been under pressure since the beginning of 1941 to perform on the radio and at NS meetings and festivities, which the majority had consistently refused to do. At the end of May, six of the leading actors at the National Theatre were called in to the Germans and threatened with dismissal unless they would give radio performances. The result was a sympathy strike among actors all over the country, which they kept going for six weeks in spite of arrests, fines and threats of many kinds. This action, which received practical support from the public, did much to intensify the attitude of the man in the street.

What was happening in Norway and in many Norwegian minds at that time can hardly be better expressed than in the words written by a Stavanger lawyer in April in *Norsk Front*, the illicit newspaper which he edited:

> The front line is to be found in the mind of every woman and man, in their unquenchable hatred for injustice and in the demand that life shall be lived in accordance with the voice of conscience. It is a front line which does not recognise compromises or admissions of a practical sort. It exists independently of German or English victory. The

struggle will be maintained along this line through our prayers and those of our children until it is won, however long that may be.

The Home Front goes underground

Terboven's answer to the forty-three organisations came on 18 June, when their leaders were summoned to a meeting in the parliament building, which had become the headquarters of the Reichskommissariat. Terboven made a furious speech: five of the signatories were arrested on the spot and led out; some organisations were dissolved by decree; and in the others — except for the trade union organisation (the LO) — the leadership was dismissed and replaced by nominated leaders. This was another clear utterance by the head of the German occupation authority, who again established a turning-point in the history of the occupation. For the Norwegian community with its democratic organisations, the making of an open protest against acts of tyranny, in which reference was made to our statutes and to international law, by representatives who had been duly elected was a natural and necessary course of action. It had indicated where the front line was during the Nazi advance, for the members of the organisations and for the Nazi authorities alike. Although later the resistance often took the form of personal protest by individual members, after 18 June 1941 it had to be organised underground and conducted by individuals whose names were not known to the Gestapo and the NS.

People were not altogether unprepared — as witness the directive to members, which was issued immediately in most of the organisations, to stultify them by individual resignations and withdrawal from functions of management. The directives were followed so faithfully that the new, nominated leaders were in charge of mere paper organisations, with hesitant members being taken in hand by more resolute colleagues. In some instances those in charge had also picked out committees of action to continue their work if the lawfully elected management was unable to function, but in most organisations such committees were first formed after 18 June and set to work separately to construct a system of secret communications and to appoint local representatives. Each of them tried to safeguard its new secret apparatus as well as possible, so a kind of blind man's buff was played during the summer until the new committees established proper contact with each other. To some extent people in R-group brought this about, but it was chiefly the leader of the doctors who co-ordinated the action-groups in accordance with an appeal which had been made to him at the 'constituent' meeting of his group. In the course of the summer months he came into touch with representatives of the lawyers, the engineers and the trade union organisation, and a couple of liaison meetings were held before the state of emergency on 10 September — the day when Terboven tried to beat down the opposition in the trade unions, and let loose terror on Norwegian society in earnest. We must therefore retrace our steps to see what happened to trade unionism after the summer of 1940.

The trade union organisation (LO): from compliance to conflict

In the first phase of the negotiations for a Council of State, the acting leadership of the unions had supported the removal from office of the King and government, but it withdrew at the close of the second phase. The 'trade union opposition' — the collaborationist wing of the LO — nevertheless continued its undermining of the lawful government-in-exile, proposing that the trade union organisation should take part in the task of establishing a 'new order' and starting peace negotiations with Germany. Leading Communists took part in this activity, which was even continued after the first wave of arrests against members of the Communist Party in mid-August, when its main newspaper was also stopped. In the period before 25 September 1940 the group was in close contact with the NS and the Germans, and the result was soon apparent. Shortly after that date, the LO's chairman was removed, and the Germans demanded that its new leader should be Jens Tangen, the chairman of the Union of Building Workers and one of the main figures in the 'trade union opposition'. The vice-chairman was pressed to retire and to recommend Tangen's candidature, while the new leadership of the LO was to agree to co-operate loyally with the NS and the German authorities. After a couple of days of intense discussion, the LO secretariat agreed to recognise a new executive, consisting of Tangen as chairman, a vice-chairman from the Railwaymen's Union who was a reliable Norwegian, and a general secretary who was a younger trade union functionary and a former member of the *Mot Dag* movement.* Tangen chose as his personal secretary a Communist who, along with the new general secretary, had been among the most active figures in the 'trade union opposition'.

In the following weeks, Tangen and his associates worked hard to strengthen their positions in close co-operation with the Acting-Minister for Social Affairs; they met scanty opposition, as most of the trade union organisation's representatives acted as if they were paralysed. The new set-up was approved at a meeting of the district trades council in Oslo on 3 October, on the proposal of a Communist and with only three 'no' votes. Then followed a demand by the Acting-Minister for unqualified declarations of loyalty to the new leadership on the part of union representatives. This was strongly opposed in some unions, but Tangen and his two 'adjutants' pushed it through by such strong-arm measures as refusing opponents access to the LO delegate meeting on 28 October, which was to pass judgment on the new situation. This meeting has been called the most unhappy one in the history of the trade union organisation. A resolution from the secretariat was moved by Tangen, 'That the delegate meeting takes note of the events which have occurred and approves the standpoint which has been adopted, since the meeting is aware that this was a matter of necessity in order to preserve the trade union organisation as an instrument to protect the interests of working people.' This was adopted without opposition, the meeting concerning itself chiefly with the economic situation, especially unemployment,† and with the situation in the Labour press.

The forces of resistance in the LO and the Labour movement generally were not, however, as feeble as this might suggest. Immediately after the *coup* of 25 September, active groups had been formed round Gerhardsen** and two other leaders, which made contact with the rest of the resistance movement and took a large part in establishing illicit newspapers and organising resistance both in Oslo and in the provinces. Members of the group were also in the Circle‡ from its initiation. Particular

*A strongly Marxist movement of 1921-36, which flourished chiefly among students.

†As late as April 1941, there were 33,556 registered unemployed.

**Einar Gerhardsen (b. 1897) was already chairman of the Oslo City Council and vice-chairman of the Labour Party; in June 1945 he headed the inter-party Government, and was Labour Prime Minister, 1945-51 and 1955-65.

‡See p.52.

importance was attached to the starting up of the paper *Fri Fagbevegelse* ('Free Trade Unionism') at the turn of the year. In the whole war I never met more devoted and consistent resistance people than its two editors and their many self-sacrificing fellow-workers, so it is something of a mystery that they had so little influence upon contemporary developments in the LO. Among several reasons for this the most important was the view that the LO was still an indispensable organ for the workers as the safeguard of their wages and conditions of employment, a consideration which was specially emphasised by Viggo Hansteen, the legal adviser to the union organisation, in a letter to the Government in London in February 1941, in which he strongly defended the line which the LO had taken up till then. Within the ranks of the organisation too, there were many who had not yet recovered from the shock of the events which had followed 9 April and 25 September, and the fear that Germany would win the war was widespread. The LO had begun to slip during the summer, both by accepting that its elected leadership was not to be reinstated and by its attitude to the negotiations for a Council of State. In addition, the historian of the trade union movement during the occupation* gives the interesting explanation that the illicit resistance groups were inhibited from sending out directives because of the strong tradition in the LO that these must emanate from the elected representatives and committees in accordance with the rules. On the other hand, resistance to the collaboration line was strong in some towns and industrial centres in different parts of the country.

In the Labour movement of 1940 the youth organisation, the AUF, had more fighting spirit than the parent body, with a leadership which was more strongly disinclined to be compliant with the Germans and the NS. On 24-25 August, the AUF held a meeting of its national committee in Oslo, at which a majority of the executive board proposed a resolution urging members to stand on guard for the national and democratic basis of Norwegian society—this was clearly aimed at the NS. A minority of two, who belonged to the 'trade union opposition', put forward a motion of their own in favour of collaboration,

*Alfred Skar (1896-1969), a prominent contributor to *Fri Fagbevegelse*, published his account in 1949, when he had become head of LO's Information Office.

but the majority proposal was carried with only a few votes on the other side; it was then sent out through the Workers' Press Office, and printed in *Arbeiderbladet* the day after the meeting. That was its final issue for the duration of the war, for it was stopped by the German security police the following day; the editor was arrested, and the premises and printing works were taken over by the NS for the use of its Party paper, *Fritt Folk*.

In the late autumn there was a change in Tangen's attitude, parallel with the worsening of relations between Germany and the Soviet Union, particularly after the unsuccessful meeting of their Foreign Ministers in November. The General Secretary, on the other hand, showed his true colours by coming forward as a member of the NS. The patriotic members of the secretariat gave Tangen the choice between co-operating with them or with the Germans and the 'trade union opposition'. He chose the former, so thereafter an 'administrative board' inside the secretariat, from which the collaborators were excluded, examined all questions of principle before they went to the secretariat. Although the resistance people had begun to get control over the central trade union organisation, some humiliations had still to be swallowed, as when the secretariat agreed in January 1941 to send a delegation — though on a somewhat reduced scale — of leading representatives to visit the 'Labour Front' in Germany. But the delegates' observations after their return were not so favourable from a propaganda point of view as the NS had expected.

There was a growing dissatisfaction among the rank and file over the weak attitude to resistance in the LO secretariat at a time when it was on the increase in the nation as a whole. *Fri Fagbevegelse* made an impression with its accounts of the strong opposition to declarations of loyalty and additional demands being made by the Nazi authorities upon the other organisations. A clear impression of the attitude of the resistance people in the LO is conveyed by a letter from Trygve Bratteli,* then a building worker in Kristiansund. After describing the unhappy developments inside the trade union organisation since the outbreak of war, he continued:

*T.M. Bratteli (b.1910) was Labour prime minister in 1971-2, when he tried to bring Norway into the European Community but failed to win the plebiscite. A recent book by O.K. Grimnes (see footnote, p.189) finds that forty-six out of fifty-two surviving Home Front leaders of all parties shared Bratteli's view on this question.

We find that the Labour movement's people are silent in face of a secular tyranny, while Churchmen declare themselves openly. We find university graduates and civil servants standing together through thick and thin to check improper pressure upon individuals in very exposed positions, while the workers' organisations look on without lifting a finger at the removal of comrades with a plainly declared attitude to the foreign tyranny being dictated from outside; nay, we have even to experience the active engagement of authorities within the organisation in the removal of such comrades...

A genuine Labour movement must fight injustice and oppression, *irrespective of how great a power stands behind the injustice and oppression.* An apparatus which does not consider itself able to engage in this struggle has thereby lost its content and meaning. The vital solidarity and will to freedom of the workers must then find other forms, whether the apparatus exists or not.

On the anniversary of the invasion of 9 April there was a big though silent demonstration in streets and roads, schools and workplaces all over the country. All traffic and activity halted for half an hour in the middle of the day, in spite of a German ban on demonstrations. This action was strongly supported by the workers, who were also embittered and incited to resist when the occupying power and the NS made a travesty of May Day.* The leadership was made aware of the members' position.

In the later part of the winter, the alliance between Tangen and the Communists on the one hand and the NS wing of the 'trade union opposition' on the other had been dissolving. This was likewise the time of the negotiations among the organisations and the protests of 3 April and 15 May, and the LO now joined the resistance front — through its vice-chairman's signature — as did several of the constituent unions through their chairmen.

Those arrested in connection with Terboven's thunderous address in the parliament building on 18 June included the vice-chairman of the LO and three principal representatives of trade unionism. Otherwise the LO was treated relatively lightly.

After 18 June, it was at first intended that the members of the unions which operated through the LO should resign. This was already being prepared in several places, when it was countermanded by the leadership, which still considered it important

*The international Labour Day was made a statutory holiday in Norway in 1947.

to safeguard the apparatus of the organisation and its substantial assets. This point of view caused a good deal of dissatisfaction in other organisations and far into the ranks of the LO's own members, where it was believed that the liberty of the organisations was the decisive matter. Instead, the LO secretariat addressed a new communication to the Reichskommissar, asking in definite but diplomatic terms for negotiations regarding a cost-of-living allowance and for the release and reinstatement of the arrested representatives. It was made clear that if these requests were not met, the members of the secretariat would withdraw from their posts. More than a month later Terboven replied in contemptuous but by his standards moderate language, and the release of the representatives immediately followed.

In the meanwhile Germany had launched its invasion of the Soviet Union on 22 June, whereupon the NS and the Germans set on foot a major propaganda offensive in Norway, 'the fight against Bolshevism'. At the same time they undertook a series of new arrests inside the Labour movement, especially in North Norway, among both Communists and Labour Party people. The LO's strongest resistance man in North Norway was taken in this round: German propaganda in general now usually regarded every opponent as 'Communist'.

The Norwegian Communists had now been given the signal to enter the resistance ranks. They negotiated with the resistance leaders in the LO for trade union directives to be issued from only one authority, which it was agreed should be formed by a group of three, including Gerhardsen. But this group did not last long.

The LO was engaged in yet another struggle that summer. The Germans, who had themselves hitherto taken charge of wage negotiations with the unions, set up a Directorate for Workers' Organisations with the defector who was the LO's General Secretary at its head. The LO's request for a cost-of-living allowance was referred to the Directorate, which was intended to be a pillar of Quisling's Corporative State. The secretariat first decided to boycott the new Nazi organ, but later in the summer it decided by a slender majority to terminate the boycott and take up negotiations over the allowance, thus causing great discontent at many workplaces. This game was broken off by the State of Emergency of 10 September.

Milk rationing was introduced on 8 September, with the

result that there were no longer any deliveries of milk to offices and places of work. Coffee had long since disappeared, and the mid-day sandwich of bread and thinly spread margarine was hard to get down. Indignation took the upper hand when the milk did not arrive, so that a large proportion of the workers at two of the biggest industrial plants in Oslo — a shipyard and a steel mill — walked out. It was a spontaneous reaction after seventeen months of tyranny and pent-up bitterness — with the further stimulus that Germans working beside them still got their bottles of milk — and both the LO leaders and the shop stewards on the spot, who were alive to the dangerous situation, urged the workers to return. But next day the strike spread to other workplaces in the Oslo area, affecting 20,000-30,000 men in all.

On the morning of the 10th Terboven proclaimed a state of emergency in Greater Oslo and let loose the terror. The mass arrests of trade union spokesmen began at dawn: the Gestapo secured every member of the LO secretariat it could lay hands on, nearly all the union chairmen, and a number of shop stewards at their work-places. At the same time the Germans arrested the Oslo chief of police, the Rector and several leading professors at the University, and the editor and several journalists belonging to the Conservative paper, *Morgenbladet*, which was the staunchest resistance element among the pre-occupation newspapers. Several of the influential resistance people who had signed the protest from the forty-three organisations in May were re-arrested, after having been at large for a time. The editor-in-chief of *Aftenposten* was dismissed along with many of the journalists, and the paper was put under Commissariat management. Other journals were also purged. The big humanitarian organisations were taken over by the NS and the Scout movement was banned.

That evening the stunned population of the capital heard the announcement on Oslo Radio that the LO's legal adviser, Hansteen, and the principal shop steward at a railway carriage works, named Rolf Wickström, had been sentenced to death by court-martial and already been executed, while several others were sentenced to imprisonment for life or terms of many years.

The days that followed brought new court-martial convictions, including several death sentences which were commuted to life imprisonment. Altogether there were more than 300 arrests, and the city swarmed with German police and SS detachments. The workers were forbidden to resign from the unions under threat of court-martial, while an ordinance of 17 September made 'disturbance of economic life or peaceful conditions of work' punishable by imprisonment or even the death penalty. No one was safe any longer, since death sentences or heavy terms of imprisonment could be visited upon anybody who dared to defy those in power. Legal rights had ceased to exist. Prominent announcements in the newspapers and public notices informed the public of the harsh threats of the occupying power and listed those who had been condemned and executed. The torturing of prisoners, which had been introduced in earnest in the spring, became both more extensive and more extreme; Heydrich, the dreaded leader of the German security police, arrived in Oslo a few days before the State of Emergency.

The Emergency was a heavy blow for the Labour movement. In addition to the trade union leaders, prominent figures in the Labour Party were taken, including Gerhardsen, and those of the former leadership in the LO and the Labour Party who escaped capture had to go into exile. Tangen was dismissed and arrested, and an acting leader was assigned to the LO. The trade union organisation had been ruthlessly brought into line with the other organisations; all future opposition would have to be organised underground.

Luckily the group which ran *Fri Fagbevegelse* had not been hit, and the new, illegal leadership of the trade unions (the FU) was largely made up of its members. The FU was set up in the autumn after consultation with the union leaders who had escaped to Stockholm and London. To some extent the situation had been anticipated — and prepared for — during the summer by a committee in the secretariat, and a circular was sent out with guidance for branch officials who could be relied upon. Before the end of the year local committees of the unions were established in Bergen, Kristiansand, Molde, Gjövik and Lillehammer.

At the end of January 1942 a new and almost paralysing stroke was directed against the illegal leadership of the Labour movement, when the *Bulletin* and *Fri Fagbevegelse* were exposed, which led to the arrest of the majority of the FU with Per Lie, its chairman, at their head. That landslide carried away not only those who edited and printed the two papers, but also many of the active young members of the AUF in the distribution network for *Fri Fagbevegelse*, including my own contacts.

When the action was over and those who were in most peril after the arrests had gone to Sweden, only two of the old Labour leaders were left to restart *Fri Fagbevegelse* and continue its expansion across the country.

The *Bulletin* was continued by two sports leaders, and our apparatus for distributing it was still intact. Yet we only just kept ourselves afloat, for a few weeks later an attempt we made to contact the new leadership of *Fri Fagbevegelse* almost brought us into a trap laid by a Gestapo agent. One of the old collecting posts for *Fri Fagbevegelse* had passed on a message that a new contact for that paper would meet us, so Alf Sanengen, who had just joined our group, was given the job of meeting him. His instinct told him that there was something underhand about the man, so without giving any information he arranged to meet him again the next afternoon in front of the entrance to the Cathedral. When the appointed time arrived, I was standing nearby, 'repairing' my bicycle. Our contact man came, looked round impatiently and glanced from time to time at his watch, and after waiting in vain for a quarter of an hour sauntered off along a busy street. Shadowing him on my bicycle, I soon saw him enter the central police station, where the Gestapo had its prison. There were of course no further negotiations with that fellow; it took us many months to find our way back to *Fri Fagbevegelse*, and the editorial link between that paper and the *Bulletin* was never re-established.

There seems no doubt that the effective blows which the Gestapo directed against the illegal leaders of the Labour movement in the autumn and winter of 1941-2 were a blood-letting from which it never completely recovered, notwithstanding the whole-hearted efforts of those who continued the struggle.

A nation-wide civil resistance organisation is constructed

The Emergency of September 1941 broke off for a short time the work of co-ordinating the action committees of the professional organisations. Contact between the resistance leaders in the LO and the others was lost after the murder of Hansteen and the escape to Stockholm of another prominent LO activist. At a meeting in the home of the doctors' action leader, probably in October, which was attended by representatives of the doctors, engineers, lawyers, clergy and the primary and secondary schools, it was decided to form a regular committee for co-operation, later known by the name of Co-ordination Committee (KK). In the course of time the KK came also to include representatives from the press, the FU, business, agriculture and the public services, as well as some members who had no professional connections; but it was not until the turn of the year 1944-5 that it elected a chairman. Closer co-operation was needed at the level of organisation; hence, when it was apparent that the network of contacts belonging to the various action groups did not cover the country adequately, it was decided to establish a joint secretariat. A young doctor, O.J. Malm, was called in to head the secretariat and to develop the common contact arrangements. In the larger towns a main contact was to be appointed, who would collaborate with district contacts for the various professions to ensure that the directives from the action groups in Oslo reached all concerned.

Malm was greatly helped by two teachers who had arranged the contacts in the primary schools, as well as by two resistance leaders in Bergen (a tax official and an engineer) who had developed an organisation covering West and South Norway. The work of finding main contacts in the different districts and instructing them was assisted by Conrad Bonnevie-Svendsen,* a clergyman whose regular work was among the deaf; he had good facilities for travel, which he used for the benefit of resistance activities of a secular as well as a religious nature. The network of contacts had been established in about twenty districts by February 1942, when it had its first serious test.

Malm appreciated that in the long run the use of couriers was too risky as a means of communication. A postal official named Lid, the chairman of the Postmen's Union, helped him to set up a system of forwarding, based on cover addresses and local or travelling postal functionaries, who were picked out by Lid on the strength of his sound judgment and wide knowledge of individuals. For further safety a simple code was adopted, together with the use of an invisible ink selected by Malm after scientific study of the available literature on the different methods. He found out through Lid what means the Germans employed in their postal censorship to detect secret writing, and then chose an ink which would be obliterated by the German

*Bonnevie-Svendsen (b.1898) later became a Vice-President both of the World Council of Churches and of Rotary International.

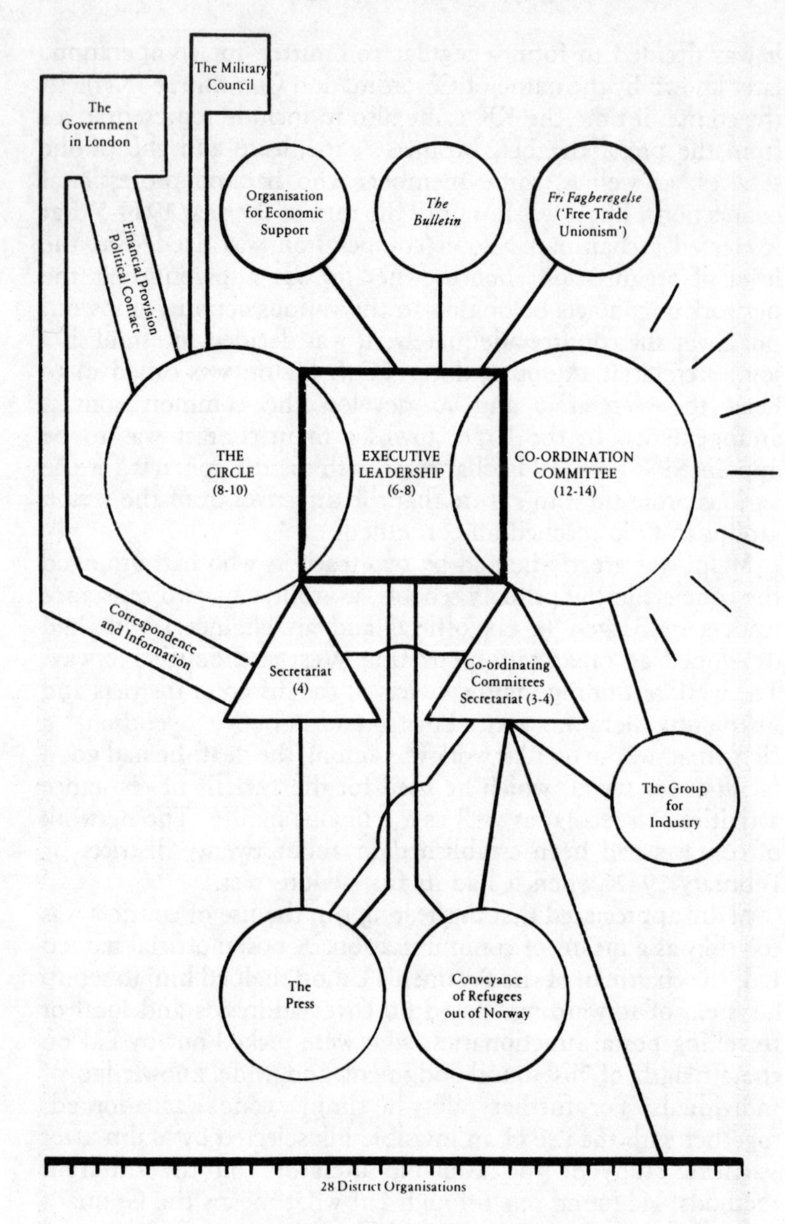

The civil leadership of the Home Front, 1942-3
(numbers of personnel involved are indicated in brackets).

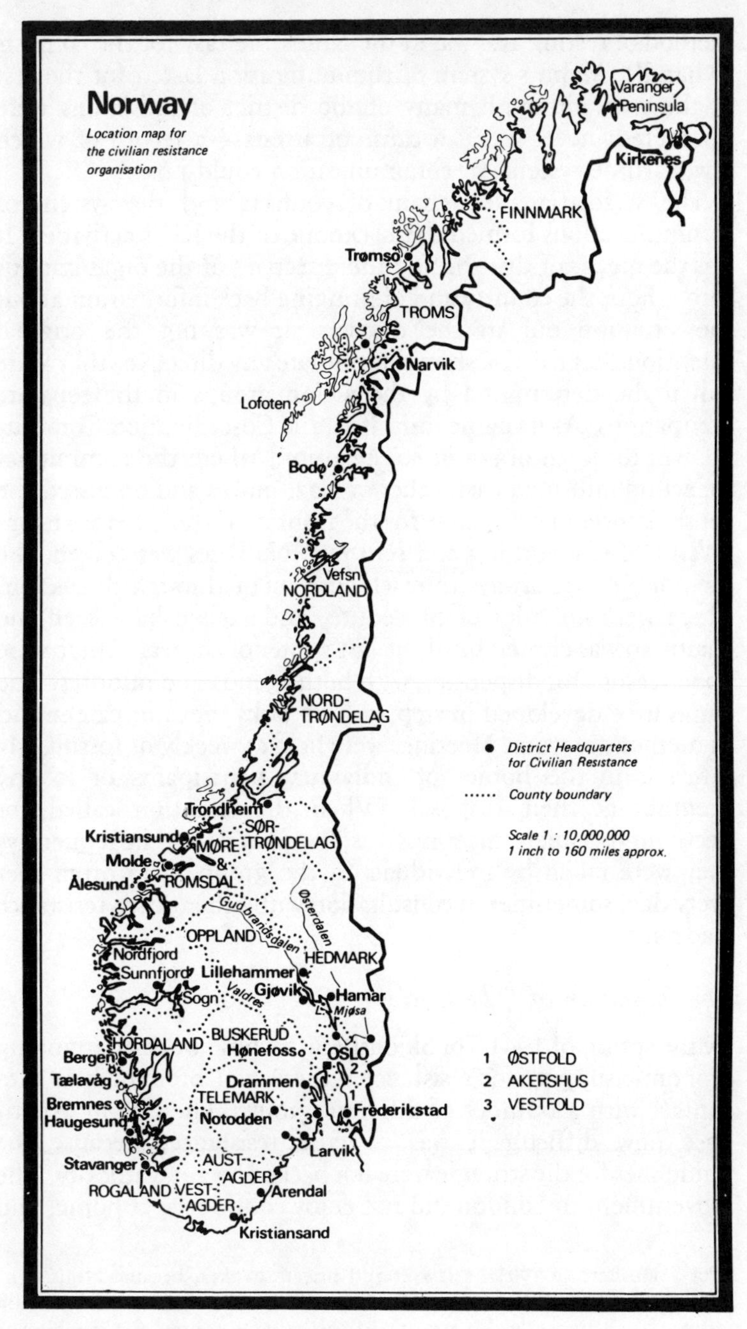

Norway: location map for the civilian resistance organisation.

method of testing and was at the same time easy for the contacts to handle. Malm's system of communication lasted for the rest of the war, although many of the district organisations were uncovered; never was it a cause of arrests — a record of which few wartime systems of communication could boast.

The secretariat, the chain of contacts and the system of communications formed the backbone of the KK's activities. It was the means of distributing the directives of the organisations throughout the country and of bringing back information about the situation out in the districts. It was not the original intention that the KK should formulate any directive; they were still to be determined by the action groups in the separate occupations. As its name indicated, the Co-ordination Committee was to be an organ of co-operation, where the committees for action informed each other of Nazi moves and discussed the consequences of a directive for the front as a whole before it was given its final wording and sent out. No votes were taken, the members trying always to reach agreement through discussion. There were no rules of procedure, and (as we have seen) no chairman was elected until the last winter of the war. There were good reasons for dispensing with both agenda and minutes. The committee developed in step with its tasks, both in extent and in methods of work. Meetings were held at weekly or fortnightly intervals in the homes of individual participants or in any premises at their disposal. When the situation called for decisions between meetings, as happened not infrequently, they were taken by individuals in the group, who often met every day, sometimes in consultation with other active resistance leaders.

The formation of 'The Circle'

By the spring of 1941 Tor Skjönsberg,* whose work of arranging economic support for resistance activity had brought him into contact with a number of different groups, knew from experience how difficult it was to raise resistance, because the guidelines for the struggle were not backed by any authority. The Government in London did not enjoy confidence at home, and

*Tor Skjönsberg (b.1903), a lawyer and private banker, became Minister of Shipping in the Government of 1945; the recollections of this highly influential resistance leader are one of the primary sources for the present book.

the Nazi powers tried deliberately to make use of this to sow discord between the lawful powers and the Norwegian people. Skjönsberg considered that this could be rectified by sending three persons from resistance circles over to London to take posts in the Government, which should include the Ministries of Defence and Justice; they would furnish the resistance campaign with a 'war cabinet' inside the Government. At that time, radio sets were still an important means of communication between the Government in London and the people at home, and there was a widespread feeling that the war would not last long. Skjönsberg had found sympathy for his ideas among the leaders of the military resistance movement, and he put them to his friend and neighbour, Consul Hans Halvorsen,* who had good connections in political and other authoritative circles and who offered to call a meeting to discuss the plan.

Skjönsberg's association with a lawyer named Thommessen over the financing of the Home Front had brought him into touch with Frihagen, the member of the Government who acted as its link with the resistance organisations in Norway at the Legation in Stockholm. He got Thommessen, when on a lawful business trip to Stockholm in May-June 1941, to present Frihagen with the idea of representation for the Home Front, and the latter forwarded the application to the Prime Minister on 23 June.

Three days before this, the Consul had collected a number of influential people at his home — those who had stood out most firmly against German pressure in the time of the Administrative Council: Gunnar Jahn, Paal Berg and Didrik A. Seip; resistance leaders from the Labour movement, including Einar Gerhardsen, and from the Conservative camp, such as C.P. Wright; Skjönsberg himself, and Öystein Thommessen. Apart from Gerhardsen, who made the reservation that he must lay the result of the discussions before his party associates, they all attended as individuals. Skjönsberg did not then raise his proposal for a 'war cabinet', previous feelers having shown that it would not be accepted, but urged the need for a more effective leadership of the Home Front and better contact with the lawful Government. The latter would best be achieved by someone from home being admitted to the Cabinet in London.

*Hans Halvorsen (1879-1974), a leading Oslo businessman and honorary consul for Portugal.

The meeting agreed to this part of Skjönsberg's proposal, but whereas he had thought of Jahn or Berg to represent the Home Front, neither of them was willing, so the meeting finally agreed to suggest to the Government that Paul Hartmann* should be sent. It was also agreed to request the Government to change the Minister of Defence, and Skjönsberg was asked to forward the proposals of the meeting through the representatives of the Cabinet at the Stockholm Legation, which he did on a further journey in the middle of July. He wrote a letter to the Prime Minister, of which he kept no copy for security reasons because of the names contained in it — an important letter which cannot be traced in the official Norwegian archives from the war period in London. Fourteen days later, a verbal reply from the Government said that 'the person concerned was welcome to London'. Before Hartmann's departure to London at the end of August, a further meeting was held, which was also attended by Schjelderup.

These meetings did not lead at the time to any formalising of the group, and no further meeting was held until the early summer of 1942; their significance lay in the establishment of contact between resistance people of different political complexions, including some who wielded considerable authority in the Norwegian community at that time. The Circle — to employ the name which came gradually into use among its members — regarded it as a main task to get rid of misunderstandings and disagreements between the fronts at home and abroad, and to obtain a united backing at home for the Government in London and its line of action. Another main task was to arrange for confident co-operation among the different shades of political belief inside the Home Front. Shortly after the meeting of August 1941, four of the participants were arrested during the State of Emergency, and a fifth had to escape; but the others remained in contact. Schjelderup and Skjönsberg were among several who threw themselves into the daily struggle. Schjelderup was continually called upon for advice in connection with the entire spectrum of conflicts in the professions and over the call to stand fast, and was the driving force on the Home Front for the first half of the war. Skjönsberg was the strategist for

*P.E.W. Hartmann (1878-1974) was finance officer in the Oslo City Council. In September 1941 he became Minister of Finance in the London Government.

organisation and had innumerable contacts. Both men attended the Co-ordination Committee and came to act as a link between the two groupings. This fact, together with their firm and well-defined attitudes, caused them to be regarded more and more as the central leaders of the civil resistance in the years that followed.

In the shadow of the State of Emergency

The autumn of 1941 was a grim time. Our eyes were turned to the east, where Hitler's armies were driving far into the Soviet Union: would the Russians manage to stem their advance? The event was to show that Hitler, like Napoleon, lost the battle against the combined forces of nature and a courageous people; but for us here at home the outlook seemed black at that period, even if the great victories announced by Hitler failed to materialise. In December came Japan's entry into the war on the side of the Axis powers, with the successful lightning attack on Pearl Harbor, the main base of the American Pacific Fleet. Our first reaction was relief that the mighty U.S.A. was now engaged actively on our side. But the Allies suffered one defeat after another, there were successive sinkings of American and British battleships and aircraft carriers, the communiqués reported Japanese victories and conquests by land, sea and air. Soon the Japanese were masters of the entire Far East, including China, South-East Asia and Indonesia (then the Netherlands East Indies), and were approaching Australia and New Zealand. These must have been hard tidings for the British, the Americans and the other Allies; for us inside occupied Europe each defeat was another cut of the whip.

The British, supported by Norwegian troops based in England, had undertaken landing operations in the Lofoten Islands and in West Norway,* and there were persistent rumours of an Allied invasion of our country. Fearing a war on two fronts above all else, the Germans struck heavily and mercilessly against all who were suspected of rendering assistance to the Allies. In the middle of September the commander-in-chief of the *Wehrmacht*, General Keitel, issued directions on Hitler's order for the use of the most drastic methods, such as

*For the raids on Svolvær (4 March 1941) and Maloy (27 December 1941), see C. Buckley, *Norway, The Commandos, Dieppe* (London 1951).

shooting of hostages, to deter the oppressed peoples from resisting the German occupation forces; capital punishment for fifty to a hundred 'Communists' was suggested as a suitable reprisal for every German soldier killed. Whereas in other parts of Europe it was the military commandants who brought the new forms of terror into force, in Norway it was Reichskommissar Terboven who took action. The state of emergency in Oslo was followed by death sentences passed on resistance groups all over the country, especially the intelligence groups in the coastal towns. Almost every number of the *Bulletin* that autumn had lists of the names of Norwegians who had received these sentences.

The full weight of this terror fell upon those engaged in military intelligence and those who helped British agents or were otherwise involved with the Allies. But the death sentences passed during the State of Emergency were a plain warning to all who resisted the master race. To know how far actions could be carried without provoking reactions which were such as to frighten those who had to bear the brunt of them into passivity or compliance, was an increasingly difficult problem for the resistance leaders.

The autumn term at Oslo university opened at the usual time, though there was tension due to the threats from those in power to dismiss a professor and other university teachers who had signed the protest of the forty-three organisations. During the Emergency a little more than a week later, the Rector and three professors whose sympathies were obviously anti-NS were removed, and the University received a NS leadership. In mid-November the Acting-Minister for Church and Education announced that the students' special committee was no longer to be elected, and a new committee was nominated by the Department. A strike broke out spontaneously among the students, but was stopped after an appeal from the students' former joint committee and from other quarters, in the belief that it would do no more harm than good.

Secret committees of action were now formed among both the teachers and the students of the University, but it took time for them to be developed and given authority. Anxious discussion continued among the students, some of whom — including their action committee — wanted the University to be boycotted by students from the end of the autumn term, while others disagreed with this, as did some of the professors. There was a sound resistance environment among the science students, but many of the active ones, especially those engaged in military intelligence, considered that it would be unfortunate for their activity if the University were closed.

Among the resistance leaders to whom the strike proposal was referred, Schjelderup was in favour of it, and Jahn and Berggrav were against. The action committee also referred the question to some members of the R-group, whom they believed to represent the Home Front leadership; at a meeting attended in addition by the Labour representatives in the group (who were against a strike), the recommendation was that the action should be cancelled, which was what happened.

It was at about the same time that the Co-ordination Committee began to function, in connection with a NS plan for compulsory membership of the professional organisations. The KK did not go in for a strike against paying dues or a new protest against the demand for membership, since this was said to result automatically from professional activity, but contented itself with a directive not to take on posts of responsibility in the organisations and to promise financial support to those who got into trouble. But it was soon to steer a different course. There can scarcely be any doubt that the cautious and hesitant attitude which found expression here and in the matter of the University was connected with the feeling which prevailed among the masses under the pressure of the mounting German terror. It also reflected the lack of a clear leadership in the Home Front at that juncture, when the R-group was greatly weakened and the Co-ordination Committee had not yet found its feet.

3
THE STRUGGLE TO STAND FAST, 1942

At the start of 1942, NS propaganda indicated that big things would shortly happen on the constitutional level: power would be taken over by the Party. Quisling's cherished dream of a State Assembly was in the air, and with it the risk of a peace agreement and the calling-up of our young men to fight on the German side 'in the struggle against Bolshevism'. The so-called 'Act of State' took place on 1 February at Akershus Castle in Oslo, when great fanfares of propagandà accompanied Terboven's appointment of Quisling as 'Minister President' and head of 'the national government'. Although the Reichskommissar certainly did not resign any significant element of his power, it was evident that Quisling had received a fresh chance to convince his German masters of his ability to rule the country. His speech that day put forward the 'authoritarian form of rule' and the creation of a Corporative State through a 'State Assembly' (*Riksting*), intended to provide a Chamber of Corporations on the lines of Fascist Italy.*

He played his first card a few days later, when a law dated 5 February set up a teachers' union with compulsory membership, to which Orvar Sæther, the chief of the *Hird*, was appointed as 'National Leader'. Two days before this, another law had made 'national youth service' obligatory: service in the NS Youth Company was required of all between nine and eighteen years of age. The connection between youth service and the new teachers' union was amplified by the National Leader at a press conference. His speech left no room for doubt: Norwegian children's education and upbringing was henceforth to indoctrinate them in the tenets of Nazism. In Germany this had succeeded to a horrifying extent, creating a new type of human

*Quisling had toyed with this idea since 1930. His enthusiasm for 'the struggle against Bolshevism' was also of long standing: cf. his book *Russia and Ourselves* (English translation, London 1931).

being, with the mentality of an Aryan master race, racial hatred, worship of the Leader and the duty of acting as an informer as its principal elements. If the NS was able to put through its demands and could be given a few years, the minds of Norwegian children might be gravely damaged.

With the teachers' leaders at its head, the Home Front went immediately to work with discussions and counter-preparations. The Church and the teachers at the University reacted at once, while the Co-ordination Committee started discussions and prepared its secretariat and communications apparatus for a major effort. The teachers were also well prepared intellectually, having conducted an almost continuous campaign on both a local and a central basis since the autumn of 1940. In 1941 the leading man in the action committee for the secondary schools, Einar Höigård, travelled the country, hammering in 'the four cardinal points': 1. reject demands for membership of, or delcarations of loyalty to, the NS; 2. reject every attempt at NS propaganda in the school; 3. reject every order from unauthorised sources; 4. reject every demand for participation in the NS Youth Company.

The discussions which took place now, and in which teachers from outside Oslo joined, were chiefly concerned with the advisability of basing the protest upon the decision that the teachers were members of the Union in virtue of their function as educators. In the secondary schools there was immediate agreement to go into action, but in the primary schools some thought that the time was not yet ripe. But when it was proposed to wait until the NS took some definite step, Kåre Norum and A. Okkenhaug — the primary school representatives in the KK — urged that immediate counter-actions were needed, especially in view of the struggle against the State Assembly, which it was rumoured would be brought into being by the NS on 1 May. The majority having sided with these two, the question remaining was how the directive should be phrased. It was agreed that individual protests from the teaching profession were the only proper thing, but should they be made against the Union or the Youth Service or both? The teachers' leaders were constantly in touch with the KK, the Circle and the Church leadership, while Schjelderup, as a main figure in the first two groups, threw himself into the discussion with his customary enthusiasm. A further asset was the work done by one of the office staff in the former Teachers'

Association, who stayed on for some weeks under the new NS management in order to keep its opponents informed of every move.

In the end the directive was hammered out at two meetings of the action committees on 11 and 12 February. It read as follows:

I find myself unable to take part in the bringing up of Norwegian youth according to the line prescribed for youth service in the NS Youth Company, as this conflicts with my conscience. As membership of the Teachers' Union, according to the statement of the National Leader among other things, lays upon me the duty of such an upbringing, and furthermore other demands are raised which conflict with my terms of appointment, I am obliged to inform you that I cannot regard myself as a member of the Teachers' Union.

Norum took the KK's directive to Malm, who immediately had it copied and distributed over the national network, the action being kept secret for a week so that the directive might be widely diffused. From 20 February onwards thousands of letters of protest poured in to the Department, and it was soon clear that the overwhelming majority of Norwegian teachers had protested.

In the meanwhile strong support had come from the Church. On the 14th, the bishops protested sharply against the law on youth service, which they called an unheard-of intrusion upon the rights of parents. Another strong letter of protest was sent by professors and other teachers at the University, while the bishops were at once supported by the big religious organisations. Thus a new popular action was brought into being against the NS, which was soon to be still more widely extended. Schjelderup co-operated with a group of leaders in the rural youth movement (*Noregs Ungdomslag*) in arranging for resignations after the elected board was removed and a NS 'leader' put in its place. Then at the beginning of March an action by parents was organised in the Oslo area to support the teachers; this was at first viewed with scepticism by the KK, which feared that the backing would be inadequate but later endorsed it to the full. A new flood of protesting letters, from between 100,000 and 200,000 parents, crammed the letter boxes of the Department. A storm passed over the country.

Quisling tried first to coerce the teachers into recalling the protests. The time-limit was 1 March, after which they would be regarded as dismissed and deprived of their salaries; at the same time they were threatened with forced labour. When this did not help, the authorities secured a breathing-space at the end of February by announcing a 'fuel famine holiday' and closing the schools for a month. Then the Germans were brought in, and from 20 March onwards more than 1,100 teachers—one in every ten—were arrested and placed in concentration camps, where they were harassed and pressed once more to recall the protest. Only a few gave in; in some individual cases the situation was almost unendurable, as a number were widowers or had sick wives and were responsible for small children. The following is a picture from the prison camp where the teachers from South and West Norway were collected, as given by Norum at a meeting after the war:

They were all paraded outside the barracks occupied by the Germans in charge of the camp. The first man to be called in to sign the statement of apology was a sickly, rather elderly teacher, who had sole responsibility for a flock of children. The others had let him know that there would be no reproaches if he signed. He dragged himself up the steps in an obvious state of collapse, which was painful to watch. Two or three minutes passed, and then he came out on to the platform at the top of the steps a completely new man. Standing in front of all 600 men, he clenched his fists and shouted: 'I bloody well didn't sign!' Then he went back to his place, and after that it was not easy for any one else to give way.

From the very outset of the conflict the teachers' leaders had emphasised that the action was not to have the character of a strike; this might provoke the Germans too much, the main consideration being to protect the children as long as possible against NS influences. The NS authorities were to shoulder the entire responsibility for the chaos created by their political demands upon the teachers. But the teachers who were still at large now faced a new situation, and some of them were opposed to the idea of going back to school as long as their colleagues were in prison. In anticipation of his own arrest, Norum had told Okkenhaug that they must stick to 'the line of legality', as he called the no-strike directive, passing him at the same time a list of people he could contact in the primary schools in case Norum himself was put out of action. But among the victims of the mass arrests were Norum and those of his fellow-workers who were on the list; therefore Okkenhaug had to send out a directive in conformity with 'the line of legality' without contacting other people in the primary schools. The directive was heavily criticised at several meetings of primary school teachers in Oslo, many of whom considered that it was now the right thing for them to strike in solidarity with their colleagues under arrest. This view was also supported in other influential quarters among resisters; but the deputy leader refused to alter the directive, which had had continuous support from the action committee of the secondary schools and also that of the Co-ordination Committee.

When the 'fuel famine holiday' was brought to an end and the schools reopened, the teachers turned up and went on with their lessons as usual, after reading out a declaration in which they repeated that they were not members of the Teachers' Union and that they would not teach anything that conflicted with their consciences.

Five hundred of the arrested teachers, whom the Germans had tried in vain to cow into submission at the camp, were sent in cattle trucks to Trondheim and packed down in the holds of an old coastal steamer, the *Skjærstad*. After a fearful journey northwards, constantly exposed to German maltreatment and the risk of Allied torpedoes, they were landed at Kirkenes, and set to work loading and unloading and doing other heavy work on a starvation diet. Inside the barbed-wire fences the majority were huddled into a cold, leaky stable with an earthen floor; later, 150 more teachers arrived from the south, who in the course of the summer were quartered in cardboard tents. Tröndelag was the only area in which the opposition of the teachers collapsed: 200 of them, interned in a prison camp, had been subjected to intolerable pressure and threats — and in addition were misinformed about the situation in other districts — so that at the end of April they agreed to sign a declaration, which the Nazi authorities required of them before they could be freed.

A couple of reports, written in telegram style and with secret ink, were smuggled out by Norum during the voyage in the *Skjærstad* and the stay in Kirkenes, and on their arrival in Oslo made an enormous impression. They were at once forwarded by courier to the Legation in Stockholm, where they did much to open Swedish eyes, and those of the world in general, to what was going on in Norway.

The Church had gone into action at the same time as the teachers. The NS people had forcibly prevented the Dean from celebrating High Mass in Trondheim Cathedral, in order to celebrate instead the 'Act of State' of 1 February with the assistance of a NS priest. When the Dean postponed his Mass to the afternoon, the police prevented the assembled crowds from entering the Cathedral, which led to inspiring religious and patriotic demonstrations outside. The Dean was later interrogated by the State Police; on the 19th he was 'removed from office' by the NS authorities; and on the 24th Skancke, the Minister for Church Affairs, received notice in writing that the bishops would no longer have any dealings with his Department. This became known just as the teachers' big action of protest was beginning, and gave the school people powerful support. The NS authorities first tried to 'suspend' the bishops and induce the deans of their sees to take over their official duties — which they refused to do. A contemporary report from Oslow relates:

'The letter of 24 February to the Department was at the same time sent out by the bishops to the congregations in the form of a pastoral letter, that to the Department being given a separate introduction. On 1 March the pastoral letter was read out in every church in which it had been received. The clergy of the parish stood in the chancel doorway fully robed, and in addition to the pastoral letter the incumbent read out a declaration that each individual priest still regarded the named bishop as his rightful bishop and spiritual father. Furthermore, a declaration from the congregational council, fully supporting the standpoint of the bishops and clergy, was read out in those places where the council had managed to handle the matter. All over the country the churches were full to overflowing, and those present felt that they were witnessing a unique event. Older people compared the day with 17 May 1905.* In many places there was great emotion, and people wept openly.'

Quisling put the bishops under police observation and raged with voice and pen against Bishop Berggrav, whom he regarded with some reason as an arch-enemy of the NS. A dozen clergymen were removed from office, but it made no difference. On Easter Day, 5 April 1942, the clergy read from the pulpits the mighty confession of faith, 'The Church's One Foundation', in which it took its stand in defence of the persecuted teachers:

If any person — in such a matter that the law cannot be invoked — is harassed and persecuted for the sake of his convictions, then the

*In 1905 Constitution Day was celebrated with special fervour in anticipation of the final breach with Sweden, which came three weeks later.

Church as guardian of conscience must stand beside the persecuted ...
So long as the conditions named continue and are carried further by new encroachments, the Church must act according to its duty on the Word of God and its confession of faith, accepting whatever may be the consequences ...

In the days which followed, the clergy gave declarations in writing to the Department that they relinquished their offices, but that they would continue their pastoral functions in their parishes. The breach between the NS state and the Church was complete.

Quisling replied with an express telegram to each individual priest, in which he compared the relinquishment of office with an act of insurrection which would be visited with the most severe penalties of the law, unless the decision was changed. Only about fifty of the 850 clergy in the country took fright, all the others standing fast in spite of the arrests of bishops and priests which were already taking place. Bishop Berggrav and four of his fellow-workers in the Joint Christian Council, who had helped him to produce 'The Church's One Foundation', were among those taken, and a number of clergy were 'removed from office'.

A leaflet of March 1942 points out the contributions which the people of the Church and the schools made to the strengthening of morale on the Home Front during these hectic months:

In the course of the last week of February the teachers have accomplished a deed which shall never be forgotten. It is not only themselves and their own independence that they have defended. They have struck a blow for the children, for our homes, for our country. And they have roused us all to a new spirit and a new courage for the fray.

One consequence of the struggle was a marked solidarity among the teachers. They voluntarily set aside 2 and later 5 per cent of their salaries for a common fund, and about 1 April 1942 they established a common leadership for both levels of education. Their organisation became the strongest and best planned among those of the various professions, and it was also one of the strongest elements in the district set-up of the Co-ordination Committee.

When the news of the struggle reached Sweden, Britain and the United States, it gave Norway a special place among the

Allies. The outside world had not rated us very highly after what had been reported in the foreign press about German troops marching into the stunned Norwegian capital on 9 April 1940;* and in the first half of 1942 Germany and Japan were at the zenith of their military power, so that the liberation of the oppressed peoples seemed very remote. That it was possible at that juncture to inflict such a complete ideological defeat upon Nazism in occupied Norway shows what strength can lie hidden in a democratic people with a national and Christian culture as its base.

Fourteen days after the Teachers' Union's proclamation, a law was made setting up a new organisation for the legal profession. This was opposed by the action committee of the Lawyers' Association. Schjelderup wrote a powerful appeal, but out of about thirty representatives who attended the first meeting on the subject, only a few supported the committee's proposal for a directive rejecting membership. However, a second meeting at the beginning of March showed that the teachers' example had proved infectious: a directive for sending individual protests against membership was fully accepted, and in the course of the next few weeks 90 per cent of the Association sent a letter declining membership of the new NS organisation. Quisling was equally unsuccessful with the ship-owners, who at the end of April protested *en masse* against compulsory membership of a new organisation for their profession.

Collapse of Quisling's proposal for a 'State Assembly'

As May day approached, there were a good many rumours that Quisling would announce his State Assembly then; but the opposition had been too strong, and the rumours gradually died away. However, there were strong indications that a Union of Labour, composed of the main organisations in industrial life, would be proclaimed on the day which celebrates the fellowship of workers. But the ceremony was cancelled at the last moment, presumably because the occupying power was afraid that the great social unrest created by the NS actions against the schools

*Leland Stowe of the *Chicago Daily News* sent highly coloured reports from Oslo regarding the passivity of the ordinary people in the streets, which were published in newspapers and magazines in both America and Britain.

and the Church might spread to the workers. Three weeks later Quisling's indignation at the turn of events was shown in an outburst at a secondary school near Oslo, when he said: 'It is you teachers who are to blame for the fact that we have not got any State Assembly.'

This was the period in which the construction of 'Fortress Norway' (*Festung Norwegen*) was in full swing, urged on by Hitler's fear of a Second Front in Norway. Although the flow of people who sought work more or less voluntarily at German building sites was unfortunately all too great, the occupying power needed a bigger labour force. As early as the summer of 1941 there had been an ordinance from the Department of Social Affairs concerning the conscription of labour for work which the Department 'finds important or essential'. The LO leadership was then engaged in the decisive round of the struggle to save the remains of trade union independence, so it paid no attention to this move. In May-June 1942, the Directorate of Labour Exchanges put out a circular calling for 15,000 men, preferably between the ages of eighteen and forty-five and without dependants, to be taken from among office and hotel workers and other groups engaged in activities which had no great importance for the Germans.

There was much bitterness in the LO over the compulsory recruitment, and its illicit leaders sent out an appeal at the end of July to refuse to go. But the appeal was signed by 'the Free Trade Union Movement', which was an unknown term; *Fri Fagbevegelse* opposed the appeal, and there was much confusion about the directive, which received little support. The illegal trade union committee (the FU) had been reorganised after the disaster in late January 1942, when a representative of the Communists was among those brought in. At Easter, Halvdan Jönsson became the new leader, and although he brought fresh strength to the organisation, it took time to restart the machinery. The intention of the NS to establish a Union of Labour was reported in March, but the proposal had been put in cold storage by the time that the FU sent out directions for opposing it; the latter included a boycott, the refusal of posts of responsibility, and a strike against the subscription. The other organisations which were intended to be members of the Union of Labour — the Employers' Association and the Federation of Handicraft Workers — took no action against the proposed Union at this time.

In May people both from the KK and from the Circle held meetings with representatives of the FU to induce them to arrange resignations of the same sort as the teachers'. This did not succeed at that stage, but the meetings resulted in Jönsson's becoming a member of the KK, and a little later of the Circle as well. The latter body met several times in June, after the Government in London had sent an inquiry about points of view on foreign policy questions, and it later functioned as a formal group. On the Labour side it was joined by Halvard Lange and Jönsson,* and by a young law student, Jens Boyesen, who with three other students had taken over and effectively organised an 'information bureau', sending regular news and reports to the Government through the press office of the Stockholm Legation. This bureau also took on the practical work for the Circle, particularly the transmission of correspondence with the Government in London.

Schjelderup's ardour and indomitable will to resist had made him the central figure in the 'Standfast' struggle. His advice was often asked by individuals and groups in the battle-line, but he was not satisfied with that role — he hurled himself into every sector where he thought he could do anything, particularly the task of strengthening the national morale. He undertook journeys — often on foot — to look up people whom he knew of through his co-operation with active resistance members in the rural youth movement. During the teachers' conflict he often attended the Co-ordination Committee, and he was one of three people who arranged for mutual contact between the KK and the Circle, even before the latter was formalised. As the telephone and post were censored, one of the enthusiasts in KK, the lawyer E.T. Poulsson, put his office in central Oslo at the disposal of the KK as a daily meeting-place for those of the committee's members who felt the need for frequent contact. The most active people in the Circle also found their way there, as did other outstanding figures in the civil resistance movement.

In July, the KK got wind of the NS plan of campaign for organising the Union of Labour, and deemed it necessary to strengthen its contacts with business organisations. It brought

*Halvard M. Lange (1902-70) as Foreign Minister after the war was largely responsible for the negotiation of Norway's entry into NATO; Halfdan Jönsson (1891-1945) died in Dachau concentration camp.

in a director to represent industry and established a special committee for the business world, consisting of two of its own members together with representatives of the shipowners, banking and insurance, industry, handicrafts, and commerce. Schjelderup composed a useful paper against the plans for the Union, which was printed and camouflaged by the title, 'Protect your valuables against fire!' He also produced new campaign papers for the farmers and the fishermen. But the illegal leadership of the LO remained so cautious that the KK expressed its impatience in a report to the Government.

At the end of August, the Home Front's spies inside the central administration picked up a letter from the Department for Home Affairs, saying that the State Assembly was, if possible, to be organised and summoned for 25 September 1942. The Assembly was to be built upon 'legalised occupational guilds' in cultural and economic life, provided that the main industrial groups were organised in the immediate future. The resistance leaders made complete preparations for the decisive battle. The KK mobilised its secretariat and special committee, and this time the counter-thrust was both quick and far-reaching. On 7 September directives went out from the action committees to the members of the Federation of Industries and the Federation of Insurance Societies, and soon afterwards to the other business organisations, and by the 20th they had all stated that adoption of the plans for a State Assembly would entail for them resignations from the associations and withdrawal from positions of trust. The FU followed with a broadly based action for resignations and refusal of subscriptions in the trade union organisation, which was a protest against both the State Assembly plans and the indifference of the acting-representatives to the demand for wage allowances to meet the rise in prices. By 22 September about 100,000 trade unionists had sent individual letters of resignation, although about one in five got no further than the branch officials.

The NS had again been rejected in a 'plebiscite', and once more the Germans were obliged to intervene to get the Party out of a fix. On 22 September spokesmen for both the employees and the employers were called in and informed that specific leading persons, who had already been arrested by the Gestapo, would be shot at stated times unless the resignations were withdrawn. With what had been experienced in the State of Emergency of the autumn of 1941 fresh in the memory, the action committees found it right to recommend withdrawal. This was done on about the 25th, which was the day when the State Assembly should have met; but the NS had made it clear on about the 20th that the Assembly was not going to be summoned, so the action had achieved its object.

Quisling's attempt to form a Corporative State as the basis for a national government had been made bankrupt for all to see. The Germans had again been obliged to intervene to prevent chaos in the labour force and get the 'ruling' Party out of trouble. The danger of a peace agreement and the consequent mobilisation of Norwegian troops on the German side was over for a long time to come. The Standfast struggle had brought success, and in its course the illicit organisations had been developed and co-ordinated, and the basis had been laid for a common leadership.

But the course of events also showed what delicate tactical problems were raised by the struggle, making it abundantly clear to the leaders that it was vital to avoid the involvement of the Germans and counter-action on their part by methods of terror, before the membership of the organisations had a chance to follow the directives. The leadership therefore strongly opposed an offer on the part of the Communists — perhaps made through contacts in Milorg* — for a sabotage action. It was seriously meant, as was demonstrated by a well-aimed action against the office of the Gestapo-modelled State Police† in central Oslo at the end of August. The Circle sent an urgent request to the Government in London for a warning against acts of violence, and on 6 September Nygaardsvold firmly dissociated himself from such acts in a talk on the BBC. Schjelderup and Boyesen tried to induce the illicit leadership of the LO to concentrate the action upon the NS's attempt to misuse the organisations for its State Assembly plans, and not to bring in the lack of wage compensation, as the Germans might regard this as being contrary to the ordinances made under the State of Emergency in the previous autumn. In his opinion it was the wage demand and the advice to withhold subscriptions which precipitated the German counter-measures. The struggle also

*From *Militærorganisasjonen* ('military organisations'). Milorg's early history is related in the next chapter.

†This political police force was established under Jonas Lie, Norway's commissarial (and first) Minister of Police, in the summer of 1941.

revealed certain weaknesses in the FU's organisation and tactics — in particular, how unfortunate it was that the Communists had not been informed immediately of the plans for action. The struggle cost the FU dear, most of its members having afterwards to retire to Sweden.

The Standfast struggle of 1942 ebbed out with the State Assembly action in September and the return of the teachers from Kirkenes in November. On the advice of the resistance leadership in Oslo, the teachers had accepted the German terms of release so as not to risk many of them dying in the forthcoming Arctic winter. The NS authorities had already been obliged to retreat on the school front, and the plans for a State Assembly were crushed. The struggle on the coast in the far north could therefore be called off without jeopardising the continuance of the campaign.

The year was to end with the greatest blot on the entire history of Norway, namely the action of the Gestapo against the Norwegian Jews, who came to share the fate of their fellows on the continent through the march they now began to annihilation in the gas chambers. The Home Front did what it could to help: the 'export' organisations used their capacity to the full — on the route from Oslo to Sweden it normally amounted to 50-60 persons per week — and new groups of 'exporters' were formed, made up of people who could not sit inactive and watch the violence done to these innocent victims. About 1,100 Norwegian and foreign Jews were taken to safety in Sweden, but of the 780 who were arrested, only twenty-four returned to Norway alive. In their work for the Jews many people, including some of the leaders, had to ignore the normal safety precautions, so a number of the helpers were taken by the Gestapo, and three of the most active members of the KK, Malm included, only narrowly escaped them at the end of November. It was then decided that Norum should take over the secretariat as soon as he returned from Kirkenes; the temporary replacement was a clergyman. The Co-ordination Committee acquired a new representative for the medical profession and one for agriculture. A year earlier the technical side of the secretarial work had been strengthened by two new recruits, one of whom was a girl, Sigrid Steinnes.

4

PREPARATIONS FOR MILITARY RESISTANCE, 1940-1942

In spite of the outright military defeat which Norway had suffered in the spring of 1940, there was a burning desire among many people, above all the young, to share in the liberation of the country from the German occupation forces. But we knew very well from experience how superior the German troops were both in military technique and in armament, even in the first days of the invasion when they had been in a weak position. Later they had employed much bigger forces to secure every centre of communications and population, and had undertaken a large-scale development of airfields, fortifications and harbours. It was therefore obvious to everybody by then that liberation could only take place in co-operation with Britain, the only one of Germany's opponents still fighting; and in 1940 its people had more than enough on their hands building up their own defences against the invasion of which the German soldiers were continually singing in our roads and streets: *'Wir fahren gegen England.'*

In this situation there were really two tasks of a military nature which could be engaged in here at home. One was *intelligence service*, for keeping our allies informed of the strength and movements of German troops, aircraft and naval forces, and of the construction of fortifications and other military installations. The second was *getting ready*, by collecting weapons and other equipment and by the formation and training of fighting groups, which could come into action when a British invasion was in progress. One or the other of these tasks was preferred according to the significance and possibilities of each particular place, but they often went on together.

Sabotage or guerrilla activities were not contemplated by anyone at this period, except in connection with an invasion. In the autumn of 1940 I joined eight or ten good friends in starting the first Milorg-squad in my home neighbourhood. We were active sportsmen, with experience from the Scout movement and life in the woods. Several of us had taken part in the fighting in the spring, and both then and later there was no lack of courage and enterprise. But in that first part of the occupation we could not see our way to doing much more in the military sphere than keeping fit and conducting some cautious field-training with a view to employing the few weapons and other resources that we had in the forest. We obeyed General Ruge's appeal after the capitulation in North Norway: wait, trust and be prepared! Hundreds of similar groups were doing the same, operating in the same night-hours in different parts of the country and mostly independently of one another. They were collections of friends from sports and shooting teams, voluntary defence organisations, and groups from Scouting or other youth movements. They would have liked professional officers as their leaders. The objectives for a Milorg group in Telemark in the summer of 1940 were valid for the others too: keep up the defence-mindedness among the young and give them training and experience — do not start a hopeless fight against the Germans — but back up any invasion and check encroachments by the NS.

Those who did not find this enough, and who were on fire to perform active war service as soon as possible, crossed the sea to the west or circled the world to the east, and joined the Norwegian or British forces in the United Kingdom. It was especially in the western coastal districts that it at once became an important task for the resistance groups to help these young people to find their way out; fully 3,500 men crossed the North Sea and about 500 went the other way in the first two years of the war.

The next stage of development was the co-ordination of the scattered military resistance groups in larger formations. Individually they could accomplish little, and especially where invasion was concerned, co-ordinated effort was essential. It usually fell to former professional or reserve* officers to be the initiators in this, even if civilians often did the organising work. According to the traditional army pattern, the intended arrangement was a separation into five areas for southern Norway, the boundaries of which largely coincided with the old divisional boundaries. North Norway also had local military groups-in-

*Under the Defence law of 1933 more than two-thirds of the cadre of officers (and sergeants) were *vernepliktige*, called up from civilian life in the event of mobilisation.

readiness in individual towns and larger valleys, but they could not be co-ordinated on a district basis, even though some of them were interconnected. The majority either died away for want of activity, or were destroyed by the Gestapo, or were absorbed into new fighting groups organised by Norwegians from England. The same thing happened to similar local groups in many places in Tröndelag and southwards along the west coast. It was only in the Bergen district and in East Norway that regional organisations developed and co-ordination was carried out on a familiar Norwegian pattern. Even there, smaller isolated groups existed for several years of the war without being co-ordinated: they were partly organised by Communists and partly such as received special tasks from SOE agents arriving from the United Kingdom or through the British military attaché's office in Stockholm.

In order to understand what happened as regards both organisation and operations, it must be appreciated that almost everywhere, but especially along the coast, the work in the military sector in the first war years was done in the expectation of an invasion in the immediate future. The driving force was the hope and belief that very soon the British would be landing. The British seaborne raids on the coast in 1941 drove expectations sky-high, and some unfortunately worded statements by senior Norwegian officers in London had the same effect. From the end of 1941 it was the assertions made to the local population by Norwegian commando troops, put ashore along the coast for various assignments, which did most to nourish the hope of invasion.

A central military organisation established

A brief outline may now be given of the development in Oslo of a central leadership for the military organisations, namely the Military Council and its executive organ or Staff (SL). Two officers who had been in close relations with Ruge during the campaign and as prisoners-of-war — Helset and Rognes — became aware after their release of the small fighting groups which were being formed. During the autumn of 1940 they discussed with individual colleagues what could be done in the given situation; they concluded that one must go to work slowly and cautiously, and that the young people should be advised to keep together in small groups or cells of from four to six men without forming any central organisation. They contacted a number of their brother-officers who were willing to guide one or more small groups, and in the course of the autumn and winter the network of officers who were disposed to help increased, often from those who took up military intelligence work. But people from the civilian occupations came to play a steadily growing part as suspicion fell on the officers, who were arrested or forced to flee. Helset was arrested in February 1941, and at about the same time Rognes and his other closest collaborator had to leave the country.

The point of view on organisation was soon modified. In the spring of 1941 it was agreed to form the Military Council ('the Council'), consisting of Lieutenant-Colonel Ole Berg, who was to lead it by remote control,* and Professor Holst, while Captain Schive headed the daily work of a group which gradually developed into a central staff (SL). In June the Council sent a letter to the King, informing him of the growth, activities and operational line of the military organisation, and expressing the desire to place a means of force at the disposal of 'an administration within the country' which had the King's approval. The Council believed in the existence of such a leadership, with which it believed itself to be in contact.

The letter caused misunderstanding in London and was much criticised, especially by British military authorities. The position was not cleared up until the autumn, when Holst and Schive had to leave the country and were able to offer further explanations and to have discussions with the Prime Minister and some members of the Cabinet. In November 1941 the Government recognised Milorg and the Council, placing the latter under the Norwegian Army Command in Britain and subsequently under the Defence Command (FO), which was reinstituted in February 1942. This was of fundamental importance for Milorg in many ways, and particularly for its further relations with the Norwegian military authorities in London. It also meant that Milorg was brought under the British Supreme Command, and later — when the United States entered the war

*Ole Berg (1890-1968) had commanded a brigade in the campaign and was therefore too conspicuous a figure to take part in the day-to-day organisation; after a period as Military Attaché in Stockholm, he was the post-war Chief of the Defence Staff. J.M. Holst (1892-1953) was a professor of surgery and head of the medical service in the campaign; J.K. Schive (1897-1969), a serving officer in 1918-30 and a cartographic expert.

— under the Allied Supreme Command, and had to follow whatever tactical directions those Commands might draw up.

The recognition of the Council by the Government did not, however, give it control over all military resistance work in Norway. Contact with the regional fighting organisations was rather poor. Moreover, British military organisations were already operating to an important extent along the coast, especially in intelligence work. Members of a Norwegian military formation called the Linge Company* had also helped SOE — the Special Operations Executive, set up by the British to bring about military resistance in German-occupied territories — to start the development of its own fighting units, which had accomplished a good deal. In the long run these stalwarts achieved great things for Norway, but they had orders to act independently both of the Norwegian authorities in London and of the central and local leadership of Milorg, which created complications, misunderstandings and dangerous situations. The Council hoped that its application to the King would result in fuller information on these activities, and preferably in some control being exercised over them. The Norwegian authorities wished the same, and early in 1942 a committee was established for co-operation between SOE and the FO. Despite this, for almost the whole of that year SOE continued to instruct the Linge groups sent back to Norway to avoid contact and co-operation with Milorg.

The summer and autumn of 1941 had brought heavy blows to the Council and its organs. First, the leadership of the intelligence work was broken up by arrests and escapes, so that thenceforth this service was managed both centrally and regionally by a special organisation, XU, though it remained formally under the Council. Then in the autumn Schive and Holst and nearly all their chief colleagues had to leave after some arrests, so that of the old group of officers, only Ole Berg himself and

*Norwegian Independent Coy. No. 1 derived its later name from its first leader, the actor Martin Linge, who was killed in the Målöy raid of December 1941. Out of 530 members, fifty-three lost their lives in a variety of exploits, including the actions against the heavy-water supply in Norway, which was potentially the most important sabotage feat of the war (see T. Gallacher, *Assault in Norway*, New York 1975). Other English references to the Company, whose gallant achievements are greatly prized by the Norwegian people, may be found in David Howarth, *The Shetland Bus* (London 1951) and *We Die Alone* (London 1955).

a couple of juniors remained. In fact, at the end of 1941 SL was obliged to suspend its activities, and in the first half of 1942 was so far reduced that contact with the regional fighting groups of Milorg was extremely poor.

Milorg activities, district by district

In *North Norway* military intelligence work always came first. Norwegians who had fled eastwards from the Varanger Peninsula at the end of the campaign of 1940 and gone into Russian service came back during the autumn of the same year, when they induced individuals or small groups to report German troops and shipping movements. After the Soviet Union entered the war, a group of seven Russians and six Norwegians was put ashore on the Varanger Peninsula, presumably as an advance party for a Russian invasion, but it was reported and eliminated within a few weeks. The intelligence work continued until 1943, when it was definitively crushed; the German reprisals were severe, the total of those executed or who lost their lives due to other causes being very large in proportion to the number of Norwegians engaged.

Military groups were to be found in the counties of Troms and Nordland, some formed mainly for intelligence purposes, others with a view to military activity when there was an invasion. These fighting groups had come into existence after a visit from Helset about the turn of the year 1940-1; they consisted of small cells which were not interconnected but were under the supervision of a younger officer in contact with the staff (SL) in Oslo. In 1941-2 an *agent provocateur* managed to knock out the groups in Harstad and Målselv; some of the other groups were likewise infiltrated, several leaders had to make their escape, and the groups lost contact with Oslo. Activity sank to a low level in the course of 1942 and did not pick up again until 1944.

In the southern half of Nordland the principal operation was in connection with parties of Norwegian commandos from the Linge Company, who arrived in fishing-smacks at the turn of 1941-2 and started preparations for an expected British invasion. They came into contact with local military groups and built up a fighting body of several hundred men. Tons of weapons, ammunitions and equipment came in by boat from Shetland and were very laboriously conveyed inland and stored in depots. The work was done in a great hurry, as the Linge people gave their local helpers the impression that the invasion was imminent, and under this heavy pressure for labour many security rules were set aside. A lot of people in the easily observable rural communities became aware of what was going on: so did the Gestapo and its efficient collaborator in Tröndelag, Henry Rinnan.* At the beginning of September, the Germans set to work and, although the Linge people and a part of their local helpers got away, were unsparing in their arrests, which in some parts of the very sparsely populated Vefsn valley included every man.

In consequence of these events, and also because of some acts of sabotage by other parties from the Linge Company both in Nordland and in *Tröndelag*, a state of emergency was declared a month later in Vefsn and Tröndelag. Twenty-four men from the Vefsn valley were shot 'for transport of weapons and assistance to saboteurs'. Ten prominent citizens, mostly from Trondheim, were executed as 'atonement for sabotage'. Every male Jew above twelve years of age was arrested, more than thirty in all, as were some seventy other persons.

Parts of the organisation remained intact and continued to function, but the Emergency had a big effect in reducing the will to resist, and it has been described as an almost irremediable blow to the resistance movement in the districts affected. The impact of the reprisals on the military staff in Oslo was so great that it sent a telegram in the middle of the month, requesting that the activities of the Linge Company should be reduced; they must not shoot, even in self-defence. It was at the same time as the parties from the Linge Company began to be active on the coast of Tröndelag that Rinnan started his infiltrations of the resistance groups. In the course of the year his cynical exploitation of the people's desire to assist the effort, cunning methods of provocation, and indubitable organising skill gave him almost complete control of the military resistance groups in Tröndelag. Military (and other) organisations under Communist leadership were likewise infiltrated by Rinnan and put out of action. Intelligence activities, directed particularly towards the German battleships in the Trondheimsfjord, were

*H.C. Rinnan was executed in 1947 for thirteen murders; he and his accomplices had instigated more than 1,000 arrests and about 100 deaths (see H.C. Adamsson and P. Klen, *Blood on the Midnight Sun*, 1964).

at a high pitch, but they too suffered heavy blows from Rinnan round the turn of the year 1942-3. He managed to place a contact inside XU, with the result that the district leader—a student at the Technical High School, a close friend of mine from childhood—jumped to his death from the Gestapo headquarters in January; only two months later, his successor was likewise arrested.

In *Möre and Romsdal* military resistance groups were organised early by a postal official from Bergen, but they were broken up or faded away after his organisation was exposed in 1941; other groups were broken up later by Rinnan. In the first years of the war most of the activity in the fishing districts of this county had to do with the traffic to Britain and with the intelligence service. A Linge party, put ashore in the autumn of 1941, formed local fighting groups with the people of the district, but these were hard hit through the exposure of the 'export' organisations at the beginning of 1942. Only a group of leaders in a remote position was able to carry the work further at a later date. Rinnan's shadow lay over Möre and Romsdal as well—it was he who eventually dealt a body-blow at the traffic with Britain from those parts. Nord- and Sunnfjord, however, possessed an organisation reckoned at 800 men in 1942; its leader had been a non-commissioned officer in the campaign of 1940, and a good many rifles and other lighter weapons had been hidden away, though with little ammunition.

In *Bergen and Hordaland*, as elsewhere along the coast, the early years were marked by intelligence work, 'export' activity and contact with couriers and commando groups from Britain. But there were also fighting groups, including those which were organised for a time by the postal official from Bergen who has already been mentioned. Soon after the end of the campaign, an army captain and the Chief Scout in Bergen began to knit together small fighting-groups in the town and environs, calculating that the war would last many years and working on strict principles of security. During 1941 this organisation was placed under the control of a major, and the total force in this part of West Norway rose to 5,000 men. Parties from the Linge Company and intelligence agents from Britain were also at work, with the little fishing port of Tælavåg, south-west of Bergen, as one of their most frequently used landing-places. Carelessness conduced to informing by local people, and at the end of April 1942 a couple of Linge men were surprised by a group of Gestapo; there was a hard fight, in which two Germans were killed and several wounded, while one of the Norwegians was killed and the other taken prisoner with severe wounds. The Gestapo afterwards burned or blew up every house and quay and destroyed all the boats; every man between sixteen and sixty-five, a total of seventy-six, was sent to concentration camps in Germany, where most of them died; and the rest of the population — 260 old men, women and children — were deported and interned. In addition, the Germans shot eighteen young men who had been arrested two months earlier in Ålesund on a vessel bound for England.

It was a further misfortune that at Tælavåg the Gestapo picked up threads which in the course of the summer resulted in heavy blows to resistance groups both in Bergen and Stavanger and in East Norway. Inter-connections had gradually been established between the West Norway organisations, with the result that Milorg in Bergen suffered damage from the discovery in June 1942 of the 'export' groups at Bremnes (near Kristiansund), which was the main centre for the traffic from West Norway to Britain. One of those who escaped to Britain at that time returned at the end of the year to renew the broken connections, when he found that the population had been intimidated by the events at Tælavåg and it was hard to discover people willing to become involved in transportation of weapons or other risky activities.

In the spring of 1943 the next blow to Milorg in Bergen was one which more or less killed all activity until the autumn. When making discoveries in Hardanger, the Germans came upon a couple of Linge men; this resulted in a big raid in Bergen, when nearly the whole of its central Milorg leadership was taken and other resistance organisations were hard hit. Some fighting groups remained intact, however, both in Bergen and outside, but they had few weapons.

As for *Rogaland* (which includes Stavanger), the introductory phase was one in which weapons were collected from the campaign areas and small groups were formed on a local basis. Otherwise military activity in the Stavanger district during the early war years was marked more strongly by intelligence work than perhaps in any other district of Norway, its traffic with Britain being bit by bit reserved for courier and other communications services connected with intelligence. The natural conditions were difficult both for this traffic and for radio transmissions, so a courier service was set up to both Bergen and Oslo. A lawyer and reserve captain, L. Lea, was the central figure, who gradually gathered most of the threads into his hands. Because of the isolated situation of Stavanger, with only two main roads leading out of the town and those easily controllable by the Germans, it was originally intended to exclude it from preparations for an eventual invasion, in which Rogaland as a whole likewise had no part. But in February 1942 Lea was requested by the central military leadership to take charge of the fighting organisation in the Stavanger district in anticipation of the first 'notified' invasion period in April. One of the steps taken was the construction with the help of telephone employees of secret lines from the coast to the hinterland.

In early May, Lea and one of his closest associates were arrested by the Gestapo through information found on the Linge soldier who had been killed at Tælavåg. Lea died in prison a few days later without the Germans finding out any more; but soon afterwards the work was disturbed by a big wave of arrests in the town, when the illegal press was discovered. Activity revived in the following autumn with the spread westwards from Kristiansand; but the Gestapo got to know what was going on and struck at the end of November, when almost the entire leadership was arrested both in Stavanger and in Haugesund and both the fighting-group organisations and the intelligence service were broken up.

The fighting groups in Rogaland numbered not more than 1,000 men at their maximum, most of them presumably in the inland and northern districts, including Haugesund. A later Milorg leader in the county says of the situation in Stavanger: 'It was not feasible to organise any army behind the Gestapo's back. What came forward in the days of the capitulation was an ill-equipped and untrained popular levy.'

On the *south coast** a considerable fighting organisation was built up in 1941 and 1942 under the leadership of Major Arne Laudal, one of the group of officers round General Ruge. He had been asked to go there by Helset after Lieutenant Odd

* *Sörlandet*, a modern name, sometimes extended to the whole of the counties of Vest- and Aust-Agder.

Starheim, who was in charge of a Linge party in the district, applied through a contact in Oslo for a professional soldier to take over the leadership of an organisation which he was forming. Starheim and some of his friends had set up a military intelligence group in the summer of 1940, and in August he and two others had gone by motor-boat to Britain, whence he returned with a transmitter in January 1941. He was going to devote himself to intelligence work, while others in his party started to build up fighting groups in the spring. Laudal had previously been in touch with such groups, formed of young sportsmen; now, in the spring, he learnt from Starheim that there would be a British invasion. The south coast also possessed a big intelligence organisation linked up with the XU organisation in Oslo, and in addition medical, pioneer and communications units. These were gradually joined up with the organisation under Laudal, which also extended its fighting groups westwards, partly by forming new units and partly by incorporating those already in existence. Laudal reckoned that in the autumn of 1942 he had a force of 3,500 men at his disposal.

Whereas the Linge parties elsewhere in Norway had orders at that time to keep away from Milorg groups, those in the south co-operated quite extensively with Laudal's organisation, especially as regards the fighting groups. There was certainly a good deal of disagreement, as Laudal put his faith in a large organisation, Starheim in the development of smaller units for guerrilla fighting or sabotage. The Milorg detachments were, nonetheless, instructed in the use of weapons from Britain supplied by air. Starheim was all the time convinced that the invasion would come, and Laudal was equally confident. A report from that period, written by one of the leaders in Arendal, runs: 'In the month of March we were told that the invasion would come at the beginning of April... April came, but no invasion... The summer went on, and at the end of July we again received a new order ... a general instruction. This included the following: "The invasion is coming. The general-in-command will publish an order of the day for the troops in a short time" ...'

Activity was gradually raised to a high pitch in all the groups, while the strong centralisation of the leadership meant that its head became more and more exposed. The summer brought some isolated but serious discoveries, as the Gestapo had gradually become aware of what was going on. A courier for the intelligence group was arrested at a place of contact in Oslo at the beginning of December, and after getting new information from Stavanger in connection with the discoveries there, the Gestapo struck by arresting Laudal and most of his close associates. Harrowing reports of torture came from the Gestapo prison in Kristiansand. Within a few days, 400-600 men were under arrest, and in the course of a couple of weeks practically the whole organisation round the coast of South Norway as far west as Haugesund was broken up. A leader who escaped describes the situation in February 1943: 'Milorg on the south coast completely shattered. There may remain individual heads of groups and squads. I cannot think of one who can rebuild it... The collapse, and the accompanying arrests, escapes, torture and reprisals, have put fear into people.' Many of those who had taken part, among them Laudal, were executed or died in German concentration camps.

In *East Norway* the intelligence service for the Allies was separated from the rest of the military resistance at a relatively early date and the work concentrated upon the development of fighting units. On the whole, the practical work of organising the recruitment and growth of such groups round the Oslo Fjord, in the counties of Telemark and Buskerud, and in the more level country up to Lake Mjösa was taken in hand by a group of army officers and civilians, led by Major H. Haneborg Hansen. They had only sporadic contact with the central military staff and worked to some extent on different lines. In Hedmark and Gudbrandsdal the groups were co-ordinated by degrees under a reserve captain who was a lawyer in Lillehammer. The organisation in this case was fairly loose, as it was on the whole in certain other parts of East Norway where the groups were only gradually drawn into the general organisation —some of them not until the later months of 1942 at the earliest. In Greater Oslo there were at first four 'battalions': one for the neighbouring districts to the north and east, two for Oslo itself (East and West), and one for the western suburbs. In addition there was a 'students' battalion' of those who took part in student athletic activities and the Students' Voluntary Military Training Corps; this later joined Oslo West.

Apart from keeping their members fit, conducting cross-country runs and collecting weapons and medical and communications equipment, the groups at first had little military

Illegal radio receiver concealed in a chopping-block.

instruction or purpose. Some exceptions were to be found, however, in the preparation for concrete actions such as attacks on railways and roads, the storing of provision, and reconnaissances with an eventual invasion in mind. It was not before the close of 1941 that reports of an impending invasion became definite, after the reserve captain and lawyer who was the chief for Greater Oslo learnt at a conference with people from London, held on the Swedish frontier, that the Allies planned the invasion of Norway for about 1 April 1942.

The work went on in a comparatively open way in the early period, so that the Germans succeeded little by little in penetrating the organisation; and after laying a trap in connection with a store of weapons in the outskirts of Oslo, the Gestapo in mid-October proceeded to arrest Haneborg Hansen and a number of his close associates, while others had to flee. In an action against the law-office of the Oslo chief shortly before Christmas, the Gestapo also got hold of an important courier to Stockholm with compromising papers in his possession; the result was that the East Norway organisation lost almost the entire stratum of central leaders through the arrests and escapes which followed. In January 1942, 125 officers were arrested and many groups lost touch with each other; this happened at a time when they were on the verge of coming to a standstill for want of directives and instructions.

It fell to one of Hansen's civilian collaborators named Knut Möyen, who had specially taken on the business of organisation among the students, to knit together once again the severed connections between groups. But he realised that this was not enough; the groups needed instruction and fresh assignments. Haneborg Hansen having been arrested, he turned to the military Staff (SL) and the Council, which however were themselves hard hit by arrests or escapes among their central leaders, so it was nearly six months before they were in a position to answer his applications. Möyen had already had proposals worked out for new guide-lines, which broke with the old mobilisation plan for large units operating together, such as the Milorg leaders with their previous military training had envisaged on the whole. He laid stress upon an adaptable construction of smaller units or 'areas', such as one town or centre of population with its neighbourhood, or a valley region. The area would have its own staff, with all necessary special services or technical sections organised in such a way that it could function as an operational unit. Instruction in staff work and the planning of *coups* and attacks on important depots and industrial concerns were begun. Furthermore, there were schemes for training the fighting groups in guerrilla warfare or 'small-scale war', as it was usually called, for which a number of directives were prepared and instructional material obtained. Thus Möyen got one of his associates, who was in hiding at the turn of the year 1941-2, to adapt a couple of foreign instruction pamphlets for the purpose, there being no Norwegian material of this kind within reach.

Alike in instruction and in his methods of organisation Möyen emphasised principles of security, denying the areas any direct connection with each other, and requiring that everybody who was to be in a fighting group should consistently keep out of any other resistance activity. Each leader, and especially ex-officers, should see to it that he had a deputy. Training should be given to none but absolutely reliable members.

Möyen had laid his proposals before the head of the East

Norway organisation in the autumn of 1941; although Haneborn Hansen was interested, the rounding-up of the leaders just afterwards meant that it was impossible to carry them out on any broad basis. Möyen introduced instruction on the new system in a couple of companies, and he tried to contact SL for its approval, as he did not want to take the responsibility for such a complete change on his own shoulders; but SL had enough to do to keep its own head above water, so Möyen's applications received no reply. At the end of March 1942 he sent another letter, saying that if he received no answer by 9 April he would take that as approval and go ahead. Some time after the limit had expired, he finally got in touch with SL and found that his scheme was acceptable; it figured in the basic document, 'Directive No. 1 to the district chief', which SL's military advisers were then compiling. In the course of the year Milorg obtained its final form of organisation, the five regional organisations being replaced by fourteen districts, which in turn were divided into sectors, areas, groups and squads.

Möyen had to work so circumspectly that guerrilla training had barely got going when he heard in the spring of a man from the Linge Company — 'Big Tor' — who had recently come home to develop separate guerrilla groups in Vestfold. As this proved impracticable in an area where Milorg was established, he contacted Milorg people in his native town of Drammen, and since Möyen urgently needed such a person to train his fighting groups in guerrilla tactics, he engaged 'Big Tor' for this through an intermediary. 'Big Tor' did a good job with some smaller groups assigned to him in the Oslo area and the county of Vestfold, but one of the two Linge people who were taken by surprise at that time at Tælavåg had to admit that he was on his way to 'Big Tor'. When the latter was arrested at the beginning of May while visiting his parents in Drammen, it turned out that he had kept a list of his contacts, and the Gestapo extracted a lot of information from him, both about SOE activities and about Milorg. Two months later the Gestapo struck at the Milorg leadership in the three counties of Buskerud, Vestfold and Telemark, but although they were on the scent of Möyen, his alertness enabled him to get away to Sweden, after installing his deputy, Jens Christian Hauge,* and arranging for the necessary contacts.

*Jens Christian Hauge (b.1915), a lawyer and in 1940-1 a Price Control

In much of East Norway, Milorg had to lie low throughout the autumn, but towards the end of the year the organising work got into its swing again. District 13, made up from Greater Oslo, was believed to amount by the New Year to fully 8,000 men, but they were badly supplied with weapons and only a few of them had received proper instruction and training. The district was also weakened throughout 1942 by lack of a leader.

In Oppland and Hedmark, the two northern counties of East Norway, the originally independent local organisations had come into contact with each other in 1941, the work in Hedmark being influenced by its proximity to the Swedish frontier, which meant that there was a good deal of 'export' activity. Fighting groups had been formed along Gudbrandsdal and Österdal; and in February 1942 the arrival of a Linge man to build up such groups on a separate basis led to a dramatic confrontation with the leaders at Lillehammer, after which SL helped to arrange for him to undertake instruction of Milorg groups in both the long valleys. In Österdal a 'trial mobilisation' was arranged at Easter 1942 by irresponsible elements, which were afterwards escorted at top speed across the frontier. By the end of the year the instruction of the fighting groups had been well started with the help of the men from Linge, but in Gudbrandsdal carelessness resulted in large-scale detection.

Informing, infiltration and activity by *agents provocateurs* arranged by the Gestapo and its Norwegian helpers were an increasing danger throughout 1941 and 1942, especially for the military organisations. Counter-measures were arranged, which in the Oslo area were entrusted increasingly to a detached group in liaison with the police force. This was started by the East Norway organisation, but after the numerous arrests in 1941 it was organised as a separate group connected to some extent with the SOE office at the British Legation in Stockholm, and after further disruption the remains of it were linked up in the autumn of 1942 with the military staff (SL). Besides smuggling information into and out of the prisons, warning people in danger, and shadowing and checking on informers, this group engaged in intelligence activities and the transportation of couriers and refugees across the frontier. Furthermore, it had

official, first joined Milorg at Christmas in 1941; after his very rapid rise in the resistance movement, he became secretary to Gerhardsen as prime minister and (November 1945-January 1952) Minister of Defence.

some energetic action units, whose bold and successful *coups* rescued important prisoners from prisons and from prison wards in hospitals. The group was in contact with the Communist action group led by Asbjörn Sunde, which was particularly helpful with the liquidation of informers.

In the autumn of 1942 a SOE party of Norwegians from London, the 'Bittern' expedition, was set down in the Nordmarka forest area outside Oslo to handle the problem of informers and the State Police. No request had been made for it from home — though such a request would not have been unnatural — nor was it properly announced to the police group in Oslo which it had orders to contact. Its leader's behaviour was rather headstrong; what was worse, one of the members, a well-known professional thief who was now going straight, was guilty of the grossest blunders in matters of security. The rumour of this spread widely in Home Front circles in the city, and — at a time when the military organisations all over the country were heavily exposed to detection — this became a serious though unjustified burden upon the reputation of the Milorg leaders. The Council for its part summed up the Bittern affair as follows, in a report to the Norwegian Defence Command in London: 'The whole expedition is an insult to Milorg.'

Changes in the structure of command

For reasons of security the structure of organisation and command on the military side, as elsewhere in the Home Front, was a secret which was protected as well as possible both internally and externally. That is why it was often supposed during the war that a clear structure of command and responsibility existed inside Milorg from an early period. As we see, down to the end of 1942 the reality was a kind of division into three parts. The parties from the Linge Company and their local organisations were subordinated to SOE in London. The regional organisations of Milorg were in the main raised and conducted on a local basis. The Military Council and staff (SL) in Oslo had some contact with what went on locally, but not a command relationship, there being no attempt from the Council's side to direct the districts. Immediately after its formation it had indeed set up a so-called 'leader-in-chief for the fighting-groups', but his functions were merely to obtain contacts and information and to give guidance; and the position was in any case abolished after its first occupant had to escape at the end of 1941, his replacement being a pair of 'travelling inspectors'. At some stages the regional leaders followed different principles from those which SL favoured; thus down to February 1941 Helset and Rognes were against the development of larger organisations, while Haneborg Hansen at this time was beginning to put together the organisation for East Norway.

The officers who started the military staff in 1941 were among those who had shown the greatest enthusiasm and capacity for war during the campaign in 1940 — the circle round General Ruge. Weakness was therefore not the reason why their communications to the Norwegian Defence Command in London in June 1941 opposed acts of sabotage and other 'over-hasty' actions against the superior German forces. Their view was that acts of sabotage would lead to such strong German retaliation against the population that both the capacity and the will for resistance would be impaired. They aimed at developing Milorg into a system of cadres for preparatory purposes, which would only become active when the British made a large-scale invasion, and thought along conventional military lines and in terms of the involvement of large formations. In their communication to London they also opposed the sending-in of weapons which did not have any direct connection with an invasion, because they were afraid that the existence of the organisations would be at hazard if they had big quantities of weapons lying about for too long before the invasion came. Yet at the same time they favoured taking care of the arms which had been concealed after the campaign. Some of the organisers of fighting groups in other parts of the country had the same outlook on the question of arms; on that of sabotage, too, the fighting group leaders long shared the outlook of the Council.

Those in charge of the British SOE thought along other lines, since they wanted to build up small local organisations which could conduct sabotage and attack German lines of communication, so that the enemy was forced to maintain large forces in Norway, Kjelstadli's dissertation* describes in detail the disagreements between SOE and Milorg at that time, but here it may suffice to say that SOE acted in a very headstrong manner

*S. Kjelstadli, 'Hjemmestyrkene I' (Oslo 1959) makes use of some generally inaccessible SOE papers, which are quoted in English.

for at least six months after the joint Norwegian-British committee for co-operation was set up in London in February 1942. The Norwegian soldiers from the Linge Company, sent in by SOE in 1941-2, spoke continually about the impending invasion. Now it was often said, and certainly with good reason, that many exposures and arrests in that early phase of the occupation were due to the average Norwegian's talkativeness and lack of experience of secret resistance work: hence, to a great extent, the success of Rinnan. But this can only slightly excuse the mistakes which were made on SOE's side at that phase in the war. Most of the big exposures of resistance were due to over-hurried work, begun by SOE, to prepare for an invasion which never came. In the small, easily observable Norwegian communities it was impossible to avoid such activities becoming too widely known.

Milorg also suffered several severe blows in cases where Linge people showed little respect for the security rules and were captured carrying names or other important information about them. It was apparent everywhere that the attempt to form separate organisations in districts where Milorg groups were already in existence was not only an impossibility but also a cause of insecurity. By the beginning of October the situation was already so critical that SL asked the military office at the Stockholm Legation for a month's intermission; and by the end of the year the circumstances recounted above were in large measure responsible for the fact that all its main leaders had either been arrested or were forced to flee. At the New Year Ole Berg, the carefully concealed head of the Council, was likewise obliged to move to Stockholm.

The many serious reverses which it had experienced in 1942 caused SOE to make a radical change of course and to opt for close co-operation with the Norwegian authorities in London and Milorg. It was agreed that in future SOE would not build up its own units, but would provide instruction and assistance for Milorg detachments. The Milorg leaders at home, on the other hand, realised that a purely passive preparatory organisation could not be kept up; the members needed to be activated by military instruction adapted to the new situation, and to be trained in the use of new weapons and methods of warfare. The reorganisation and training methods at which Möyen worked in the autumn of 1941 and the first half of 1942 were the first definite signs of a change of course.

Other sides of the resistance were also hit by the big exposures of Milorg in 1942. With the incomplete knowledge of the structure of responsibility and command on the military side which people had at that time, Milorg's central leadership unavoidably received the blame and was discredited in the eyes both of the rank and file and of prominent personages on the civil front. The reverses even led individuals to doubt whether the military resistance activity served any useful purpose.

In January 1943 the Council was reconstructed. One of its first tasks was to answer an enquiry from the Norwegian Defence Command in London (FO) as to its view of what Milorg could contribute in the event of an Allied invasion, and especially as to how it thought the population would react to German reprisals resulting from such a contribution. Jens Christian Hauge, who at the end of 1942 had been made chief of the military staff (SL), drafted a reply which the Council considered should be laid before the civilian leadership for approval. In the mistaken belief that such a leadership was represented by a 'Civil Council', with which the Military Council had contact through one of its members, the answer received from that source was treated as approval by the civilian leadership, and the Military Council sent off the letter. Its evaluation of the reprisals question ended with the statement that German counter-measures would be hard but ought not to hinder Milorg from making a contribution in the phase of liberation. Four conditions must be fulfilled by Milorg if its contribution was to have military value: it had to be intact, to possess the necessary supplies, to know the objectives selected by FO for the operations, and to be informed whether its participation was to take the form of localised actions or of an 'uprising in all districts'. Finally, the Council stated that it was of national importance that the militant youth of the country should share in its liberation, so that it should not only be a gift from the Allies.

The letter was shown to Schjelderup just after it had been sent, and his reaction was in accordance with his own temperament. As he himself puts it: 'With the great Standfast struggle of 1942 just behind us, the section of the letter (i.e. about the national importance of a military uprising of the Home Front) was like a red rag.' After a meeting with Paal Berg and two other members of the Circle, he — together with Boyesen — composed a letter from the Circle to the Government, criticising Milorg's letter in mordant terms. The Council's evaluation of

Milorg's ability to contribute to the liberation struggle was also attacked, and great doubt was expressed regarding its estimate of how German reprisals would affect members of Milorg and the people at large. In the light of the situation in which the organisation was placed at the turn of 1942-3 and the short time remaining, as many supposed, before the expected invasion in the west, a good deal might be said about the representations of the Council. But the criticisms in the letter from the Circle went much too far, and they were expressed in a form which made them doubly distressing to the authors of the communication from the Council, who indeed believed that it had been approved on the civil side before it was sent.

It has been claimed that one of Schjelderup's objects in writing so sharply to the Government was that he wanted to indicate once and for all that it was the Circle and the Co-ordination Committee which represented the civil leadership of the Home Front. Such a result was fully achieved, and it is certain that the Circle had resented the failure of the Government at that time to send all correspondence direct, a part coming through military channels instead. At the end of March, meetings were held on the initiative of Biering and Helset which cleared up some of the misunderstandings about the position of the 'Civil Council'. The Military Council added Schjelderup and Halvorsen to its membership from the Circle, and in the course of six months the Council and the civil resistance organisations reached agreement on the main lines for conducting the struggle. In May, negotiations between the Council and the Norwegian Defence Command (FO) showed that on several points the latter must damp down Milorg's ambitions. The Defence Command was unable to answer affirmatively regarding any of the four conditions which the Council had laid down in its January letter as requisite if Milorg's contribution to an Allied invasion was to be militarily effective. But the place of Milorg in the common struggle against the enemy was emphasised, since everyone recognised the value of having fighting organisations through which the urge of the nation's youth to contribute to its liberation could find expression under responsible leaders.

5

TOTAL WAR—THE 'NATIONAL LABOUR EFFORT'

In the late autumn of 1942 the fortunes of war at last began to turn. At the beginning of November the British forces in Egypt inflicted a definitive defeat on the German Afrika Korps at El Alamein; a few days later British-American forces made their landing in North Africa; and after another six months the whole of the German and Italian forces in Africa had been overcome and 250,000 soldiers taken prisoner. On the Eastern front the German summer offensive had stagnated after reaching the oilfields of the Caucasus and the Volga bend at Stalingrad, where towards the end of the year the Red Army succeeded in encircling the German Sixth Army, originally more than 300,000 strong; when its remnants capitulated on 1 February 1943, they numbered about 100,000. In the days which followed, the Nazi leaders in Berlin set in motion a new propaganda campaign against 'Bolshevism'—Europe was in the utmost danger, the German troops were the bulwark defending Western culture, and the rest of Europe must at the very least contribute to the struggle with its labour force. In Norway the NS leaders followed this up with speeches and appeals, and pointed out that thousands upon thousands of those employed in offices and institutions formed a reserve labour force which could be used in 'the struggle for the destiny of Europe'.

On 22 February Quisling announced 'the law of the common national labour effort', which introduced the obligation to register and to work for every man aged between eighteen and fifty-five and for women aged between twenty-one and forty years. The Home Front leaders had heard rumours of this shortly beforehand, and sent urgent telegrams to the Government in London to the effect that there was going to be a mobilisation of Norwegians for labour service in Germany; the Government was requested to ask the Allies for help in pressing Sweden to prevent transit. On the 23rd, the day when the announcement of the labour service appeared in the newspapers, the chairman of the NS Student Union called a meeting in the Great Hall of the University 'to discuss the situation'. The students felt that their position was now particularly precarious, so at least 400 of them turned up and the hall was filled; they were then given disingenuous promises of escaping more serious matters if they would take on the University's wood-fuel supply, which they agreed to do. Next day the papers were able to report in heavy type that the students had shown support for the 'national' labour effort. But a counter-action was started at once, in which more than 2,500 of the 2,700 students on the registers sent individual protests and declared at the same time that they did not recognise the Student Union as their representative.

There were other ways too in which this was an awkward business for the resistance movement. At that juncture not many people, even inside its organised groups, had any clear idea of how the Home Front was led. Some believed that the directions for the struggle came from the King and Government in London. It was certainly supposed that people in the particular occupational groups stood behind the successful actions during the Standfast struggle of 1942; the illegal newspapers usually waited to give directives to occupations until they had been received from the appropriate sources. But for questions of a more general nature, the editors often thought it their duty to give directions as quickly as possible, which was what happened in the present case. Barely two days after the announcement *London News*, the largest and most influential BBC-based paper* in the capital, launched a directive with this wording: 'Those who are taken for national labour duty in agriculture, forestry, fisheries and transport shall do their duty to the full for the preservation of the country. All services which ... imply obligations for the people to take part in military operations against the fatherland *shall be refused*. Service outside the country's frontiers *shall be refused* ...'

The same weak directive came in slightly different wording

*In the autumn of 1941 the Germans had ordered the confiscation of all radio sets (except those of NS members) — a unique tribute to the ascendancy of the BBC over broadcast services under NS and German control. This action gave a great impetus to the free press, whose editors henceforth reproduced mainly material from the clandestinely heard Norwegian-language bulletins of the BBC.

from *London Radio* and *Radio News*, the other big BBC-based papers in Oslo, and from several of the smaller ones. *Fri Fagbevegelse*, the principal organ of the resistance leaders in the trade union organisation, was very cautious in its first comments, made on 27 February: 'According to the "law" given by Quisling on the national labour effort, neither he nor the Germans have ventured in the first instance to talk of transferring Norwegian workers to Germany. That will possibly come later. Our attitude, too, must then be taken up for reconsideration, but until that happens the sacrifices needed to offer a united opposition to the compulsory mobilisation which is now taking place will be too great.'

This utterance, and the reports which reached the Government from the leadership in Oslo in the first period after the announcement, indicate that the labour effort was now thought to have been somewhat overdramatised beforehand. The terms of the 'law' had damped down the intense fear, originating in rumour, that the labour force would be compulsorily transferred to Germany — a relief which was encouraged by confidential information from the public offices that those conscripted would be employed in purely Norwegian activities. The Circle accordingly telegraphed to the Government in early March that the labour mobilisation would not be nearly so far-reaching as the German conditions originally made it. Public opinion, which at first was almost panic-stricken, setting off a big increase in the refugee traffic to Sweden, became calmer. For the time being no one was drafted, while the NS propaganda machine played hard upon national feelings about 'self-sufficiency'. Reports picked up from the NS administration a little later in March indicated that in the first instance — up to September — 35,000 men were to be called up for road and railway building and for the *Organisation Todt*, which had charge of military installations in Norway.

In reality, compulsory mobilisation of labour was not something new. As early as the summer of 1941 there had been an ordinance for drafting workers to activities which the authorities found 'important or essential', and in May 1942 the Directorate of Labour Exchanges called for 15,000 men from commercial and office employment for more 'necessary' work. The action committees for the other occupations at that time regarded this as a matter for the illegal leadership of the trade union movement (the FU). For most people, what appeared to be new about the situation in 1943 was its wider scope, the additional occupations affected, and its special background as a source of support for a wavering German front. But there were some who viewed it more seriously, even after the cautious formulation of the 'law', believing that it was the beginning of a compulsory mobilisation of Norwegian youth for the German side in the war. Among the leaders it was Skjönsberg who saw this most clearly, but he found little support for his view in the first rounds of the discussions in which the Co-ordination Committee drafted directives and guidelines for the struggle; nor was he supported by the members of the Circle.

At the beginning of March, when it was urgent to adopt a standpoint regarding the first stage in the mobilisation — namely the registration of those liable for service, which was to be completed on the 20th — the Co-ordinating Committee (KK) sent out a directive that a maximum of false returns should be made, so as to create chaos in the official records. This was followed to a quite considerable extent, witness a letter from the Labour Directorate in the middle of June: 'Oslo Labour Office received about 43,000 returns from male persons, of which about 10,000 were seen at first scrutiny to be false. At later callings-up a number of further returns, about 25%, were found false... How much work this costs us can easily be imagined.' On the whole, however, the registration went on unhindered, and on a national basis it comprised 300,000 people.

It took the committee a long time to reach a final standpoint regarding guidelines for the attitude of those who were drafted. The majority considered that, on the basis of the available information, particularly from sources in the administration, the draftees were going to be put into agriculture or into Norwegian places of employment, and that therefore it was not right to aim for a complete boycott. A directive to this effect would not have many followers and would reduce people's respect for subsequent directives. As the matter most closely affected the workers' organisations — public services were for the time being exempted from mobilisation — the committee, in accordance with its usual practice, gave great weight to the view of the FU's representative. He still held firmly to the line which *Fri Fagbevegelse* had immediately adopted, namely that the situation was not ripe for unconditional refusal. The teachers' organisations likewise were of the opinion that no firmer opposition was possible. And the fact that 200,000 Norwegians had already found employment in German undertakings would not make it any easier to convince the man in the street that a strong directive was reasonable.

The question of international law also came prominently into the discussion, having been touched upon by many of the illegal newspapers, which in general used it as an argument for refusing to be mobilised. The difficulty, however, was that the regulations for land warfare in the Hague Convention of 1907 did in fact give to an army of occupation the right to exact individual contributions and the performance of work from the population; and the University's legal experts, on being asked their advice, had few words of comfort to offer to the resistance movement in defining the limits of the occupying power's rights in the existing situation.

It was not only the civil resistance movement which had problems to contend with in connection with the 'national' labour effort. The illegal organisations, especially the military ones, included among their members many young people of the age for labour service, and in 1943 few saw any alternative to mobilisation except crossing over the frontier to Sweden. If this happened on a large scale, the organisations would be so badly depleted that they might risk being unable to operate. Accordingly, as soon as the 'law' was announced, the Military Council issued a directive that the *chasseurs** of the fighting groups should not leave the country for the time being; but 'if the mobilisation led to comprehensive draftings of young Norwegian men to foreign countries, the Council must take its position on whether the time had come for a complete or partial uprising of the fighting-groups.' After this was written, the Council contacted the Circle, and the leaders of both discussed the problems created by the labour effort. The view of the Council, expressed in a notice to the heads of districts on 7 April, was that the *chasseurs* should do everything in their power to evade the mobilisation, but they must not leave the country.

This attitude accorded with the attitude reached by the Co-ordination Committee after the first round of new discussions at the beginning of April. A good deal of impatience over

**Jegerne*: literally 'hunters', but used in Norway since 1788 for élite regiments of light infantry or dragoons.

the absence of clear guidelines had been expressed both out in the country and in the illicit press of the capital, as when *London News* wrote on 12 March: 'Complete obscurity now prevails about the labour mobilisation.' Yet opinion was still divided, both inside the Co-ordination Committee and in the country at large. Thus a courier was sent from Ålesund pressing for a strong directive, whereas a representative from the no less active resistance leaders at Hamar pleaded with the leadership not to decide for a directive which could not be followed up. The result of the discussions at that stage was a Notification on the 'national' labour effort, giving no concrete directive; as Schjelderup put it, 'it was thought sufficient just to *point* to what we considered must be right.' This Notification was so obscure that none of the BBC-based papers printed it.

Greatly perturbed over the result of the meeting, Skjönsberg had a new one called on the 13th, by which time new information had also arrived, some of it from a 'school for drivers' at Svelvik, where the draftees were put into German uniforms. On this occasion Skjönsberg managed to secure agreement to a directive for *unconditional* refusal, both of registration and of mobilisation. His own account may be extracted from a letter he sent to the author during the preparation of this book:

I had no doubt that the drafting for labour service was a camouflaged call-up of Norwegian youth for German military service, and that it must be combated as quickly as possible by every available means. It was not hard to appreciate that an active line was a very dangerous step, and it was easy to find arguments for failing to do anything. It would be impossible to provide quarters for all who withdrew from the service; they were not wanted in Sweden; there would be reprisals against relatives; hostages would be shot — to mention some of the arguments. My opinion at that time was that we must not let these possibilities frighten us, but that we must accept the full responsibility for what would necessarily follow a plain directive to resist. Any other procedure would only lead to worse results on the next occasion.

In my view we had experience enough after three years of occupation to know that each action by the Germans and NS began with caution and then gradually developed on harder lines if they experienced no opposition. We had never achieved anything at all by compliance and by indulging in the hope and belief that the worst could not happen. There was also at that time a common impression that this would not lead to serious consequences, and that therefore one ought not to proceed to serious counter-measures ...

There was a further consideration which counted heavily with me. The absence of a clear directive brought uncertainty and a disintegrative tendency throughout the resistance movement; our position as leaders was on the verge of collapsing. This would have extremely serious consequences, since at that time no other leadership existed with the organisation and authority which were needed to hold the resistance together. We were in the position that we, and only we, could give the word required.

As the days passed, the situation became more and more unendurable. Even when we got to know that the boys at Svelvik were equipped with uniforms, a number of our friends persisted in their unwillingness for action....

In the end it was resolved to send out a directive to evade service. The clergyman Alex Johnson wrote in a letter just after the war: 'What eventually aroused me and others was the information about Svelvik; we now understood for the first time that the labour mobilisation was a purely military undertaking, which we ought to have understood at once, as Skjönsberg did.' The new directive was accepted at once by the illegal press, and emphasised a week later, on 21 April, by an audacious act of sabotage against the conscription office in Oslo, committed by a group under Communist leadership; two of the five men involved were immediately arrested and later executed. In addition, the directive received the blessing of the Church, whose emergency leadership sent a strong letter of protest against the call-up to Quisling at the beginning of May; this cost the freedom of the Church's two remaining leaders, Hallesby and Hope.

As further alarming items of information came in one by one, the Co-ordination Committee sent out, in May and early June, a number of special directives and re-emphasised the main directive not to attend. In mid-May the Labour Service called up girls of eighteen for duty, whereupon the women's service was boycotted, appeals being made to the parents, especially mothers. But the directive received no great support, one of the reasons being the continued toleration of the Labour Service (AT) for men.

At the beginning of the year the committee had sent out a directive, proposed by Skjönsberg, against applying for a number of public positions, in order to slow down the persecution and dismissal by the NS of officials who stood out against them. When the labour conscription was extended early in May to include people in public employment, the directive for a boycott was likewise extended to the posts which had previously been excepted.

Employers in commerce, handicrafts and industry received directives not to assist in the regulation of their concerns by the NS for the purpose of procuring labour for the compulsory levy. Finally, in the middle of June, the police received directives from their illegal leadership not to assist in fetching draftees who refused to come forward. The persistent campaign, which was conducted by the Committee with the help of the illegal press after the adoption of the directive for refusal, gradually took effect in the capital. In mid-June the Directorate of Labour states: 'The conscription for the national labour effort in Oslo must be said to have given a meagre result.' Furthermore, the maladministration of the labour effort under the NS authorities meant that very few of those who did come forward reached any place of work.

At the end of May 400 men from East Norway were called up to be sent to work for a German artillery regiment in Tromsö. A member of the Circle's secretariat, Hans Engen, wishing to find out what was going to happen, went right into the lion's den, namely a school in Oslo where the enrolment was taking place under heavy guard. He afterwards made a report on his experiences, part of which was printed in the illegal press: the draftees included an agricultural worker, which sufficiently showed up the NS propaganda about mobilisation to increase the food supply, and of the 400 called out by name only seventy-one — or less than 20 per cent — were present. When Engen was on his way out after completing the assignment, one of the guards made a gesture to stop him for searching; the reporter roared out in German that he was interpreter for the Labour Service, whereupon the guard clicked his heels and said 'Passieren'.

At about the same time the resistance leaders informed the Government that the attendance in Oslo and Bærum was around 25 per cent. The situation was worse in the country at large, partly because the directive came so late; but in small, easily observable communities it was in any case more difficult than in big towns to carry out a directive of such an uncompromising nature. In some districts, too, the population was still under the influence of the State of Emergency and other acts of intimidation in connection with the uncovering of Milorg in the autumn of 1942.

Moreover, it was hard for the district organisations to reach the masses through the usual system for distributing directives —a task which would have been best accomplished by the illegal trade union leaders of the districts, but they seem to have made little effort. A further hindrance to the spreading of the directives about the country at this time was the ordinance of November 1942, making it a capital offence 'to be sent or to possess' illegal publications, which had heavily reduced the transmission of illegal papers through the post.

In Trondheim and Bergen the illegal leadership was seriously affected at this critical juncture by arrests and discoveries. Trondheim in April strongly deprecated any action against the labour effort: 'One lives almost on a volcano here, and comprehensive sabotage will undoubtedly result in drastic measures. The means of distribution are also so small for the moment that on that ground alone a successful realisation of the plans is impossible.' In Bergen the directive was not sent out, even after the activity had got going in June. This appeared to be due to the fact that one of the teachers' resistance leaders in Oslo, who disagreed with the directive, had sent a counter-message.

The action against the 'national' labour effort in the spring of 1943 had disclosed a quantity of weaknesses in the way in which the Home Front was organised. Some of these were put right during the struggle. Contact was established at the top level between military and civil resistance, and discussion took place concerning the main lines of guidance for the movement. Contact between the leadership and the free press had broken down for some weeks during February and March, but was re-established and improved.

A new round in the struggle against the NS's youth service

At the beginning of 1943, the NS made a fresh attempt to introduce compulsory service in its Youth Company, which the Party had had to abandon in the previous year in face of the massive opposition from teachers, parents and the Church. But here the Co-ordination Committee met it on familiar ground, by establishing a special action-group of people in the schools and the Church, who prepared directives and information material, and supplemented the district organisations where the pressure from the NS was most severe; at the same time the committee employed its distribution network to disseminate the directives, of which extra stocks were laid up in the districts. The NS achieved little or no result in that round, either. It was particularly impressive that resistance was so good in Kristiansand, where the Gestapo terror during the large-scale discovery of Milorg was still felt keenly by the population.

The year 1943 was marked as a whole by a stubborn resistance by Church and school people against continually renewed attempts by the authorities to find a breach in the firm front against NS interference in the affairs of Church and school. This roused many homes in the towns and the countryside all over Norway for the struggle against the NS, which steadily deepened the cleavage between the Party and the people created by the acute conflicts of the previous year.

Civil preparations for the period of liberation

About the turn of the year 1941-2 the Military Council took up the question of how various civil functions should be organised in connection with an eventual Allied invasion, a possibility which just at that juncture was very much to the fore on the military side of the Home Front. In the following autumn the members of the Circle had begun to discuss the question of a civil administration, but the Circle did not take the subject up seriously until January 1943, with Schjelderup as the driving force. The next month, it received an important communication from the Government, which cleared up their mutual relations by announcing that as soon as Norway was liberated, the Nygaardsvold Government would give place to a coalition Cabinet, to be formed after discussion between the King, the outgoing ministers, and leading personalities at home. The letter also confirmed that the Government had never tried to give directives for the activities of the struggle on the Home Front.

This same letter of February 1943 stated that during a reconquest or a German collapse, Norway had to reckon with an Allied occupation, which we must try to avoid by having a Norwegian civil administration ready on which the Allies could rely. Its intended members must therefore have shown a patriotic attitude and be suitable to take part in secret preparations under the eyes of the Gestapo; and the Circle accordingly concluded that they must be nominated, and proposed a system for this which took care to preserve the political balance in the local councils. Before it was sent to the Government in May, the proposal was submitted to the Co-ordination Committee, which supported it, with emphasis on the importance of keeping the balance of parties and nominating the maximum of persons who had previously been elected. Finally, the committee made the assumption that the interim period before the holding of proper elections would be kept as short as possible.

The proposal from the Circle crossed with a provisional ordinance from the Minister of Justice in London on local government arrangements for the interim period. It was apparent that five of the Cabinet favoured a system of nominations such as the Circle had proposed, but a majority of six preferred that the old local government authorities should be summoned again, omitting members of the NS. The Circle found the majority proposal unacceptable, since it could not be prepared for without great risk of detection by the Gestapo, while in some places it might result in local authorities lacking the confidence of the population, which in turn might lead to conditions which gave the Allies an excuse to set up a military government. After further exchanges, in which the Prime Minister still persisted in the majority proposal, the Circle gave notice at the end of July that it would not take responsibility for any further developments in the matter, whereupon the Government gave way and accepted with minor modifications the arrangement supported by the Circle.

A former chairman of the Oslo city council named Nilson, having learnt of the matter through one of the members of the Circle, joined with one of the teachers' leaders, Edmund Haug, to start an agitation against what the Circle had proposed, partly by means of a chain letter in Norway and partly through applications to the Government in London. The Circle knew of this, and in connection with its refusal in July invited the Government to contact other Home Front organisations. In declining to do so, the Government stated that it had attached no weight to applications from other sources, after which the Circle could begin to operate the new arrangements by nominating county committees and choosing people to conduct the functions of the *fylkesmenn*. Individual members of the Circle, especially Skjönsberg and Biering, travelled round and instructed them, while the connection with them was established through the secretariat of the Co-ordination Committee and its district contacts.

My own new task

In June 1943 Jan Jansen inquired whether I could consider taking over the leadership of the organising apparatus of 'a committee called the Co-ordination Committee', which had charge of the civil struggle; this was the first time I had heard the committee's name, and the duties sounded interesting. A couple of months earlier I had been under arrest for a week in connection with my work in the intelligence service, and even though the interrogations showed that on this occasion the Gestapo had struck at random, it occurred to me that a change in my field of illegal activity might be sensible. So I accepted the assignment, on condition that my identity should not be known to the committee. This was agreed, and on Midsummer Eve I was conducted through several intermediate stages to an apartment which was used as cover, where I was to meet my predecessor and obtain the necessary contacts and detailed information on my duties. When the door opened I immediately recognised the man who appeared, despite his camouflaged appearance. He gave a smile of recognition in return and was just as surprised as I was: he was Kåre Norum, who had been my teacher before I left primary school at Ski, and I had then liked him very much. He appeared pleased to be handing over the baton to a former pupil, and introduced me to a young woman inside the flat, Sigrid Steinnes, who under the name of 'Elisabeth' had been the right hand of KK's secretary since the turn of 1941-2. For practical reasons it would be necessary for us to know each other, so it did not really matter that we already did so, as she had been one year my junior at the Oslo Cathedral School. I was then given a brief survey of the situation; Norum was to depart for Sweden the same evening. I was told of the composition and work of the committee, its district organisation, the system of communications and other practical matters. I was to take part in the meetings of the committee, act as secretary, and see that its resolutions were carried out. Apart from Sigrid Steinnes and myself, the secretariat consisted of only one full-time worker, Erik Bratsberg; Sigrid had the help of another girl, who worked for the head of the press as well.

Thus it was not a large staff, but I soon realised that no fellow-workers could be more energetic and skilful. Sigrid might have been made for the job, intelligent and alert, persevering and fearless; as Norum once said, she did the most dangerous things with the same nonchalance as if she was dusting. Erik was only a young lad, but a magician when it came to illegal activity, who never admitted that any task was impossible. If a duplicating machine was needed and could not be obtained in any other way, he would go to the nearest office-equipment company, take the machine under his arm, say good-bye politely, and walk out again with the most natural air of ownership on his freckled boyish face.

More than a year of hectic activity had given the working arrangements of the secretariat their weaknesses with regard to security. All too many of the committee members knew Sigrid by her real name and were aware of where she lived, so I asked her to find a cover address as quickly as possible. In order to contact us, the members of the committee were to announce themselves under cover names according to an agreed system, at a shop which we contacted a couple of times a day. Our place of work was my apartment, which was particularly suitable because in 1941, some time after I had moved in, the block had been occupied by the NS authorities for the use of party members moving into town to work in the central administration. I had taken the apartment so as to have undisturbed quarters for illegal work, and saw at once that, if I could dig myself in, the place would be proof against raids; so having discovered that the confiscation had no legal basis, I refused to be turned out and was allowed to go on living there. My neighbour was the caretaker, whom I gradually discovered to be a trustworthy citizen and from whom I obtained all sorts of help. What was of most value was an oil-fired boiler in the cellar, which had to be put out of operation because there was no oil and which provided me with ample space for secret files, while for short-term safe-keeping I had several secret spaces in the walls and floor of my apartment upstairs.

The system of communications, which had been skilfully built up by Malm and further developed by Norum, still functioned very well. Its key man was the postal official Lid, with whom I had long been co-operating over the distribution of the *Bulletin*. His innocent exterior — he looked like a kind, rather elderly uncle — concealed one of the most inventive and ingenious circumventers of the law that I met during the entire war. His thorough knowledge of the methods of dispatch in the postal service was invaluable for modifying or extending our system; and when our district organisations were being tracked down, the fact that Lid had fellow-workers in the service all over the country meant that he could often help us to find out what had happened and assist in getting the work restarted.

Representatives of the district leaders had hitherto to a great extent known the names of the secretaries in the Co-ordination Committee, and could seek them out directly when visiting Oslo; they now got a couple of contacts for couriers, to which they should report. Although it did not take long for these security measures to show their usefulness, they were not popular at the outset either with the members of the Committee or with the district contacts, this being a slower system than the old one. My reason was in a sense quite simple: people can always be found to sit on committees, but it is much more difficult to reconstruct an illegal organisation which has been broken up. That had happened in the spring to the district organisations in Bergen and Trondheim.

As soon as I had settled in my new job, I travelled round to Bergen, Ålesund, Kristiansund and Trondheim to give information to the Committee's main contacts and to the representatives of the illegal trade union leadership (the FU). It was instructive for me to discuss the situation in the struggle and what work might be done with our people in these places. There was still a need to reinforce the opposition to the 'national' labour effort. I was surprised that in some places the trade union leaders took little interest in this; instead, they preferred to listen to news from Oslo and London and discuss post-war problems. That was indeed a tendency which also showed itself in other sectors of the Home Front in the course of 1943. The occupation had lasted for more than three years and was beginning to wear us all down. Even though the tide of war had turned, the terror, the food shortage and the political pressure in Norway were worse than ever. It was not surprising that it told both upon people's spirits and upon their will to follow directives at the cost of personal sacrifices.

The leadership and the free press

In such a situation the contribution of the free press was more important than ever. These papers had sprung up on the initiative of individuals or small groups, and they were in an exposed position — as was shown by the shortness of the lives of most of them. The Gestapo had many means of getting to grips with them, so the editors naturally tried to isolate themselves as best they could; on the other hand, they needed money and material help. Even if editors had a great urge to be as independent as possible over the contents too, most of them realised that they needed to be in touch with the leadership of the Home Front for guidelines in the struggle and for directives.

While the leadership entirely respected editorial integrity, it had to be able to put forward its own directives and so prevent the papers from giving different and contradictory ones. Because of his own comprehensive work for the economic support of the illegal organisations, and through the help of a resistance leader among the Oslo municipal functionaries, Skjönsberg had been brought into contact with many newspapers in the capital. At the beginning of 1942 they agreed to put one of their own people in charge of the contact with the press, but their nominee was arrested in another connection in February 1943, and in mid-March the municipal functionary was also obliged to flee. However, the latter put Skjönsberg in touch with Herlov Rygh ('Steen'), the editor of *London News*, who agreed to take over as contact with the press, for which purpose he brought with him four or five of his closest associates, handing over the editorship of his newspaper to a new group.

Rygh was a masterful and energetic man, who applied himself to his new task with great vigour and was soon known as 'the press chief'. He established connections with many leading personalities in the Home Front, and was well informed; besides acting as the link between the leadership and the press, he with his associates provided local editions and a fortnightly national edition of *London News*. In addition, he began at once to inquire into the conditions under which the illegal press were working in the rest of the country, partly on his own account and partly in co-operation with the KK secretariat. At the end of March 1943, Norum sent a letter to every point of contact, asking for information about press conditions and offering technical help if it was wanted. The regulation announced the previous autumn, allowing capital punishment for the production, distribution and reception of illegal papers, made people living in more easily observable circumstances than those of Oslo reluctant to increase their effort in this field. However, when I took over, some places had become more interested in the offer, so before his departure Norum instructed me to arrange a further discussion with the press chief. At our first meeting he asked for the names of our regular contacts along Lake Mjösa and in Trondheim, as he would send someone to discuss press matters with them direct. For security reasons I flatly refused to comply, but promised to send a request to our contacts to indicate a representative with whom he could be put in touch. The very temperamental press chief gave me a dressing-down, but he accepted my offer all the same, and the inquiry went out at once to the towns he wanted.

During the autumn of 1943 the free press reached what were probably its largest printings, something like 500,000 copies a month. Early in that period our district leadership in Trondheim gave warning that a man who had started an illegal paper and was in contact with Rygh was in fact serving the Gestapo. I passed the information on at once to Rygh, who after a short time decided that it was a false alarm. However, when the press chief under a cover name met this man in Trondheim, the Gestapo checked the train on which he returned to Oslo, thus establishing his identity. The immediate sequel was that the Gestapo struck in the middle of November, capturing Rygh and all his fellow-workers.

At the desire of the press chief a small press council had been set up in the course of the autumn to support his operations. It was while Rygh was on his way to a meeting of this council that he was taken, and when he did not arrive the other two members, Skjönsberg and Jansen, feared that something had gone wrong, so they left the rendezvous. That evening the Circle was assembled at Skjönsberg's home, when Biering was informed by telephone during the meeting that Rygh had been arrested. 'I have seldom felt so uneasy,' Skjönsberg wrote in a recent letter to the author. 'The Gestapo could be expected to surround the house at any moment, and I had a lot of trouble in getting the others away; they did not appreciate the seriousness of the situation and were more interested in the discussion than in reaching safety. I was relieved when I could leave the house in company with the last of them.' He had reason for his disquiet; the way in which Rygh and his associates were taken showed that they had been shadowed for several days.

The press chief and the others were severely tortured to disclose their connections, but the arrests did not lead at once to any further discoveries in Oslo. Nevertheless, many of the civil resistance leaders had to go into hiding, for fear that their correct names were known to — and might therefore be extorted from — those in charge of press affairs. One of Rygh's co-workers had been on a tour round the coast between Bergen and Oslo, and discoveries followed immediately in several of the coastal towns. Our main contacts were taken both in Kristiansand and in Arendal, and the discoveries were so far-reaching that in Kristiansand it took almost an entire year to set up new leaders; in Arendal, things moved more quickly, but there were frequent changes in the leadership later on. The south coast region suffered something approaching a mortal wound that autumn. The discoveries in Kristiansand led on to the arrest of Alex Johnson, who was one of the representatives of the clergy on the Co-ordination Committee. As he had acted as secretary during a short interregnum between Malm and Norum, so that his name was known in that connection to the main contacts, things at first looked black. However, we learnt that his betrayal had only been in connection with a route for refugees from Kristiansand, and the danger passed. This was the second occasion in a short time that this happened to a member of the committee, a lawyer having been taken in October who was one of the four or five who formed the original nucleus. Again it was not in relation to KK business, and the only consequence of the arrest for the committee was the loss of one of its good supports. At about the same time the representative of the secondary schools came into the danger zone and had to go abroad, his successor being Magnus Jensen.

Blow upon blow

Another black day in the history of the occupation was 16 August 1943. A few days earlier, the head of the civil section of the Oslo police, Inspector Gunnar Eilifsen, was arrested for refusing to fetch in some young Oslo girls who had not reported for labour service. A new 'law' was made, under which Eilifsen was brought before a 'Norwegian' special tribunal and condemned to death. This was on Sunday, 15 August; on the previous day every official and member of the police force in Oslo received orders to parade in the yard of the police barracks on the following Monday at 6 a.m. When they were drawn up, the barracks was surrounded by armed German detachments; Police Minister Jonas Lie and the head of the German security forces, General Rediess, then appeared; and Lie mounted the rostrum to announce that Inspector Eilifsen, having refused to carry out an order, had received sentence of death, which had just been executed, so it was necessary to demand a declaration of loyalty from every man. Then Rediess made a menacing speech, after which the policemen were called out individually to sign. The NS leaders of the police signed first, but the other police officials went past the table without signing, as did a number of the rank and file. Those who refused their signatures were sent down into the cellar, where they were accused of mutiny and threatened with court-martial and the same fate as Eilifsen. Most of them gradually gave way, but fourteen held out to the end and were taken away in German cars.

The murder of Eilifsen made a deep impression. We had indeed been hardened in the two years which had passed since the execution of Hansteen and Wickström, but this was the first time that a Norwegian had been condemned to death by his fellow-countrymen, after a summary trial and by the use of a 'law' which had been given retrospective effect. In the autumn of 1940 Eilifsen had been among the many policemen who let themselves be hustled into the NS; he had quickly regretted it, and resigned early the following year. By his upright behaviour in 1943 he not merely corrected a mistake but set an example to the entire Resistance.

The action also showed how little the NS could rely on the old Norwegian police force, in spite of the number who let themselves be cajoled or frightened into the NS Party in the autumn of 1940, many of whom had in any case resigned in 1941. Yet it is undeniable that the NS achieved part of its object, which was to make the less resolute of the police still weaker and deprive others of the desire to put up an opposition.

The illegal leadership of the police put to the Home Front leaders the question whether the police ought to be given a directive to withdraw from the service and go underground. The answer was that until further notice they should remain in service, so as to be able to help the population and fend off acts of tyranny, even if they must to some extent carry out unlawful orders.

The action on 16 August had the further object of sifting out the resistance men in the ranks of the police. At the end of the month there was a fresh attack, in which about 500 men in all parts of the country were arrested according to a list drawn up by the head of the State Police, Karl A. Marthinsen. Several

Grini, the wartime place of detention of 19,000 Norwegians.

hundred of them were sent to a 'retraining camp' in Germany.

Yet it was not the police alone who were to feel the mark of the Nazis' iron heel on that day. In the course of the preceding night more than 1,100 officers were arrested, to be treated later as prisoners-of-war. Already 200 were behind bars, so more than 1,300 were now in German hands. Warning of the arrests had gone out in Oslo and its immediate neighbourhood, so a good part had gone into hiding. Quite a number of these decided later to report themselves, while others ignored the warning and let themselves be taken. Individual officers excused their attitude in this situation by reference to the lack of directions from the Government, the Defence Command and the Military Council. Others were afraid that members of their families would be taken as hostages if they made off.

In the country at large, to which the warning of the arrests did not penetrate, individual key men in Milorg were taken. But the situation had been foreseen, civilian reserves were ready to move in and Milorg suffered no mortal wound from these arrests. More than 1,100 officers were sent to a prisoner-of-war camp in Poland.

However, the late summer of 1943 brought other news of a different kind. In July, Mussolini was overthrown and soon afterwards Italy capitulated. On 29 August Denmark terminated its existence as 'Hitler's little canary' and put up an ever stronger resistance.

A warning-shot for members of the NS

The increasing number of acts of tryanny, the waves of arrests, the ruthless proceedings of the authorities against more and more groups of the population, and especially the use of terror and torture by the State Police as the year advanced, roused strong feelings among the people. Hatred for the enemy's henchmen, the members of the NS, might become so strong that, when peace came, a judicial settlement might be anticipated by a 'night of the long knives'. So it was necessary to make a start on the preparation of a judicial settlement, and accordingly a small committee in close touch with the Circle undertook this in collaboration with the Government in London. It was also high time for NS members to be given a clear warning of the fate which would be meted out to them; this would have been rather useless earlier on, but now that the tide of war had turned, there was a hope that some of them would think twice.

One of my associates from the earliest days of the war Arvid Brodersen, brought me the draft of a letter to members of the NS which he had discussed with Bishop Berggrav, then under house-arrest at his country cabin outside Oslo. It was shown to some of the members of the Co-ordination Committee and of the Circle, a part of whom were against it and others doubtful; in particular, it was urged that it was wrong to hold out expectations to members that to leave the NS Party now would have a mitigating effect when the judicial settlement took place. Therefore the draft was not sent out on the leadership's behalf. I undertook to re-edit and tighten up the document, so that it should be quite clear that only positive actions, involving great personal risk, for the benefit of the national resistance struggle would modify the account on the day of settlement. Afterwards the secretariat had thousands of copies printed under the title 'Warning to those who help the enemy', which were posted to conspicuous members of the NS in all parts of the country; it was also reprinted in many illegal newspapers without any pressure on our part.

The first point in the letter was a reminder that Norway was at war with Germany, as had been repeatedly confirmed by the Germans, most recently through the taking of Norwegian officers as prisoners-of-war. Much emphasis was laid upon the responsibility of NS members for the Party's collaboration with the occupying power in a series of offences against international law and in the oppression and intimidation of the people. Attention was drawn to the increasingly brutal methods used by the Party leaders, such as the murder of Eilifsen, and to the object which lay behind the arming and weapon-training of male members of the NS. They were reminded that even before the war Norway had definite penalties for treason, to which a number of additions had been made, including in 1941 the penalty of death for particularly grave cases and in 1943 the penalty of a fine without a top limit. It was made clear that the state would carry out a judicial settlement and that taking the law into one's own hands would not be tolerated; in return, punishment must be severe enough to meet the reasonable demands of the community for just retribution. Finally, the letter addressed a sharp warning, not to those who were already doomed to the heaviest penalties of the law, but to those for whom the account was not yet closed.

The letter caused considerable unrest in the ranks of the NS, and one of its legal backers was set to write reassuring articles in the controlled newspapers.

Brodersen continued to concern himself with the possibilities for driving in wedges to split the ranks of our opponents. He knew the German mentality well and had good connections with anti-Nazi circles in the *Wehrmacht*. In 1944 at his suggestion we started an 'opposition' paper, called *Norsk Hird*, of which he edited the first two issues. Our secretariat undertook the printing and distribution, and found a new editor after Brodersen had to leave the country.

The closing-down of the Oslo University

The discussion of counter-measures to NS control over the university authorities and the students' committees in the autumn of 1941 had revealed marked differences of opinion in the centre of our academic life. These concerned matters both of principle and of practice, which may be simplified as follows. One wing, represented by most of the deans of faculties and many professors, accepted practical co-operation with the new acting-head (Pro-rector) of the University, the NS professor Adolf Hoel, whom they regarded as the least dangerous of the possible candidates for the post. This wing, which at several junctures proved to be the more numerous, considered that it was right to keep the University in operation for as long as possible and regarded its position as distinct from the resistance struggle at large. The other wing, represented by a secret committee of action, wanted a fully consistent line of resistance in keeping with the Standfast struggle elsewhere, even if this might affect the University's existence.

Opinion among the students was likewise divided. Many were chiefly concerned to complete their studies; others belonged to illegal resistance groups with special objects, such as intelligence activities, and wanted to keep the University intact as a workplace and centre for organisation; others again had a part in the Standfast struggle, as in the publishing of illegal newspapers, and wished the University to be in the front line of the struggle and not to come hesitantly behind. After the discussion about a strike in the autumn of 1941, a number of those who were ideologically most concerned absented themselves, at any rate for a time, which no doubt contributed to the scarcity of qualified resistance leaders, which was apparent in student circles in some critical situations. But early in 1942 the students themselves established an illegal leadership; both this and the action committee of the University teaching staff came gradually into contact with the Co-ordination Committee.

At the beginning of 1942 the Party authorities tried to push NS students ahead of their proper turn into the faculty of medicine, which had been limited for want of space. Teachers and students resisted strongly, but were not entirely successful. Just before the start of the autumn term, the Department sent a new demand for NS students to be given preference for medical studies. The dean of the faculty took the matter up with the Pro-rector, Hoel; later, he and the dean of the faculty of mathematics and natural sciences also met Skancke, the Acting-Minister of Education, but no solution was reached.

Meanwhile the committee of action was working for a joint protest from the faculties, of which the text had been completed, and the representatives of the students and other interested bodies in the University were ready to give it their support. But after a meeting between the two deans and Quisling, backed by the NS leadership in the University, which began with sharp controversy, a provisional solution was reached. This prevented any preference being given to NS students for the time being by throwing open the lectures for the restricted courses, while certain compulsory parts of the curriculum were postponed for a year. The acceptance of this solution by a majority of the

University teaching staff knocked the bottom out of the well-prepared protest action. The supporters of 'the deans' line' in the University also tolerated the arrest and removal from their posts of two of the professors of medicine in succession.

In February 1943, as previously mentioned, the students were caught off guard by the NS student leader in connection with the announcement of the 'national' labour effort, but a counter-action went ahead and prevented the blunder from having lasting consequences. It was a valuable lesson for the students, who from then onwards were more watchful.

The final crisis for the University came in the following autumn, when the assembling of students was postponed until 1 October, so that they could help in the harvest. The University was confronted a month in advance by new regulations for admission, formulated by the NS Department of Education, which included a rule that the Rector (and not, as hitherto, the separate faculties) was to determine admissions and that 25 per cent of students were to be admitted on other criteria than their marks. It was not hard to guess what was meant by 'other criteria', and the regulations were to come into force for the first admissions in four weeks' time. The crisis was acute.

Contact between the illegal action committees and the leadership of the Home Front had now been strengthened. The University teachers' committee had had Schjelderup as an adviser from an earlier period, and now received direct contact with the Co-ordination Committee through Alex Johnson. I myself had all the time been in touch with the committee of action through Jan Jansen, and now the illegal leadership of the students was likewise put in touch with me.

The proposal for a statement to be put forward through the faculties was discussed with representative teachers from all of them, and was approved by the Co-ordination Committee. It contained a point-black rejection of the proposed new regulations, and aimed at bringing the University on to the same consistent line of resistance as had been followed previously by the Supreme Court, the Church and people in the schools. After the preface to the protest had been to some extent modified, it was approved by all the faculties against the votes of a few NS professors. This was in the middle of September; but a week later the deans were summoned to a meeting with Skancke and Hoel. After a preliminary exchange of views, in which the deans stood firmly by the rejection of the new regulation, a

The rounding-up of students at Oslo University, 30 November 1943.

fresh round of negotiations was begun, which had gone a long way when it was broken off by Quisling. The next day, 15 October, ten professors and fifty to sixty students were arrested.

The deans protested against this, but opposed an action of protest by the rest of the teaching staff, which was therefore held off for four weeks. It was supported at once by an organised action on the part of the students by means of individual letters; this was very badly received both by the NS authorities and by the principal negotiators among the deans, who considered that the action blocked a release which the Pro-rector had promised. Then on 28 November an opposition group from outside University circles set its Great Hall on fire — which was extinguished before any serious damage could be done. In leading quarters on the Home Front it was believed at the time that this must be a typical piece of Nazi provocation: a Norwegian 'Reichstag Fire'. At any rate it was used as such, for Terboven now found that the time had come to direct a decisive blow against the University.

For a long time Brodersen had been supplying me with information about the internal affairs of the Germans in Oslo from a group of anti-Nazi officers, led by Lieutenant-Colonel Theodor Steltzer in the transport command of the *Wehrmacht*. On the evening of 29 November Brodersen brought a warning from Steltzer that at 11 a.m. the next day the Security Service, with the support of SS detachments numbering 300 men, would go into action against the University, which was to be closed; all male students were to be arrested, collected in a camp in Vestfold and sent to Germany. Some members of the action committee of the teaching staff, who had been informed some hours before, had found that it would not be possible to save all the students because of recent detections of the 'export' organisations; so provisionally a warning should only go out to organised resistance groups in the University. I doubted whether this was the right course, and during the night I fixed up a meeting of a number of key people in the leadership of the Home Front, including the head of our 'export' organisation, Aage Biering. After an earnest canvassing of the situation and the chances of snapping up several thousand persons as it were out of the jaws of an all-powerful Gestapo, we agreed to arrange a general warning. The deciding factor was Biering's firm belief that the organisations could manage the job of getting the students out of the country.

The action was prepared and set going by our little secretariat with the help of one of my closest associates at the University, Alf Sanengen. In the early hours of the morning we managed to get the warning through in a satisfactory way to all the University's places of instruction around the capital. In the new science blocks the students to a great extent took heed of the warning and got away when the German forces went into action at 11, but in the old buildings down in the centre of the town there were many who took the chance of its being a false alarm. Some of the teaching staff did not pass the warning on to students who were taking examinations, and other 'well-informed' professors who had sided with the deans reassured students who asked their advice that the warning was not correct. All through the day and the following night German police with motor-cycles and cars were busily rounding up the students by street controls in the centre of the town and visiting of the places where they lived. Altogether more than 1,100 students were arrested on one of the grimmest days the capital experienced during the occupation.

The action took us by surprise, which may sound strange in retrospect — and indeed we had an inkling that something was under preparation, especially after the Gestapo earlier in the autumn had gone through the registers of students at the

University. But it is a wrong view which has been maintained after the war, that we who were 'activists' in the dispute about the University wanted it closed. What we did want was to put an end to the policy of negotiation and collaboration with the NS authorities, which was favoured by a majority of the deans and by many professors, and which gradually brought the University out of step with the rest of the resistance movement. No individual group could be permitted to conduct a policy in relation to the enemy and the NS authorities at variance with the general line of conflict, for this might easily have large and disastrous consequences all along the front.

That the dissatisfaction with the line taken by the deans was keenly felt among the Home Front leaders was shown in a statement from the Co-ordination Committee in March 1944. It had been asked to put a question from Norwegian professors then in Stockholm concerning the education of the Norwegian students in Sweden to one of the two deans who had headed the negotiations with the NS authorities. The committee prefaced its answer with the following: 'Before we express ourselves on the matter, we call attention to the fact that we have found no reason to lay it before Professor N.N., since he as little as the other deans enjoys the confidence of the Home Front... We have ascertained, on the other hand, that the view of the matter which we express below is shared by those who are at present within the range of University teachers who have fought for a firm and uncompromising attitude at the University ...'

By a great effort on the part of all the 'export' organisations, those students who had evaded arrest were brought to safety in Sweden, where many of them joined the Norwegian police troops which were being set up.* After a short interruption, the research work at most of the University institutes could be resumed, in the shelter of which much of the illegal activity previously developed there was continued. As for the students under arrest, about half were gradually released, while the remainder, numbering about 700, shared the fate of the policemen who had been arrested some months earlier, as they were sent to a 'retraining camp' in Germany.

The German action against the students at Oslo University in

*On 23 November 1943 the Swedish Government authorised a restricted form of military training for and by Norwegian nationals, who might later be used to preserve order in Norway in the event of a German collapse. About 14,300 refugees took part.

the autumn of 1943 made a deep impression in the outside world, particularly in Sweden, where it did much to rouse both public opinion and those in government circles to an understanding of the true meaning of German mastery in Europe. The Swedish Government appealed to the German Government in vain to stop the action and not to deport the students.

The organisation and leadership of the Home Front in 1943

In the course of 1943 and the first half of 1944 Milorg was slowly and surely re-established and extended, while the plans for organising it which dated from 1942 were carried out, so that in Southern Norway it comprised fourteen districts and more than 30,000 men. The Military Council was made more representative, with two members from the Circle and the head of the War Police — the secret organisation in readiness for the period of liberation which was formed in co-operation with the Government in London. A member from the workers' illegal organisations had already been added to it early in 1942. What was more important, however, was the expansion of the Council's central military staff (SL) and the district organisations. Under the leadership of J.C. Hauge, the SL was turned into an effectively centralised and departmentalised organisation; Hauge himself became a member of the Council in the autumn of 1943, and his authority and efficiency made him the most influential leader of Milorg for the rest of the war.

In London co-operation at last functioned properly between the Norwegian military authorities, represented by the newly established Defence Command (FO), and the British SOE organisation, which included the Linge Company. This disposed of the earlier disagreement about guidelines and forms of organisation for the military activity in Norway as led from home and as inspired from London. In May 1943 there was a meeting across the border in Sweden between Helset and Hauge and representatives from the FO and the Norwegian military office at the Legation in Stockholm. The lines of guidance and the command structure for Milorg's further activities were then fixed in accordance with the strategy determined by SHAEF — the Allied Supreme Command. Milorg had to accept a reduction in the intended scope of its contribution during the period of liberation and lost the power to start actions independently. The Norwegian Command in London was to regulate Milorg's co-operation during an eventual invasion, and direct communication was to be established between it and the Milorg districts. In return the FO would not, except in special cases, establish military groups in Norway apart from Milorg. Instructions and organisational guidance were formulated in accordance with the agreement, and strict discipline was required in Milorg's ranks.

This was the best year for the Gestapo in its struggle against Milorg, with detections on a large scale in every part of the country. It was also the year when the noisy agitation for guerrilla warfare which the Communists set going — and which was combined with the rousing of suspicion alike against the Western Allies and the leadership at home — created considerable disquiet among the young. The fact that discipline held out and Milorg continued to grow testifies to the strength of the central leadership, the district staffs, and the rank and file.

The agreement of May 1943 gave the Norwegian military authorities in London decisive control over Milorg in Norway. Yet although the Military Council and Central Staff had formally renounced the possibility of giving fighting orders on their own account, they strengthened their position inside the country by establishing a good working relationship with London and seeing to it that the resolutions from the meeting in May were promptly executed in the districts. Their co-operation with the FO also gave them the chance to influence the distribution of weapons, instructors and communications personnel to the various districts, and they could affect the shaping of the tactical guidance formulated by the FO. Nevertheless, the arrangement meant that the command over Milorg was no longer allocated to any leadership inside Norway. This situation was known to only a few people on the outside; I myself did not know it until the last phase of the war.

On the civil side there was no development of the resistance front in 1943 to correspond with that of Milorg. 'Sivorg' was a term used exclusively by Milorg people who needed a common name for the rest of the Home Front activity. Inasmuch as the work of civil (*sivil*) resistance was all the time directed outwards and shaped the daily struggle in the eyes of the people, 'The Home Front' was the customary designation for the conglomerate of civil organisations. Its nucleus was still the illegal organisations within the separate occupations. On a national basis the most important element was the Co-ordination

Committee, its secretariat, and district organisations covering the entire country from north to south and east to west, while in relation to London and Milorg the Circle and its secretariat occupied the central position. Inside the capital the pattern of organisation was decentralised and complex. The leadership fell to small groups and to individuals, mainly people whose hazardous organisation work and wide network of contacts gave them from one day to the next the necessary information on the enemy's actions and intentions, so that they were in a position to decide on the required counter-measures and set them in operation. In 1943 this category of leaders, which never acquired a name but can best be described as an executive leadership, comprised eight to ten men.

From that year, the pressure upon the major unorganised groups of the population was an important element in the Nazis' tactics, particularly with the object of procuring labour and other help for the ever more exhausted German war machine. The need for a more centralised leadership was therefore increasingly evident, and one was developed on an informal daily basis, composed according to the changing needs of the situation, from those who from 1942 onwards had been meeting inside the offices of a lawyer, E.T. Poulsson. Skjönsberg and Biering still had charge of the financing of resistance activities, and they also worked together in many other fields; both of them had good connections with Milorg and with the prison and security service. Biering in addition took a special interest in the 'export' of refugees and the supply service and had many contacts in the police, while Skjönsberg was the link between the principal committees, was concerned with the activation of the future civil administration, and communicated directives and guidelines for the leadership of the press. Boyesen and Engen conducted comprehensive intelligence activities on the civil and political front to keep the Government informed, and co-operated with the press office at the Stockholm Legation in passing the correspondence between the Circle and the Government; this was microfilmed and — with the help of the train staff — hidden in a screwed-down container under one of the carriages on the route between Oslo and Stockholm.

Bonnevie-Svendsen — the missioner to the deaf who was the linch-pin in the illegal Church organisation — conducted a many-sided activity which one of his contacts epitomised thus: 'His church for the deaf had food from Denmark inside the altar rail* and weapons in the crypt!' In the first half of 1943, Kåre Norum, who had been in charge of the organisation of the Co-ordination Committee and was one of those who set the tone for the teachers' front, was among the most industrious labourers in the illegal vineyard, as talented in the practical work of communications as in the formulation of directives. When he departed at midsummer, Magnus Jensen became the principal spokesman of the teachers in the group. Jan Jansen figured quietly and steadily among them all, as contact man with the academic front and the mysterious set behind the *Bulletin*. That the peaceful, modest Reader in Anatomy alone constituted that set, writing both authoritative leading articles and shrewd military surveys which appeared to demand the highest professional qualifications, was surmised by nobody. Schjelderup still frequented the company of active leaders, but he was absorbed in the new tasks imposed by the preparations for the civil administration at the time of liberation. This description of the category of leaders remains incomplete, for the action committees of the occupational organisations included people who were engaged full-time on their own front, where their leadership of important sectors was relatively independent.

The directives were fixed, as before, by those who led the action within the separate occupations, but as the centre of gravity in the struggle moved from them to larger sections of the population, the directives became to a greater extent a matter for the Co-ordination Committee. Those who represented their occupations there acquired more authority and had increased influence on the making of directives inside their own groups as well. The illegal press became by degrees a more important instrument for the dissemination of directives, while the various auxiliary organisations for supply, security and the transportation of refugees mattered very much more to the individual resistance organisations as the Gestapo increased its pressure. Thus the executive leadership, which gathered together all the threads and either controlled or strongly influenced both the resistance organisations themselves and the auxiliaries, became a link in the workings of the Home Front which was at least as important as the committees which took the formal decisions.

*From the autumn of 1941 the Danes sent food to relieve distress in Norway and covertly to help the Home Front; the total was 32,716 tons.

The system of leadership and the pattern of organisation on the civil side in 1943 had grown out of the exigencies of the situation, and the division of responsibility was largely dependent on the militancy and field of interest of the individual, with the result that overlapping and duplication of work were not infrequent. In some respects this was advantageous at that stage of the war, and it was one reason why the Gestapo, in spite of big advances, did not figure things out and could not so easily crush the Home Front. But the co-operation had been going on from the first years of the struggle, and most of those concerned knew each other's names and positions: if the Gestapo got hold of the right thread, great disasters might follow.

When I took over Norum's duties for the Co-ordination Committee at midsummer, I was drawn into this set, all of whom gave me help and support. For many practical purposes Biering was of most assistance: he had any number of contacts and could get hold of almost anything in a capital city which had been generally stripped. Jansen continued to be my daily adviser, whose patience in listening to his young associates was endless, while his powers of judgment gave us confidence during the daily turmoil.

The Communist line on the struggle

The average Norwegian Communist had very much the same view as other Norwegians of the German invasion on 9 April 1940. But in the occupied areas, especially round Oslo, it was not many days before the leading men in the Party had shown a much greater willingness to co-operate with the enemy than those who represented the other parties. This struck the rest of the population so forcibly that the Communist Party (NKP) leaders in the then still unoccupied county of Troms published in a local newspaper on the 16th an appeal to support the Nygaardsvold Government, with the heading: 'Communists are Norwegians!' and the following explanatory remark: 'As there have been a lot of questions about the position of the Communist Party in the existing situation ...'

The party line, which was defined in a number of leading articles in the Communist organ *Arbeideren* and in many appeals from the secretariat in the spring and summer of 1940, admits of a rough comparison with that of the French Vichy Government after the collapse on the Western Front that June.

It was most plainly visible in practice among the many Communist or 'fellow-travelling' representatives inside the Trade Union Opposition in the LO during 1940-1. The line was carried further, though with declining vigour, after the Communist Party was banned in August 1940 and some of its members arrested (mostly for brief periods), and right up to the German invasion of the Soviet Union on 22 June 1941. It is not fanciful to claim that the NKP followed directives from the Comintern after the signing of the Hitler-Stalin pact of August 1939, so that it was not a cordial relationship but a policy of opportunism which the leaders acted upon in 1940-1. There is also no doubt that individual party members were unable to swallow it and by degrees joined the resistance. In the Bergen area some Communists had entered the resistance organisation at an early stage.

On the other hand, the NKP did not join in the agreement of the other parties in August 1940 for the abandonment of political agitation on a party basis for the duration of the war. The Marxist objective was indeed damped down in favour of a supranationalist phraseology in their appeals and newspaper propaganda; active resistance people often joined Communist-organised groups without at first noticing the element of party politics. It was a typical Popular Front policy which Peder Furubotn* launched and got accepted at a party meeting at the turn of 1941-2, when he secured the rejection of the old leadership and filled most of the key positions in the central committee with people of his own. In fact it was not until the spring of 1943 that the NKP came forward as a resistance organisation under the party name, having worked for the two preceding years under cover of organisational names such as the League of Norwegian Patriots, the National Guard and National Front. Furubotn's closest associates included some of the foremost Communist representatives in the 'trade union opposition'. At the beginning of 1942 a proposal was put forward for an 'agreement of unity' in the Labour movement, which was so full of phrases and big words about the need to create 'a united national will of the people, a truly heroic will to fight', and about making the national front into 'a heroic and unconquerable force', that the following comment on the

*P.E. Furubotn (1890-1975), a Bergen carpenter and pioneer Communist, had worked in Moscow for the Comintern from 1930 to 1938; he left the Party in 1949 after a dispute between fractions.

guidance given understates the case: 'The terms employed were so general that no one could take exception to them, but they were marked by an ultra-patriotic tone which was not attractive.' Nor did it make a very good impression on us, when we first saw the document in 1943, that those strong words about the need for national unity in the struggle came from the party which in the first years of the war, when it was a matter of life and death for our nation to stand together against the occupying power and the party of treason, had consistently pursued a policy of division. Nevertheless, after the party finally decided to enter the struggle, it did so in a way which commanded considerable respect.* It organised an effective illegal press and a skilful 'export' apparatus, and it possessed military action groups which had performed several bold exploits.

Yet Furubotn arranged his affairs in a way which limited his freedom of operation. He set up his successive headquarters in out-of-the-way valleys or mountain-pasture neighbourhoods and had only advance posts of his organisation in or near Oslo, connection with which was maintained by couriers, as was also the connection with their representatives in Stockholm and the Soviet Legation there. Our opinion on the Home Front was that the opposition must be led from Oslo, where we were best able to follow the enemy's movements and keep in touch with all the big resistance organisations. A system of communications which was founded on individual couriers quickly showed itself to be risky, and in the autumn of 1942 the Gestapo came on the track of the Communists' organisation centre not far from Oslo; this they attacked at the end of October, when one key man in the Party was arrested and two were shot. Immediately afterwards 200-300 German police went into action against Furubotn's quarters in the high mountains, and although he and the rest of the central committee got away at the last moment after shots had been exchanged between the Gestapo and the outposts, in the later part of the war the central committee was kept on the move between different remote locations.

For a long time the sabotage operations in Oslo and East Norway were headed by a veteran of the Spanish Civil War,

*At the election of 1936 NKP received only 4,376 votes (0.30%); in 1945 — when the military triumphs of Soviet Russia were a contributory factor — it reached a peak of 176,535 votes (11.89%). The widow of Viggo Hansteen, who had himself left the Party early in 1940, was one of two Communists in the inter-party Government after the liberation.

Asbjörn Sunde (commonly known as 'Osvald'), but these too did not begin until the Soviet Union entered the war. A series of actions at the turn of 1941-2 were rather unsuccessful, and the Gestapo traced the groups; in the following August an otherwise successfully completed attack on the State Police offices in Oslo was immediately followed by the capture of most of Sunde's closest collaborators by the Gestapo, with executions as the result.

In the course of 1942 there were negotiations between a Communist-led military organisation and Milorg in East Norway. In Oslo, however, the connection was severed after the East Oslo section of D13 lost its entire leadership in January 1943 during a big wave of detections which started with arrests of Communists. The co-operation had been slow to develop, the Communists being chiefly interested in establishing contacts with the Linge Company and obtaining weapons, without wanting any real co-ordination. After that the central military staff was against any fresh attempt to co-operate. In district 15 — the county of Vestfold — Milorg received loyal support from some units of an organisation called the National Guard, which was partly controlled by Communists. In West Norway Communist action groups were equipped with weapons and trained by Linge people who otherwise worked for Milorg district D20; these groups carried out several bold and valuable actions in the Bergen area and Stavanger, sometimes with heavy losses, and in general worked loyally according to the guidelines which applied to Milorg. In 1942-3 Milorg was in contact with Sunde's action groups through the police group in Oslo; the action against the Oslo Labour Office in April 1943 had been approved in advance by the Military Council.

Sabotage under Communist leadership increased in the following autumn, attracting a good many young people who did not realise the political background of what was being done; their sole desire was to fight for their country, and they lacked the patience to submit to the guidelines which at that time Milorg had to follow in order to obtain arms and other help from the Allies. Some of the actions were useful; others, directed against railway lines and generator-fuel factories,* had no particular military significance but resulted all the same in

*These prepared billets of wood for use as substitute fuel in motor vehicles, etc.

heavy counter-measures by the occupying power. So the male population in the places where these actions occurred were compelled to go on 'railway guard' or 'civic guard', answerable with their lives for any fresh acts of sabotage. A number of raids which they directed against small savings bank branches were likewise not particularly popular, and gave the authorities rather too good arguments in their propaganda against 'bandit operations', as the Nazi-controlled press called them.

Conflict over lines of action

By degrees the Communist newspapers started to agitate against the line of action which the Home Front had followed so successfully during the Standfast struggle. Even though some strokes had gone wrong early in 1943 in relation to the 'national' labour effort, these had been to a great extent corrected; yet in the course of the autumn the front showed increasing signs of weariness. These were due to the heavy blows which had fallen on us at short intervals and which we had only small means of parrying, but also to a general disappointment over the fact that the expected Allied invasion in the west had not materialised in the past summer. This was a situation which could not be set right by propaganda talk about 'awakening the giant powers of the people' — to quote one of Furubotn's favourite expressions. Nor was there any political offensive from the NS side just then; the Home Front was often at its best under pressure.

Milorg had been significantly developed during the year, thanks to a vigorous effort by the district leaders up and down the country and the energetic work of the central staff under J.C. Hauge; the force now numbered 30,000 men. Co-operation with the British was well under way, and members of the Linge Company were functioning in many districts as instructors in the handling of weapons and as communications personnel. But so few weapons had yet arrived that there were not even enough for purposes of instruction: Milorg was still mainly an army without the means of warfare. Sabotage by Linge groups showed a systematic increase, but it was done without any overtones of propaganda. The enemy knew who was behind it, and executed without compunction — and in conflict with international law — the Norwegian and British soldiers whom they occasionally caught; but as a rule reprisals against the population were confined to those cases where it was suspected of having assisted.

For the sake of arms and other support, Milorg was bound by the instructions which were issued from time to time by SHAEF as the Allied supreme command. In 1943 and the first half of 1944, this meant the practice of self-restraint and patience. Norway was then overshadowed by the main theatres of war, and SHAEF did not want a situation to develop in Norway which might disturb Allied operational plans.

The Communists started an increasingly vociferous agitation for guerrilla warfare, combined with a sowing of suspicion alike against the Western Allies, the Government and the leadership at home. For a long time the Home Front leaders took the agitation calmly, in spite of the strain it imposed on those with a bent for action, both in the leadership and among the young. Economic support was given to the activities of the Communists in connection with the illegal press and the transport of refugees, and on several occasions Home Front people helped Communist action groups with accommodation and possibilities of work. The support which the Communists received was sent through various channels, and amounted altogether to larger amounts than went to any other organisation except Milorg.

In September the Communists sent the Home Front leadership a request for increased economic support for their press. Skjönsberg and the press chief then met two of Furubotn's closest associates, to whom support was promised on condition that the Communists followed the Home Front's guidelines in the struggle.

Shortly afterwards, on 7 October 1943, a Communist action group, headed by Sunde, attacked a main-line train near Drammen, causing the deaths of two Germans and a larger number of Norwegians. This was met by extensive raids in the Drammen district, the arrest of sixty hostages, and threats from the Gestapo that a number of them would be executed unless prominent local representatives sent out an appeal denouncing acts of sabotage. The population was panic-stricken, and an appeal against sabotage, placed in the local papers by some worthy citizens, received the spontaneous endorsement of thousands of local people. Five of the hostages were afterwards executed by the Gestapo. This happening was an obvious setback for the Home Front, and a little later the Circle sent an evaluation of the action against the train and its consequences to the authorities outside Norway, saying: 'We too condemn most severely the senseless acts of sabotage of which we have recently seen several examples — while at the same time strongly favouring all sabotage with a purpose, including acts of violence which genuinely damage the German war effort.'

Skjönsberg and Biering arranged another meeting at the ending of October with representatives of the central committee of the Communist Party, at which they met the two from the previous occasion and one other person. This time there was a heated discussion, in which the representatives of the Home Front leadership pointed out that what had followed the recent railway sabotage showed that ordinary people did not accept that form of 'activist' militancy. To conduct active warfare demanded support and sympathy from the population, in the absence of which it would quickly collapse without having achieved any military significance worth mentioning. The terror with which the enemy at that time would confront an 'aggressive line' would affect the Standfast position, the very heart of our struggle, and would put great obstacles in the way of the military and civil preparations. The Communists maintained, however, that such attacks as that near Drammen aimed at inciting reprisals from the enemy, which in turn would rouse the people to further efforts. But Skjönsberg insisted that he could only promise continued economic support so long as they refrained from such attacks, and the two Communists in charge accepted this. At the same time the Communists put forward proposals for the reorganisation of the Government, the setting up of a 'unified political centre' to conduct the struggle at home, likewise of a people's court, and presented our representatives with a large collection of documents. The proposals were rejected immediately.

In the Home Front, too, this affair occasioned a debate on principles, which resulted in complete agreement between the civil and military sectors regarding the guidelines for the struggle. A draft drawn up by Hauge was used by the Circle, the Military Council, and the leadership of the Police for a lengthy letter to the Government, in which the question of a modification of campaign methods was thoroughly examined. It reached this conclusion: 'We are convinced that what serves everybody best is for the Home Front to continue its struggle against the enemy along the lines followed hitherto, and that to activate the campaign by attacks on the enemy at the present juncture would be a fatal mistake.'

Nevertheless, agreement did not signify that the leadership

was contented with the state of affairs in 1943. The Coordination Committee was uneasy about individual breaches of the front at the end of the year, such as the paying of subscriptions to the NS dentists' association and the weakness of attitude among parts of the commercial community. It was particularly Poulsson in *News for Lawyers* and Jansen in the *Bulletin* who showed tireless energy and great literary skill in the struggle to combat war-weariness and lack of backbone. In September Poulsson wrote an article entitled 'It is not enough', challenging the trend towards compliance:

> The question today is whether you are making an active effort to hinder the advance of Nazism. The question is whether you are willing, in the concrete case now actually presented and not merely in something on a big scale at some future time, to adopt a standpoint which at any moment may land you in prison. The question is whether you can see the large in the small, the significant in the insignificant, the matter of principle in something casual. If not, you too or else your son may one day be a Nazi soldier on the Eastern Front. That is what Hitler wants to use Quisling for.

In the issue of the *Bulletin* for February 1944, Jansen wrote an article on 'Balance of mind', which included the following:

> We have been under a heavy strain for a long time now, our nervous strength has been drained for nearly four years, so it would not be strange if our mental balance were somewhat unstable. It would be understandable but it would be unfortunate, and we must guard against it ...
>
> The fluctuations are particularly marked between optimism and pessimism over the events of the war, not as regards the eventual result, for that has never been in doubt, but as regards how long the war will last. After a couple of stimulating events at the front, people are convinced that it will all be over in two or three months, but if fourteen days pass without particularly striking events, they suddenly see no end to the misery ... The Home Front is not served by such uncontrolled, uninhibited fluctuations. We need a steady course and balanced people.

6

THE SPECTRE OF MOBILISATION

The central question for the Norwegian Home Front at the end of 1943 and the beginning of 1944 was not what pinpricks our few, ill-armed action groups could inflict upon superior German forces. It was how to prevent tens of thousands of our young people of military age from being compelled to fight on the enemy's side on the Eastern Front, where the German troops were on the retreat and the need for reinforcements was obvious. The rumours that the NS had offered to provide 50,000 men from Norway were more and more persistent as the year drew to an end, so in mid-January 1944 the Co-ordination Committee took the matter up for thorough discussion. It was a meeting I shall never forget. Our fear was that the Nazis would be able to use the Labour Service (AT), originally a voluntary organisation started by short-sighted idealists at the time of the Administrative Council, the object being that the youth of Norway should take part in the country's reconstruction. In reality it was a semi-military organisation, which after the NS came into power had been made compulsory and discreetly converted into a tool for the authorities by such means as the introduction of NS officers into the top positions. It was only slightly involved in the political struggle, and its efforts to help with food production and wood-cutting had gained it considerable sympathy and support in the countryside. Its rolls contained the names and addresses of tens of thousands of young people of prime military age.

Information was given at the meeting of the committee, which suggested that the Labour Service was going to be called up earlier than usual and in considerably greater numbers than the 5,000 taken in each previous year. There was no difference of opinion about the desirability of stopping AT, the discussion centring instead upon the extent to which a directive on the subject would be followed.

Poulsson strongly favoured a boycott, which he supported

with a battery of arguments, while the engineers' representative leaned most heavily to the other side; he believed that most people saw no particular danger in the AT, so that it would be impossible to get adequate backing for the directive, and several members agreed with him. By degrees the debate became both sharp and heated, until there was an intervention by Skjönsberg, who had sat listening for a long time in silence. Quietly and powerfully, he cut through the doubt which gnawed at all of us: we must not hesitate any longer, but must take up the struggle against the danger which the AT represented for the nation's youth. We must go forward and show the way — 'by day in a pillar of a cloud, by night in a pillar of fire'. His contribution made a great impression on all of us, and we resolved to resist the Labour Service.

In addition, we considered the matter to be so important for the position of Milorg that it ought to be laid before the Military Council. Poulsson was asked to draft a directive and contact Milorg, and a week later we were notified that Milorg was in agreement. At about the same time we had got hold of a copy of a letter, dated 17 January 1944, in which the 'Minister of Justice', Riisnæs, made an offer to a German SS general to mobilise five annual age-groups of Norwegian youth for service on the Eastern Front. As one of the most revealing documents in the history of the occupation, this letter deserves to be reproduced here in its entirety:

MEMORANDUM

Every since New Year 1942 I have considered and maintained that Norway ought to be wholly or partly mobilised, and the troops set in on the Eastern Front. I am convinced that it can be counted upon that the great majority of the soldiers will be reliable in battle against bolshevik Soviet Russia.* On the other hand, in my opinion reliability cannot be counted upon as a general rule in the employment of Norwegian troops on other fronts.

As time has passed and the struggle against Soviet Russia has become ever harder, it can be counted upon that the reliability has become steadily greater. Nevertheless, a mobilisation is a measure which in the event must only be undertaken with the exercise of great caution and observance of all the necessary security arrangements. *A successful completion depends absolutely upon the utmost discretion, care, and energy being shown at every point of contributory service.*

*NS propaganda had succeeded in enlisting at least 5,000 Norwegian volunteers for the Eastern Front.

1 There are to be mobilised in the first instance at least five age groups (18-23 years), which will amount to about 75,000 men.
2 The Norwegian authorities are to be supported to the greatest possible extent by *the German civil and military authorities*. The mobilisation will be carried out in exact co-operation.
3 In good time before the first day of mobilisation:
   (a) the frontier towards Sweden must be barred by the greatest possible muster of military formations and police.
   (b) The watch along the coast must be increased.
4 The announcement of the mobilisation of the five annual classes will take place thereafter first and foremost by poster. The posters will be put up everywhere in the entire country *simultaneously*. The troops are required within a precisely fixed time-limit to meet at a fixed place (assembly centre). The time-limit must be fixed differently according to local conditions. In the towns and densely populated areas in the country twenty-four hours, otherwise from two to five days.
5 Those who *fail* to meet will be fetched by *commando detachments of soldiers and police* as soon as possible.
6 At the assembly points the troops will be sifted politically. Communistic elements will be taken out and placed in internment camps (Berg, Bredtvedt). The spokesmen for Nasjonal Samling in the area should therefore be present at the assembly points.
7 From the assembly centres the troops should be sent in detachments to the quarters, and from there as quickly as possible to the training camps in Germany. It will be desirable (but not essential) for the troops during their stay in the quarters and before departure to Germany to be
   (a) medically examined;
   (b) put into uniform (jacket, trousers, cap, boots, shoes, stockings, underwear, belt);
   (c) immediately set to introductory training.
8 *They ought not to be given arms here in the country*. The transportation to Germany must take place as quickly as possible and be carried out *in the course of 14 days*.
9 The troops will be put into formations *belonging to the Waffen SS*. They will wear SS uniforms and should be informed that they are not German but Germanic soldiers.
   The Norwegian troops should never constitute more than 50% of the unit concerned (*platoon, company, battalion, regiment*). The other 50% should be German troops.
10 In the case of the three northernmost counties (Finnmark, Troms and Nordland) the transportation should be if possible via Kirkenes to *Russian Karelia*, where the troops will be placed in training camps and established on the front from Murmansk and southwards.

11 Apart from the Communistic elements being taken out and interned, the mobilisation ought to comprise *all troops of the annual classes decided upon.*
As regards industry of military importance, there ought to be no exceptions (exemptions) allowed. What we are concerned with here are the youngest age groups and there are *practically speaking no skilled workers among them.* Industry of military importance will therefore not be affected. Should there exceptionally be found troops who work at plants of military importance, these must be replaced by requisition from the Labour Exchange. The mobilisation also assumes that female labour will be requisitioned from the Labour Exchange to a greater extent than is the case at present.

This letter was obtained by a circuitous route through a member of Milorg, who got a copy from a girl he knew who worked in Riisnæs' office. It gave the best possible evidence that AT must be stopped, and banished the last remaining doubts from the Co-ordination Committee's minds.

In the executive leadership we considered that there was another point of danger — the civic guard. Under various names, such as railway guard and quay guard, the occupation authorities had from the earliest period of the war compelled Norwegian civilians to keep watch on threatened lines of transport and communications. In the autumn of 1943 Quisling produced a 'law' on civic guard, and the call-ups for that purpose increased. Not only did the civic guards relieve the Nazi police and military forces, but it was also conceivable that the Nazi authorities would be able in this way to lay hands on parts of the population which were fit for fighting; it was certain in any case that the civic guards freed German troops from guard duties. At its meetings in mid-January 1944, the majority of the Co-ordination Committee would not agree to a complete boycott of the civic guard, so only a restricted directive for refusal was sent out. But after Riisnæs' letter with the proposal for mobilisation had become known, we got to hear alarming rumours about new Nazi plans for the civic guard, and it was decided at a hurriedly summoned meeting of the executive to send out a directive for a full boycott. When the committee itself next met, we who had done this had to swallow hard words from certain members who claimed that we had acted disloyally and impaired the authority of the committee, whereas our opinion as the guilty party was that this was a situation in which those who conducted the day-to-day struggle had to act on the spur of the moment when new information was available. The criticism caused the work inside the leadership to be more definitely formalised. However, we were soon to have something else to think about, for at the beginning of February the Gestapo embarked on a major action against the civil resistance movement.

The Gestapo tries to break us

We had received an advance warning. An agent deserting from the Gestapo had crossed the frontier at the close of the previous year and told representatives of the Norwegian Legation in Stockholm that the Gestapo had information enough to strike down the whole of our press; as an example, he gave an address where the Gestapo believed the main Communist paper *Friheten* was printed. We passed the warning on through the channels at our disposal, and tried to set up a new, somewhat less centralised contact with the press. It looked as though Rygh and his associates had managed to conceal their successors in the editorship of *London News*, but for safety's sake the latter had changed the place where they worked and printed and had gone under cover. We therefore took the risk of nominating Petter Moen, the editor of *London News*, as Rygh's successor, but he was to share the post of press chief with Viggo Aagaard, who edited *London Radio*.

In the first days of February the Gestapo began the second round of 'the press disaster'. The editors, printers and principal distributors of most of the illegal papers in Oslo, except the Communist ones, were arrested in the space of one week. Both Moen and Aagaard were taken, as were Moen's closest associates, so the saga of *London News* came to an end. But in spite of bestial torture Aagaard managed to cover up his fellow-workers, nor did he betray anything about his work as press chief. In *Fri Fagbevegelse* all the individuals at the centre were arrested except the editor, and two of them lost their lives during the wave of arrests and the prison tortures which followed. Another important Labour paper, *Vårt Land*, was also discovered; when the press disaster was over, the *Bulletin* was the only survivor of the papers co-operating with the leadership of the Home Front.

But it was not only the press that the Gestapo was after. They looked for Biering, but he was in Stockholm on a legal business journey when the Gestapo knocked on his door in Oslo. He was one of the major figures in the field of illegal work, and was later greatly missed by all of us whom he had helped. However, we had felt for a long time that this Scarlet Pimpernel of the Home Front was in a very exposed position, so we were more than relieved that he was safely beyond the clutches of the Gestapo.

On the night of 3-4 February the Gestapo nearly made some big catches on the Home Front. They were looking for Jens Boyesen,* secretary to the Circle and much else, who lived with his parents in a block of apartments in the western district of Oslo. That evening he was holding a little party in the apartment with three members of the secretariat for a friend who was about to leave the country. When the Gestapo came in by the main door, Boyesen slipped out by the back, which led into another street, and so escaped. The guest and one secretary pretended to be casual callers and disappeared arm in arm through the main door. The other woman secretary was caught with a gas pistol and a manuscript for an illegal paper on her, but managed to get out by the back way after being given permission to go to the lavatory. The man who was left behind, Hans Engen, had shown on several previous occasions that he had unusually good control over his nerves, which he now demonstrated to the full. The Gestapo men had quite naturally become somewhat cantankerous as one after the other of the party slipped out of their hands, and regarded the last one who remained with great scepticism. But he started a conversation with their leader in fluent German, explaining that he rented a room in the flat and had merely been mixed up in the party by chance. He had of course no idea that he was in the society of such undesirables as they appeared to be. The Gestapo leader was so overwhelmed by his eloquence that in the end he took his subordinates with him and left the place. The back door was quickly reached, whereupon the last of the Circle's secretariat was safe.

Next morning I was warned of what had happened by Skjönsberg, who explained that important sections of the Circle's archives lay in a concealed space in the kitchen floor of Boyesen's flat and must be got out. The caretaker in the block

*J.M. Boyesen (b.1920) became adviser to the Norwegian delegation at the UN General Assembly, and in 1955 was appointed as Ambassador to NATO and OEEC (later OECD).

knew where it was, so we went along with Sanengen. As the caretaker was not at home, it was proposed by Skjönsberg, who also knew about the hiding-place and had keys, that we should go up ourselves and take it out. It flashed through my mind what a senseless thing it was for Skjönsberg, the central person in the leadership of the Home Front and the father of three small children, to take part in such a risky action; but there was no time for such reflections, we had to act quickly — if the Gestapo were not back already, they might come at any moment.

We agreed that Skjönsberg and I should go up, but Sanengen should keep an eye on what went on outside from a convenient vantage point. It was too daring to go straight ahead without first finding out whether the Gestapo were in the flat. While we were considering how to set about our task, Skjönsberg noticed a Home Front man whom he knew, who was the proprietor of an electrical business in the neighbourhood, passing by. He was told what was happening, and was at once ready to go up and find out; if challenged, he would say that the family had asked him to repair an electrical fault. We waited anxiously, but fortunately he was soon able to come down and report that the way was clear, whereupon we rushed up the back way at top speed. I sat on guard in the corridor with our only weapon, a pistol of the smallest calibre, while Skjönsberg disappeared into the kitchen like lightning and heaped the contents of the secret space into a rucksack, and we sped together down the back way as if the devil was at our heels. Well outside, I snatched the sack from Skjönsberg, hurried by a roundabout route to a surburban station, boarded a train, and brought it to safety in our own 'underground' files out in Bærum. We had acted at the right moment, for the Gestapo were soon back again to the spot and took one of Boyesen's fellow-workers who had gone inside.

The following weeks were hard in more ways than one. It was evident that the Gestapo possessed important information; its nature and extent were unknown, and many others in the executive group went into hiding and lived under great nervous pressure. There was a risk that some of the press people who had been arrested knew their names, and reports of the torturing in the prisons created a justified fear that in the long run they would not be able to keep silent. Then there had been other arrests which might have dangerous consequences. In mid-January, the chairman of the FU, who was a member of both the Co-ordination Committee and the Circle, was taken; he died later in a German concentration camp. In February several other leading people on the Labour front had to go abroad because of the detection of *Fri Fagbevegelse*, among them a veteran who was a member of the Circle. There were also waves of arrests out in the provinces, though in the first round our people kept clear. The pressure on the 'export' apparatus was heavy, especially as many of its principal people were imperilled as a result of the arrests over the newspapers. As I myself could feel safe — none of those arrested knew my name — it became my job to keep the wheels turning as much as possible, procure information from the prisons, and find possibilities of 'export' and other help for those in danger. My right-hand man in this work was Erik Bratsberg, who had got himself good contacts in the police, while Sanengen, who had taken over my job for the *Bulletin*, also assisted and moved naturally into the staff.

We had based our campaign against the AT to a great extent upon the illegal press, and the directive was to have been sent out in the middle of February. As the papers had disappeared, the presentation had to be altered so as to build upon the Norwegian broadcasts of the BBC, relations with which had been complicated in the previous year by the uncertain attitude of the Government in London to the Home Front leadership. The action had now to be postponed for a month, for although Boyesen's technical arrangements for communicating with the Government via Stockholm were still intact, a new group had to be formed to conduct the work in Oslo. Boyesen asked Jansen to take it over, which he did without giving away even then his solitary role in the editing of the *Bulletin*. However, as we had collaborated for many years, I naturally helped him in various ways and took on the writing of the reports to the Government. Under such a pressure of work it was good to have Sanengen at one's side, so I proposed to the Co-ordination Committee that he should relieve me as its secretary. No one knew him, and for security reasons the committee did not want any extension; but it was agreed to with some murmuring, and before long he had acquired the respect from them that was needed. I could then devote my time to reorganising the contacts with the press and 'export', and help with the reconstruction after the discoveries. The need for contact with those under arrest and for a better system of warning was more urgent than ever, and we had to put a lot of work into improving the system of security in the organisations.

Reconstruction and extension on the organising side had to go on at the same time as the campaign against the AT, which in itself required a lot of organising work. Meanwhile the leadership continued to lose good people. The representative of the local government officials on the KK, a man with many valuable contacts, had to go abroad, and at the end of March the bell tolled for Poulsson, an inspiring and centrally placed figure, who had likewise to tread the heavy path across the frontier. Among the members of the Circle, Hans Halvorsen had to depart, and a few weeks later the time was up for Schjelderup as well; it was the end of an epoch in the Home Front struggle.

Over to the offensive: the campaign against the AT

The agreement to campaign against the AT did not mean that we underestimated the difficulties ahead of us. Three days before the directive was sent out in mid-March over the BBC, we wrote to the Government: 'It is expected here that it will take 2-3 months before the directive for boycotting the AT operates effectively, as the AT has been tolerated for so long, and positive misuse is as yet little recognised ...' Nor was there any lack of warnings. One of our principal contacts in the West wrote to us on 8 March: 'The campaign against the AT ... is regarded here as inopportune and dangerous.' The reactions from other illegal quarters, including the press, were also negative. A comprehensive service of information and advice was required, and the district organisations had to be alerted and stimulated. At the suggestion of Magnus Jensen, the Co-ordination Committee resolved to entrust this task to a special anti-AT committee, consisting of five men from those spheres of life with most experience of youth work, namely Church and school, agriculture and public service, together with Sanengen from the secretariat, who had the day-to-day charge of the committee and was its contact with the KK. Both individually and in meetings, the members of the group worked under high pressure, and from the end of April sent out a veritable flood of directives, articles, and appeals addressed to the recruits, the registrars of enrolment, the parents, the farmers, the doctors, and other groups, as well as instructions and advice to the principal contacts and the special spokesmen whom they were urged to bring into play for the action.

Reference has already been made to the war-weariness which was more and more prevalent in the autumn of 1943 and the ensuing winter, and which found expression partly in reduced backing for particular directives. The near-total destruction of the illegal press did not make it any better, so it was our opinion in the secretariat that people must now learn that the directives were sponsored by an authoritative leadership. Skjönsberg agreed, but in both the Circle and the Co-ordination Committee there were strong objections to the idea for a long time, especially from the security angle.

When the AT campaign was started, Sanengen and I again appealed urgently to the leadership to come forward in connection with the launching of the directive against the AT, but at first we were only half successful. When the directive was broadcast by the BBC on 15 March 1944, we were allowed to preface it with the words 'The Home Front announces'. This helped to some extent but, we believed, not enough; so the next time we were to send a directive over the radio, without consulting anyone else we instructed those in charge of the broadcasting in London to announce it as 'from the leadership of the Home Front'. The effect on our contacts both in the districts and in the capital was unmistakable — and this time we received no reprimand for disloyalty or for taking the law into our own hands. By that time the Circle and the Co-ordination Committee had agreed to a proposal from Skjönsberg to publish a proclamation from the leadership of the Home Front.

It was our opinion in the executive that it was insufficient merely to stop recruitment to AT; we must destroy the registers for the service, which comprised four earlier age-groups, 80,000-90,000 men in all, and were the most important instrument for the Nazis in the event of a mobilisation. Acts of sabotage against the AT records would also convey to the young people whom the campaign concerned that the directive was backed by vigorous organisation, and would have a disturbing effect on those in charge of the service, who would be receiving a directive to leave it. We received support for these views in the Co-ordination Committee, which agreed to ask the military staff (SL) whether Milorg was willing to undertake the destruction of the records. We had to wait two or three weeks for the answer but when it came finally at the beginning of March it was in the affirmative, although conditional upon the approval of the FO, and after another two or three weeks Milorg received clearance from London. The contact between our secretariat and the SL went at that time through several links and took too long. We therefore asked for a quicker system because the matter was urgent, and the SL went so far as to allow contact through a box in one of the larger banks in central Oslo; we could now reach one another in the course of a few hours, as long as the banks were open.

It fell to me to plan the acts of sabotage, which were to be quite comprehensive, as it would not be sufficient to destroy only the main registers, which were maintained on a punched-card system and could if necessary be reconstructed with the help of the records for the ten counties and for Greater Oslo; these, therefore, had to be included in the action. The first thing was to find out where and how the main registers were kept and what security arrangements had to be penetrated. For this I brought in a young lawyer named Risting, who had been working with Sanengen and a few others since the previous autumn on special intelligence projects. In determining the lay-out of the registers, we had of course to work very cautiously in case any one should get wind of our purpose.

By a lucky chance, one of the girls who worked with us was able to tell me one day that she knew a reliable fellow-citizen in the Oslo firm which possessed the punch-card machine used by the AT in connection with the enrolment, and he in turn knew the AT officer in charge of the enrolment and had a general idea of where the registers were. I immediately established contact with her acquaintance, who unhesitatingly agreed to help us, and who played a significant part in the subsequent developments. He told me that the central records were stored in three places, the majority being in a vault on the top floor of the AT headquarters close beside Oslo Town Hall. It would simplify our task considerably if all the records could be assembled in one place, which would naturally be the headquarters, and he thought he could find a pretext for arranging this by the beginning of May, when I thought the operation ought to be carried out. The vault had two keys, of which the officer in charge of the enrolment held one, but he thought that the person in question would be willing to co-operate and arranged for me to meet him.

I was in some doubt as to whether this might not be a trap, and asked Bratsberg to take one of our two small pistols and place himself as near the rendezvous as possible. The officer seemed very nervous, but I thought I should take the risk and we agreed that he should deliver his bunch of keys to me after office hours on the day of the action, in return for which he would at once be sent over the frontier to Sweden. The bunch included all the necessary keys from the street entrance up through all the floors and into the vault, except for the ante-room to the vault, which was an office belonging to the State Auditors. Risting was going to try to get a key to this office without anyone discovering our intentions. After making some enquiries, he sent a friend of his a few days later to the State Audit office, where he asked for a bookkeeper called Larsen. On being told there was nobody of that name, he said it was rather strange, as he had been given it by a mutual acquaintance. He stood there shifting from one foot to the other and explained that he needed to go to the lavatory, so could they lend him a key? They thought they could help him to that extent, and gave him one. He went quietly out, but once outside he dashed to the lift and a nearby ironmonger's, where Risting had arranged for assistance. He had discovered that the office and the lavatory had identical keys, so a duplicate was quickly filed; a few minutes later, he handed the original key back to the office with warm thanks for their help in his moment of need.

Reconstruction after 'the disaster to the press'

Preparations for the action against the Labour Service took a lot of time, but a general reconstruction needed to be carried on simultaneously at full speed. Biering had kept all the threads for our 'export' organisation and supply service in his hands, and trying to pick up the many loose threads again was a complicated and risky task. However, Bratsberg proved to be so well adapted to this that he gradually took over the current contacts between the secretariat and the 'export'. An engineer named Harald Bryn, who had worked with Biering, was in touch with a number of 'export' groups, but he had to work very cautiously as the Gestapo were at their heels; he came relatively quickly into the danger zone and had to go abroad in April. In Biering's time we had had a good many refugees sent on the Communist routes, and after his arrival in Sweden I was instructed to pay a considerable sum to the Communist 'export' organisation in the person of a man with the cover name of 'Winther'. But we only managed to get a few refugees away by his routes, a fact for which I did not receive any explanation. At last Bratsberg and I went to 'Winther's' office to ask for a plain statement, but when we arrived there we were told that he was away. By chance the door of a side-room came open, and there sat 'Winther', who hurriedly tried to get out of sight; I had now had enough of this trickery and broke the contract. Since the war I have established that 'Winther' was identical with a man who at that time was in charge of the economy or finances in the central committee of the Communist Party, and the report of a Gestapo interpreter after the capitulation states: 'This transport group was a profitable business for the NKP.'

Later on, the 'export' activities of the Communists were paid by our 'export' organisation at a fixed rate for each refugee who was helped to leave. We continued to help the Communists' 'export' group with transport and supplies. The 'export' of refugees was often conducted at this time by individual groups, most of which were co-ordinated in three principal organisations, belonging respectively to ourselves as 'Sivorg', to Milorg, and to the NKP. There were, however, many cross-connections, and the person in charge of a particular route might work simultaneously for more than one of the organisations. In addition, those in charge of some routes worked independently and had their own apparatus. One of these was Reidar Vold, whose routes conveyed small numbers through the forests east of Oslo Fjord; what he undertook he performed with great precision and the minimum of expense, so that we had gret confidence in him, often entrusted him with getting our most important people across, and by degrees developed co-operation in several fields.

A valuable helper at this time was Finn Haugland, an official in the State Pension Fund, who was one of Biering's earlier co-workers and had a number of good contacts for supplies. He was also in the leadership of the illegal group among public servants and a key man for getting information from the Labour Directorate and other links in the NS administration.

The replacement of Bryn by a new management for our 'export' affairs coincided with a black day for the export groups in the forest areas south-east of Oslo. On 21 April three parties of refugees, two on Milorg's and the third on the Communists' route, came up against a strengthened frontier control. The drivers and guides belonging to the Communists shot their way through and managed to get the refugees across, leaving one guide dead; he was the father of eleven children, with his wife expecting a twelfth. In the second party likewise the majority got away, after an exchange of shots, but the whole of the third party was captured. The different strands of the refugee traffic were so inter-connected that important parts of our own organisation were unavoidably pulled into the net as well. The man in charge of the route, who had kept up a bold and efficient export of refugees ever since 1941, only escaped the Gestapo at the last moment, and the land routes in this area, which had hitherto borne the main weight of traffic, never regained their importance. Before his departure Bryn had started a route by sea from the Vestfold shore of the Oslo Fjörd while also resuming activity through the forest area on the east side.

We had arranged our offensive against the AT with its starting-point in our own nationwide organisation and the broadcasts from London, and we had asked our action committees in the various professions to activate their illegal 'trade periodicals', such as *Lawyers' News, Engineers' News*, etc. At the same time, we needed all the support we could get from a free press, although considerations of security prevented us from taking steps ourselves to organise the setting-up of papers. This, in any case, was unnecessary, as they grew up again spontaneously: the demand for uncensored news was so tremendous, that it virtually drove people who had the will into starting new papers or reviving old ones which had not been knocked out completely. But those concerned were desperately in need of help with equipment, such as radios, paper, typewriters and stencilling machines — and money.

One of our biggest difficulties was to find our way to those who were editing the new free papers and make safe arrangements for contact. The Gestapo at this time was also trying to start illegal newspapers of its own, and although the pretence was usually transparent, one could not be too careful. The many skilful organisers of illegality who had been lost in the press disaster were hard to replace, but while we were looking for a likely man to manage the new press system, chance came to our aid. In the latter half of March a student named Paal Brunsvig returned from Stockholm; he had been drawn into many illegal activities while still at school, had become one of press chief Rygh's close associates in his home district, west of the Oslo fjord, and was obliged to cross the frontier after Rygh's arrest.

The press office at the Norwegian Legation had now asked him to travel to Oslo and arrange new transport routes for bringing in its propaganda material, as the organisation which had previously looked after this had also been broken up during the press disaster. Jansen put us in touch with Brunsvig on his first visit, and it did not take us long to discover that he was just the man we needed for organising the press. After rapidly completing his assignment and reporting back to Stockholm, he returned to Oslo and took up his new work.

It was not an easy matter, as there was a natural scepticism about anything which might smack of a new centralised press system, and precautions had to be taken on both sides so that, if one side were detected, it should not affect the other. But Brunsvig had the right qualifications — experience and a tireless energy — and set up a system of contacts which proved capable of standing the strains which came, and which were bound to come on this front as time went on. The system safeguarded not only the line between ourselves and each individual paper but also that between one paper and another; even if the Gestapo still managed to kill off particular papers, there was no further press disaster. By the time the great stroke against the AT was to be brought off, which was a month after he took up his new work, Brunsvig had established connections with the most prominent of the new illegal papers, and the illegal press could again take up its advanced position in the front line. And by the end of the summer we had a firm arrangement for contacting eighteen or twenty papers in the Oslo area — virtually all the free papers except those associated with the Communist Party.

One desperate matter during these months after the press disaster was our almost complete lack of small arms for self-defence. In our task of picking up contacts with the survivors of groups which had been decimated by the Gestapo, we often had to go to a rendezvous which it might have under observation, so we were just as likely to find a Gestapo agent at the door as the person we were looking for. Reports of the torturing in prison of our former co-workers spread a very sinister atmosphere over that period. On 19 April Aagaard wrote to us from prison:

... I was of course driven straight to the Terrace, where for a full week I was treated quite severely in regular examinations. It was something of a strain, you know, but I think on the whole I can say that I managed it. 1) *"Sonderbehandlung"*, as I received it, consisted partly of the following: arm twisted behind my back; repeatedly lifted up by my hair so that tufts fell out, pressure on the cavities behind the ears; ears twisted (bloody for three weeks afterwards); blows on the head with all sorts of instruments, flogging with heavy ropes and blows with iron rods over the entire body. Result: a completely black body. Threat of 2) *castration* by drunken interpreter with knife, actual attempts at the same with baton, jumping and stamping all over the body — and much more which I do not care to mention. Altogether there were eight men at it, and on one occasion — the worst — all of them at once ...

This letter, passed to us by helpers in the prison service, is the record of a man who stood up to torture better than most; so in the light of such reports we found it opportune to circularise the illegal press with an article by a woman doctor, newly released from the Grini prison, which gave good advice and said that some of the torture was not much worse than a woman's childbirth pains. We also sent urgent requests to our people in Stockholm to obtain pistols or other small arms for self-defence, but much time passed by before anything useful arrived, and for the whole spring and summer we went round almost unarmed, having a total of two small-calibre pistols which Bratsberg had dug up in the forest early in the war. We could not understand why our allies were unable to help us in such a simple matter, and we rather thought that it was due to an ineffective Norwegian administration in London. We later learnt that not even our Defence Chief could procure pistols in England at that time.

An attack from the rear

The prison doors had only just been slammed behind our arrested press people in February that year when the Communist Party press started a frenzied agitation against the Home Front leadership, which it accused of conducting a passive campaign, representing reactionary views, and preparing a *coup* against the constitution. The heaviest accusations appeared in the paper *All for Norway*, published by the central committee with a name — King Haakon's royal motto — taken from a very early Home Front paper which had been suppressed in 1941. The Communists demanded the establishment of a 'unified' leadership, a Freedom Council on the Danish model,* which

*Established in Copenhagen 16 September 1943, one of its six founder-members being a Communist newspaper editor (see J. Hæstrup, *Secret Alliance*, Vol. I, Odense 1976).

would take charge of all resistance activity, including the military forces, set up courts, raise a state loan, and manage the country after liberation alongside the Government. The agitation was supported by certain emigrant circles in Stockholm and by the People's Radio, 'Freedom of Norway', which transmitted in Norwegian from somewhere in the Soviet Union.

We did not engage in any sharp polemic against the attacks from the Communist papers; we had more than enough to do to make good the damage after the press disaster and to prepare the action against the AT. But when Skjönsberg received a letter in March, immediately after the attacks on us had begun, in which a member of the NKP's central committee referred to their conversations in the previous autumn and asked for continued economic support for the party press, he replied a few weeks later in terms which strongly deprecated the attitude of the Communists and rebutted their criticisms. In spite of the irritation we naturally felt at their agitation, the demands of the war still caused us to search for a *modus vivendi* with them. We rejected the proposal for a Freedom Council, but went on helping them with ration cards and other practical support. When the NS made preparations in mid-May for a 'plebiscite' against Communism, we sent out a directive opposing participation, and asked the Government to broadcast it at once over the BBC. In addition, we engaged in an attempt at local co-operation. But in the course of the summer we sent statements to the Government and to the spokesmen in the districts, explaining our choice of tactics and our rejection of the proposal for a Freedom Council.

There was another group as well which was by no means backward in seeking to discredit us; its leaders, Edmund Haug and Trygve Nilsen, had displayed great activity in the summer and autumn of 1943, particularly in circulating a chain letter denouncing the local government arrangements on which the Cabinet in London and the Circle had agreed for the transition period at the end of the occupation. The situation had been explained to both of them by Paal Berg and Schjelderup, with documentation of the Prime Minister's warning in August against what they were doing; and Schjelderup, in the hope that Haug would abandon his opposition if admitted to the leadership, got him into the Co-ordination Committee as a representative of the teachers. All the same, he continued his agitation in private, and without informing the committee of his object, summoned the teachers' district representatives to a meeting in Oslo in November 1943, at which he made a tendentious and misleading attack on the local government arrangements and their sponsors. In consequence of this and other information on his disloyal attitude towards the leadership, he was excluded from the Committee the following January, but he still had a strong position in the teachers' front and remained very active. Chain letters went the rounds, containing accusations that a *coup* was being prepared, and the Home Front leaders were stigmatised as 'neo-Nazis'. Thus it was easy to deduce who was supplying the Communists with ammunition for their attacks on us; Haug even copied and circulated parts of the secret correspondence between the Circle and the Government. The gossip which the agitation created was bound eventually to have effects on security. In the course of March the persons nominated to take over as *fylkesmenn* in two counties were arrested, several of the people in the leadership had to go under cover, and one had to flee abroad. At the end of the month Haug and his closest associates were likewise arrested, he himself being let out again after only three days.

In a report to the Government immediately afterwards, I wrote as follows: 'We know nothing of the reason either for the arrest or the release, but are actually not surprised that he got out, if the police know of his work.' We soon received confirmation through a report made by a refugee to the Legation in Stockholm; from conversations with one of Haug's close collaborators, he was able to tell that the security police had found at Haug's home three of the pamphlets he had written against the local government arrangements, while the report also confirmed the co-operation between the Communists and Haug and his flirtation with the proposal for a Freedom Council. It may be remarked that it would have been much more difficult for Haug to win a hearing for his agitation if, in the course of the autumn and winter, the Government in London had sent word home about the matter. But after the retreat *vis-à-vis* the Circle in August, the Prime Minister did not answer any of its numerous letters until the following March — a *de facto* seven months' strike. 'Old Man' Nygaardsvold, who commented ironically to Trygve Lie* upon the sulkiness of the

*Trygve Lie (1896-1968), formerly legal adviser to LO and a member of Nygaardsvold's Cabinet since 1935, was foreign minister from August 1940

the Circle in this matter, himself took offence with equal ease.

In the month of January 1944 Norum returned to Norway and had a series of meetings with the district contacts, at which he expounded the agreement between the Government and the Circle; in addition, he had a fruitless meeting with Haug. At the end of the month the KK sent the district contacts an account of the preparations for civil administration, explaining the co-operation and agreement with the Government and the opposition which had arisen. This merits an extract of some length:

The underlying principles are pure and clear. The temporary local government authorities are going to be organs of the size of the executive committees.* They are to consist of persons experienced in local administration whose national attitude is beyond doubt. The composition of these temporary authorities will lie as close as possible to the composition of the local authority after the last election.

By carrying out the arrangement approved by the Government, we shall avoid having in our country any foreign control of our civil administration, even in the very first period of transition.

As mentioned above, it is obvious that all preparatory work has had to be done on the quiet. It is very regrettable that this work has been taken up for discussion at the present juncture, and especially so that suspicion should be thrown on it as involving an attempt at a *coup*, so that democracy would be in peril. The approved settlement of local government administration for the time when military conditions prevail in the country is a necessary part in the liquidation of the war our country is involved in, and ought not at present to be the subject of discussion.

The enemy is interested in every clue which may lead to the bringing to light of this administrative apparatus just before it is to come into operation or when the situation becomes critical for him. Whoever contributes to the possibility of such a disclosure is in reality doing the enemy's work.

For the next period — namely after the military liberation has been carried out and the King and Government have returned — the Government has provisionally pictured the recalling of the complete local authorities, in order that they may elect the committee which shall conduct the local administration until public elections can take place. The number shall be the same as in the temporary nominated

until his appointment as first Secretary-General of the United Nations in February 1946.

**Formannskapene*: one-fourth of the total membership of the local council, which varied with the population of the area.

committee, but the old local authority will thus be able at that time to undertake a replacement of individuals if desired.

The question whether the Storting elected in 1936 is to be recalled has also been thrown into the discussion. The temporary local government settlement approved does not in any way touch this question. To what extent, and if so when, this Storting is to meet, lies in the Storting's own hands ... '

Magnus Jensen held a number of meetings in the teachers' organisations, which in March disclaimed responsibility for Haug's activities and his misuse of their apparatus. In September he was removed from the teachers' leadership, and later presented us merely with a security problem.

The anti-AT campaign approaches its climax

The Labour Service recruits of 1944 had received notice to assemble in the middle of May. In most parts of the country they were warned not to do so by a barrage from our organisations. Teachers and clergymen got the names and addresses of recruits from school and church registers; spokesmen were picked out from among them to inform and influence their companions; and the old committees of parents from the struggle against the NS Youth Company were set in motion again. The teachers again accepted a large burden of work for the resistance struggle. The anti-AT committee produced information material all round the clock, while the secretariat toiled under high pressure to activate the district contacts and forward instructions and propaganda to them. In Greater Oslo a special organisation was set up by Sanengen in collaboration with the action committees of the occupational groups.

In its applications to the district organisations the secretariat emphasised the seriousness of the situation: 'We must exert our full strength in the campaign against the AT. This will be a touchstone for the attitude of the Norwegian people, and the result of the action will determine the line to be followed for the future in the struggle here at home.' Both as regards work and security the campaign put a heavy strain on these organisations: the business of informing and advising was on a bigger scale than ever before, and there had to be a huge expansion of the technical equipment for the duplication and distribution of directives and other explanatory material.

We also took up the task of breaking down the AT from

inside. The staff was sifted, and those who were deemed reliable from a national standpoint received warnings not to remain in the organisation.

The editor and announcer for the Norwegian broadcasts from London. T. Öksnevad, rendered a particularly skilled and valuable service to the Home Front by defining and commenting on the directive against the AT. In spite of his long absence from Norway,* he had an intuitive understanding of the situation at home and excelled others over in London in finding the right words.

Quisling attempted a counter-move, by maintaining in the press and on the air that the AT would only be arranged in the normal way and by denying allegations of an impending mobilisation. This had some effect, appeals being made to us from various quarters to reconsider the action against the AT. Instead we hoisted full sail and made ready to engage the enemy. A message went to Milorg for the action against the AT records to take place at midnight on 4-5 May. The military staff received the key to the ante-room of the vault in its headquarters, and it was agreed that the leader of the action should fetch the officer's bunch of keys before the end of office hours that day; in order to follow the situation, I asked our own action group to keep the building under observation on the preceding days as well.

The sabotage actions went awry at the very outset, for the bunch of keys was not fetched at the agreed time, though I was warned and got hold of them at the very last moment. It is well known that the criminal finds it hard to keep away from the scene of the crime, so by 11 in the evening Bratsberg and I were at a convenient spot a couple of hundred yards from the AT headquarters, waiting for the bang. We heard nothing, and an hour after midnight we had to leave as we had an agreement with Risting for him to meet us in the west end of the town with a report from our watch group. There we were very lucky to avoid a Gestapo motor-cycle patrol which rushed round and lit everything up, evidently on the hunt for someone. The next morning's report from our watchers at the AT headquarters was

*Toralv Öksnevad (1891-1975), a prominent figure in the State Broadcasting since 1933, had been sent to London in August 1940 from Stockholm, where he was temporarily press attaché.

laconic: nothing special had happened, no action group had done anything.

Never since the days of April 1940 had I been so angry and disappointed. It looked as though the sabotage in Oslo had either failed or been cancelled; it could not be repeated. The sad facts were confirmed to me at a masked meeting later in the day with the head of the military staff (SL), J.C. Hauge. He explained that there had been a mishap with a hand grenade in the action group just when it was due to go into action against the AT headquarters. At the same time it received a report that the action against the records of the county of Akershus elsewhere in the town had gone wrong, three guards from Milorg having been taken, though the Linge men shot their way through. Finally, the action group for the headquarters had had a report that a body of Germans in uniform had entered the place, so in the belief that the Gestapo had put in reinforcements for its protection they cancelled the action; this was a misunderstanding, as the German military had offices of their own in the building. Hauge took full responsibility on himself for what had happened, having undertaken to co-ordinate the actions. The chief blunder lay in the fact that the three Oslo actions were supposed to be simultaneous, whereas the one against the headquarters should have been slightly in advance; he greatly regretted the mistakes, but they had taught Milorg a lesson. Hauge's way of squaring matters melted my indignation, and instead the meeting proved to be the prelude to good co-operation between us.

The actions against the AT offices outside Oslo, too, did not go particularly well; they were carried out against the records in no more than four places and with varying success.

So the general result on that occasion was not much to cheer about. A good many AT recruits had apparently chosen to overlook the Home Front's appeal for a strike; there were only a couple of places, mountain districts in East Norway, in which the directive was almost universally followed, but there the local organisations had also done particularly good preparatory work. Our estimate at the time, especially after information came to us from a refugee camp in Sweden, was that the directive received about 30 per cent support, which on a nation-wide basis is presumably too high, as there seem to have been many places where support was considerably smaller. The campaign was to cost the lives of four of our own people. At Notodden, where the district leadership had conducted the action against AT with great vigour and effectiveness, a young man was sentenced to death by a special court and executed on 22 May for having influenced recruits to absent themselves. This was immediately followed by the execution of the three Milorg lads under arrest in Oslo who had taken part in the abortive action against the county records for Akershus.

Wrestling with the enemy

On 11 May Quisling started a propaganda campaign on the front pages of the entire Nazi-controlled press, with huge headlines in heavy type claiming that a bolshevik occupation of Norway was official confirmed from England. The campaign, which continued right up to the 20th, reached its climax on the 15th in a big propaganda meeting in the forecourt of the University, at which Quisling ended his speech: 'I therefore declare that Norway, in close co-operation with Germany, will help with increasing vigour in the organising and mustering of the strength of Europe, and that we in Norway will apply all our sources of assistance to the common struggle for Europe's safety and future.' Such words, coupled with the Riisnæs memorandum of 17 January and a rumoured offer by Quisling to Hitler at the end of the same month, inevitably weighed much more heavily with us than the assertions of the controlled press that only those who had missed serving in the AT were to be called up, and only for service in Norway.

On 12 May Haugland picked up a report from the NS administration of the Directorate of Labour about the intended call-up for national labour effort of the three yearly classes for 1921-3 — the precise age-groups which had been in for AT service. He warned us at once, and we immediately sent a warning to the district contacts. The directive, 'Mobilisation is coming', was formulated under high pressure and transmitted immediately to the illegal press and the contacts for the districts; it was likewise sent by the quickest route to London. The directive ends as follows: *'No one meets for registration, not even those who are offered the enticement of provisional exemption from service*. Our day is soon coming. Remember General Ruge's last appeal to his soldiers to hold themselves in readiness. If you find yourself in a German camp by then, you have no chance of joining in the liberation. Be true to your country, your king, and your people. *Refuse to register*, whatever the cost may be.'

At the same time Sanengen had set his entire apparatus in motion, both in the country at large and in the capital. In the Oslo area alone, the directive was spread within a few days as a circular with a printing of nearly 100,000 copies. The teachers, both in Oslo and in the provinces, again put the biggest effort into the work of distribution, both by getting the names and addresses of those liable for registration, disseminating directives, organising groups of parents, and strengthening morale by good advice and assistance.

On 17 May 1944 the controlled press contained the first announcement of the call-up. On our side the day — our national holiday — was celebrated by intense preparations for the impending battle, but in the afternoon I had intended to visit my parents and friends at Ski, whom I had not seen for a long while. But I was overtaken at the railway station by Bratsberg, with the news that the authorities were preparing to use the punch-card machine (already mentioned) for the impending registration, whereupon I sent a special message to the central military staff that the machine must be destroyed. The office where it stood was blown up by a gang from the Linge Company on the night of the 18th-19th — the latter being the date for the registration announced in the press. In addition, after office hours on the 18th two Linge men entered the corridor of the Oslo Labour Exchange, where the call-up would begin next day; placed a suitcase containing dynamite; lit the fuse; and warned staff who were working overtime that they must get out in a hurry, as it was about to go off. And so it did, with results — shattered windows and torn awnings — which were visible from the street.

It was evident that Milorg wanted to have their revenge for the defeats earlier in the month. Their arrangements for action in Oslo had been reorganised with the establishment of Sönsteby's Oslo Gang,* and its successful supporting-operations continued in the days which followed. The last punch-card machine which could be used for the AT's card records, though under heavy guard on the premises of an insurance company,

*The title of chapter 7 in Max Manus, *9 Lives Before Thirty* (New York 1947). By the autumn of 1944 Captain G. Sönsteby was in full charge of a number of Linge personnel who had been sent to East Norway independently.

was badly damaged in an action in the middle of June. The acts of sabotage conveyed the message that the directives were backed by an organisation which had both the will and the power to use the requisite means of force when the situation demanded.

It was in these hectic days of mid-May that the proclamation, which the leadership of the Home Front had drawn up in April, was broadcast over the BBC. HL thereby presented itself formally to the people of Norway; defined its war objectives — the immediate restoration of democracy, free speech and legal security, and free elections; and appealed to all Norwegians to follow the directives issued. It undoubtedly heightened the effect of the proclamation that it had the full support of the Government. It was first broadcast on 18 May, having been delayed for a month due to a misunderstanding in Stockholm; but although the delay certainly weakened the campaign against the AT at first, the proclamation nevertheless came very opportunely at the same time as the directive against registration was made known by the BBC, the illegal press, and our nation-wide network of communications.

The fight for our young people now entered its last round, and on the first day for enlistment the excitement in our camp was at boiling-point. When Sanengen was able to inform us well on in the day that the assembly place was almost deserted, we began to have hopes; when evening came and only a score of the thousands due to report had actually done so, it was hard to conceal our delight. Months of uphill work was now producing results, for when the days for registration were over, it had proved a complete failure in Oslo, and reports from the provinces, with a couple of regrettable exceptions, told the same story. We had won an important round, young people had followed our directive and refused to report.

But a new and critical situation had arisen: the Police resorted to round-ups in the streets, arresting any young men of suitable age whom they came across. The youth of Oslo area and the towns in Buskerud, Vestfold and Telemark, thousands in number, left their homes and went into hiding among relatives and friends in the country, or else in the forests round the towns, where they established themselves in primitive camps of tents, built lean-tos out of branches, or made use of any shelter available. It all happened spontaneously and was improvised by the young themselves, who forthwith became popularly known as 'the lads in the forest'.* A report based on interviews with youngsters liable for registration, who arrived in Sweden during the summer, gives this description of life in the camps: 'The atmosphere in the camps and the spirit among the boys seems to have been excellent. They all emphasise the good comradeship. Even the three weeks of rain in July, when many were still living in huts made of branches, so that clothes, food, and everything else were wet through, did not succeed in lowering their spirits.'

Help, however, was essential, for they had neither food nor equipment for the situation they were in. In the first instance it was the family, relatives and friends who helped, with others gradually joining in, and supplies also came from wholesale firms, shopkeepers and farmers. This spontaneous effort was a great assistance and encouragement, both to the lads and to us. But the situation was dangerous; we could not maintain such camps for any length of time, and they might also fall an easy prey to *agents provocateurs* and informers. We had at once to make a survey of the position, arrange contact with the individual camps, organise a supply service on a safe and adequate footing, and then get them wound up before autumn and winter set in.

Sanengen took on the leadership of this work, arranging for supplies from Swedish and Danish Relief stocks through Bonnevie-Svendsen, while Haugland secured some from other sources. Sanengen also got in touch very quickly with a girl and a young man who had independently set about the risky task of reaching the camps and taking in supplies. The girl became a linch-pin in the later work with 'the lads in the forest', and the two of them succeeded in finding their way to the majority of the camps in the woods round Oslo. But after a while they became so exposed that they had to be taken out of the search, and in this precarious situation we had to ignore the usual security considerations in bringing in my brother Odd, whose activities in cross-country running and Scouting had familiarised him with large parts of the Oslo woodland. A special supply committee was set up under Haugland, which with the help of good backers in such places as the Directorate of Rationing quickly got an effective service in operation.

**gutta på skauen*: this half-romantic name was later applied to units in the Home Forces which set up secret bases in connection with the dropping of Allied supplies of arms, etc., and Milorg's plans for fighting in support of an eventual liberation.

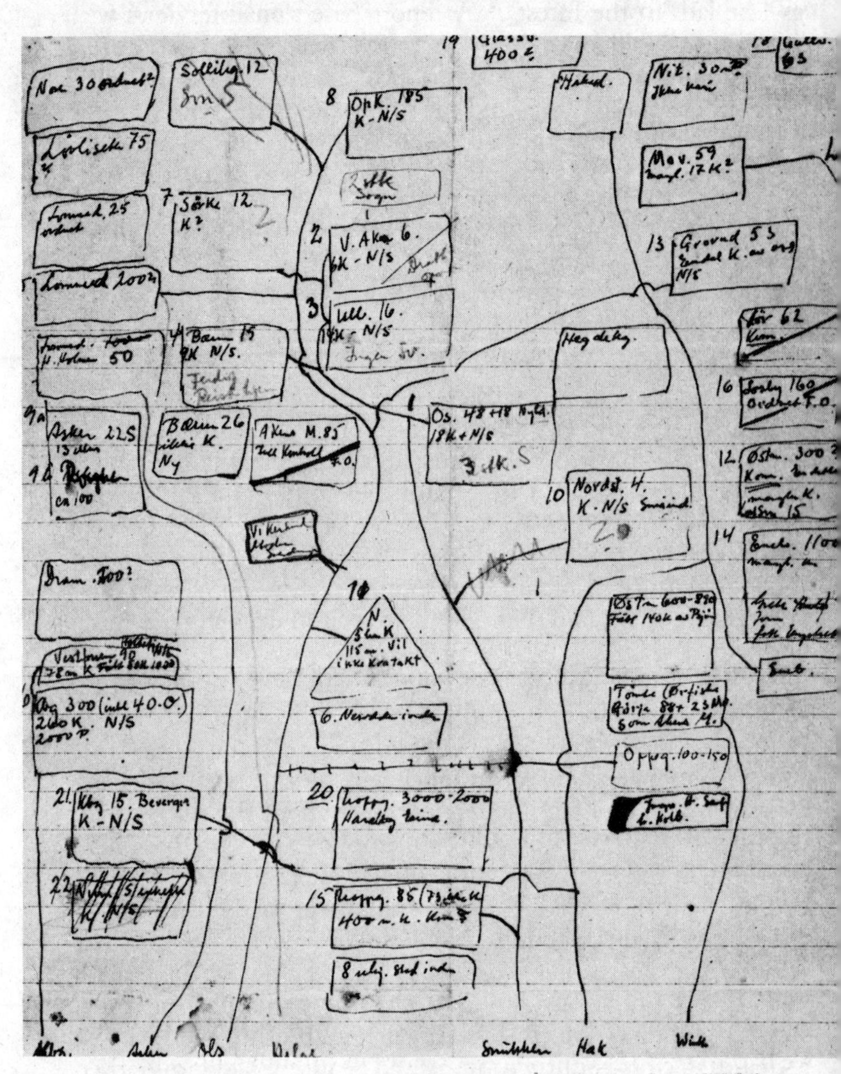

'The lads in the forest' — sketch-map of locations by Odd Gjelsvik, made in the summer of 1944.

The first reports suggested that about 10,000 lads were in the forest in the Oslo area alone, but the checking gradually enabled us to eliminate a good many phantom figures, while some of the young people removed themselves. After 2-3 weeks we concluded that there were about 3,000 men in the Oslo woodlands, 1,500 in Lower Telemark, and some hundreds in other districts adjoining the built-up areas of East Norway. The illegal trade union committees in Oslo and other towns in East Norway gave splendid help in tracing and assisting 2,000 men, while the 1,500 in Lower Telemark were taken in hand by a local committee, in which both Milorg and the civil resistance organisations were represented.

The directive to those who had been registered was first and foremost to lie low and not to undertake anything desperate; help would be coming.

After a few days, disquieting news arrived: in some of the camps, groups organised by Communists were agitating for the formation of partisan detachments, with promises of arms and equipment. It was in exactly these days, which were the most critical for the youth of Norway, that the Allies at last crossed the Channel and attacked the Germans' Atlantic rampart. The jubilation because the liberation of Europe had now begun in earnest could not blind our eyes as responsible leaders to the fact that the weapons now dropped over Europe must go to those underground forces which were in the actual battle areas. The Norwegian Milorg was still extremely badly equipped; most of its members were still unarmed, and so remained until well into the coming winter. When carefully picked groups could not be supplied with arms, it was an irresponsible act to promise them to haphazard collections of young people.

We had to reckon with most of the rural population gradually getting wind of where the camps lay, and there would then be a risk that German troops would soon be on the track. At the first possible moment we arranged a meeting with the leaders of Milorg, and there too the conclusion was that only the most suitable of the lads could be included on a rather longer view in the 'cells' which Milorg was establishing; its representatives went round the camps and picked out the relatively few for whom there was room in the Milorg 'cells'. For the time being we had to try to scatter the remainder in rural neighbourhoods. The anti-AT committee arranged for the farmers to receive directives and be prevailed upon to help as many as possible with work and house-room; the young men got ration cards and money to take with them.

We also sent an immediate enquiry to Stockholm as to whether the youths could not be included in the Norwegian 'police troops', which were being organised there under Helset's command. At the beginning of July we were notified that 2-3,000 could be accepted there, so we made the necessary arrangements for them to be sent over. With the 'export' organisations working at high pressure and setting up new routes so as to get as many as possible away during the summer season, more than 1,500 men arrived in Sweden by the end of August. On the civil side a new division was introduced directly under the secretariat, to prevent undesirable elements from insinuating themselves among those who were to be sent to Sweden. This system of control was still employed in sending people over the frontier later on, not only on security grounds but also to ensure that the illegal organisations were properly informed when one of their people had to flee, and that equipment left behind might be brought into use instead of being confiscated. Meanwhile we were continuing the work of establishing control over the camps, which in most places was not very difficult, as the young men displayed an exemplary discipline and the directives from the leadership were followed everywhere. The exception was provided by some camps under Communist leadership, which, according to my brother's estimate at the time, had a complement of about 300.

The 'lads in the forest' are to be starved out!

But danger was now threatening from another quarter. Alarming reports came in from our contacts in the NS central administration that the lads were to be starved out. Instead of the head of the household being able to collect ration cards for food and clothes for all members of the family, each individual would now have to fetch them from the rationing offices in person. We had heard rumours of this as early as the beginning of May, and alerted our contacts in the Rationing Directorate; its head and several of his closest associates being in Home Front organisations, they used the fact that the issue of cards for the third quarter was almost due as a pretext, so that in general the order was not enforced on that occasion. However, a warning shot had been fired; if the order became operative for the fourth quarter, the food situation for many of the young men would become critical.

After four years of occupation and scantily doled out rations, our homes were drained of reserves and people were dependent on what the authorities provided. There had been a tacit understanding on both sides of the front line in Norway during these years that the rationing system should not be attacked. Accordingly, at the beginning of 1944 the Home Front leadership had opposed a directive of Communist origin for the fixing of 'reasonable' prices for goods on the Black Market, which would thereby become a legal institution in the eyes of patriots. And now, in the following summer, there were clear indications that the Nazis were going to use food as a weapon of war. Skjönsberg, Sanengen and I, who had already discussed the question during the scare in May, asked our authorities in Stockholm and London in June whether ration cards for the next period could be printed there. We sent over matrices, specimens of paper, and other material as requested, but were not confident about the solution, so Sanengen undertook preparations for securing the cards needed by a *coup*; his plans were in readiness, but they were put in cold storage in the first half of July, when we were notified that cards would be made available from London.

The camps in the forest had now been in operation for some two months, and their existence had by degrees become a little too widely known. There had also been a couple of episodes in which NS sheriffs (*lensmenn*) had come upon the boys, and after the arrest of some of them in the country of Buskerud the local sheriff was liquidated by a Home Front group in the area. In mid-July the NS authorities issued an order to sheriffs to intensify the search for the camps. After consulting Sanengen, I therefore took the responsibility for sending out on my own account a slightly toned-down version of a draft directive which had been devised by the anti-AT committee. The gist of it was as follows:

The directive is not to be understood as a *recommendation* but as an *order* from the highest authority in a time of war. Further developments will determine whether persons disobeying the order will be court-martialled or will be sentenced in accordance with the Norwegian Government's ordinance of 22 January 1942, section 1 of which prescribes definite and very severe penalties for assisting the enemy... The leadership of the Home Front demands in the name of the Norwegian people that the sheriffs refuse any complicity in the persecution of our youth. Any sheriff who misjudges who they are that constitute Norway's sole lawful authorities and his own lawful superiors, must be prepared to take the consequences. The war has now entered its final phase, and the Home Front does not shrink from using the strongest measure in this conflict, where the future of the entire nation is at risk. Sheriffs who infringe this directive may expect to meet the same fate as police inspector Lindvik and sheriff Horgen* ... We repeat: *No Norwegian youth is to be arrested because he does his duty to his fatherland.*

Both Sanengen and I considered that the situation was so dangerous for the lads that such strong words were justified, and we were not exactly sorry that the authoritative committees could not handle the matter in the holiday period; it is questionable whether the majority of their members would have approved the directive, even in the modified form. Yet it proved to have useful effects, both upon the sheriffs and not least upon the 'lads in the forest', who got a feeling that the Home Front would go to any length to protect them.

In planning a *coup* to secure ration cards for the last quarter of 1944, Sanengen had found out that the final chance was on 8-9 August when the last lorry-load of cards — those for the Oslo region — would leave the printing-works for local distribution. When Sanengen and I arrived for our routine morning conference at Skjönsberg's office on the 4th, we were shocked to learn from Stockholm that the Government had declared itself unable after all to supply us with the promised cards, as they had not got hold of the right quality paper. Our contacts in the Rationing Directorate, like most of the members of the KK and the Circle, were on their summer holidays, so we had to take an immediate decision on our own. Sanengen was given the all-clear for carrying out his plan, on which he started at once; and it would be wrong to say that we took the decision with regret, for we had all three been thirsting for a long time to give the authorities the proper reply to their challenge in using food as a means of pressure in the struggle.

The plan was thought out to the last detail, and Sanengen had good contacts in the printing-works where the cards were stocked. On the morning of 9 August, as soon as the lorry had left the works in the Old Town, Sönsteby and two other members of the 'Oslo gang' jumped on to it at a cross roads; put pistols into the backs of the drivers and guards, who were driven off in another car; and took the vehicle down into the most tightly packed central district. There it was backed into a yard where another gang was waiting with a second lorry, of which

*An officer of the State Police in Oslo and the Buskerud sheriff whose liquidation has already been mentioned.

the number plates were covered up; the boxes with the cards were at once transferred; and a new driver emerging by a different gate brought the boxes to safety. We now had 70-80,000 cards in our possession.

In spite of rewards of 200,000 kroner tax-free for putting the police on the track of the culprits, the authorities received no information from the public, although the *coup* had been brought off in the very heart of the city on a busy working-day. We put aside fully 13,000 cards, and while the NS Supply Minister's head was still reeling with the shock of the impudent action, we got in touch with him on the telephone and offered to return the rest of the cards, if the order to appear before the supply committees in person was rescinded. He accepted our demand unconditionally and in the course of the month sent the required instructions to the committees, whereupon we returned the cards in successive quantities of 10,000, while he on his side reduced by stages the restrictions which he had laid upon the population on behalf of the authorities. In the end all that was left was the cancellation of the liquor and tobacco ration for the quarter, a penalty which the people of the city and county accepted with composure. The authorities made no further attempt during the war to use the food supply as a weapon.

Meanwhile we continued with the business of winding up the camps. By the end of October the original ones in the Oslo area contained only fifty young men, and elsewhere in the country they were wound up still more quickly.

The fight was over and the victory won; but we did not feel secure, and we warned those who might still be taken to be on their guard and if possible unavailable at their homes or places of work. And the victory was exploited for a continued struggle against AT and the 'national' labour effort as long as the war lasted. AT was beginning to disintegrate — increasingly, both officers and other ranks quitted the camps. But the significance of the victory in the campaign against 'the labour mobilisation' is best expressed in the words of Reichskommissar Terboven himself: 'Quisling's old standing demands (i.e. peace, sovereignty, military honour, mobilisation) ... have been finally buried.'

In these crucial summer months, criticism of the Home Front leadership quietened down. The Home Front had made a great impact by using active methods of warfare in such a way that people could understand and respect the objective. The large numbers, even among good patriots,* who at the start of the campaign against the AT had not believed that any mobilisation was impending and had therefore been lukewarm in their reaction to the directive, could now see the truth with their own eyes. From now on, the Home Front leadership had a firm grip on its troops, an authority which could no longer be shaken. On the inside, too, the co-operation which had been achieved between ourselves and the military staff created a mutual respect and understanding, which did a great deal to weld the Home Front together.

*Literally 'Jössingfiord people', with reference to those Norwegians who approved of the British breach of neutral rights in that area on 16 February 1940, when 300 prisoners were rescued from the German ship *Altmark*. Hence 'patriots', in contrast with 'quislings'.

7

CONSOLIDATING THE POSITION

A joint secretariat for the Home Front leadership

In the autumn of 1943 the secretariat of the Co-ordination Committee had been entrusted with the service of internal communications for the Circle in connection with the preparations for the civil administration. Then before Jansen's departure, on one of the hectic days in mid-May 1944, he asked me to take over the charge of the Circle's 'foreign office': I had already assisted him in various practical matters and — as previously mentioned — taken on the writing of surveys for the Government of the situation on the Home Front. Skjönsberg, Jansen, Sanengen and I worked together so closely that in practice a common secretariat for the KK and the Circle had existed since Jansen succeeded Boyesen in February; in May this was formalised as the secretariat for the Home Front leadership (HLS).* The extension and consolidation of the organisations during the spring and summer also made the notion of 'Sivorg' more of a reality than before.

When the AT campaign had passed its climax, Sanengen took over entirely the greatly increased activities of the old KK secretariat and proceeded to strengthen the district organisations, and therefore some development at the centre was urgently needed. The Supply Committee, which had worked under Haugland for the 'lads in the forest', continued as a common committee of supply for all the main organisations in the Home Front, while Sanengen, who was still its link with the leadership, set up an additional supply service for our personal needs, so that we could devote all our time and energy to resistance activities.

Whereas Sanengen headed the internal organisation of the HLS, I was responsible for the greater part of the co-operation

*The peacetime associations of the word 'secretariat' do less than justice to the exact functions of HLS, which was the civilian counterpart to SL — the military staff instituted by Milorg.

with Milorg and the other principal illegal bodies, as well as relations with the illegal press and the 'export' organisations. In September Milorg and Sivorg set up a joint information committee, particularly for the elucidation of questions from the Government in connection with the transition period at the close of hostilities.

The work in the press section underwent a marked increase after the Allied invasion of France and our dramatic campaign against the 'labour mobilisation' in the early summer of 1944. The papers wanted more information — about the course of the war, the sabotage activities, the Government's work with supplies and other preparations for the transition period, and about the discussion which was going on abroad over inter-Allied co-operation to secure peace after Germany was defeated. The interest in post-war problems sometimes got the upper hand to such an extent that we found it necessary to remind people that we were still deeply engaged in the struggle against an enemy who remained predominant in our country. In other sections, too, the business expanded greatly in the course of the year, so that by the autumn the number of full-time workers in the secretariat had increased tenfold — a nucleus of six (Brunsvig, Sigrid Steinnes, Bratsberg, Risting, Sanengen and myself) and, by the end of the year, about sixty others, of whom nearly half were women.

The heavy blows which the Gestapo dealt us in the autumn of 1943 and the following winter had shown the need for a better security service, and in the spring Milorg, XU, Sivorg and the Police Organisation agreed to unite their efforts in this direction. The various contacts with the police and the prisons, which each of us had formed or linked up with independently, were transferred in the course of the summer to a special group taken from the Police Organisation, which developed the service further. In the end, its many ramifications reached within prison walls and the barbed wire perimeters of the concentration camps, and extended to the tapping of telephones, the opening of the correspondence of the State Police and the Gestapo, and the copying of interrogation records and other police reports — to mention some of the most important. Useful information also came in from the judicial office at the Norwegian Legation in Stockholm, which engaged in comprehensive intelligence work for our protection against informers and *agents provocateurs*. The central security group was linked up for the passing of warnings to each main organisation, which might develop its own internal precautions. The mutual security service functioned well and deserves much of the credit for the fact that the organisations later avoided large-scale exposures, even if every one of us still had to put up with heavy blows.

Once a week, or more frequently if the situation required, a representative of each main organisation met with the head of the security services to examine questions of principle arising in that sphere — a group in which I represented Sivorg. Work which bore so closely upon the Gestapo was not without risk and on one occasion the Gestapo got on the track of the place where we used to meet. The warning given did not reach me in time, so I went there unsuspectingly, and had raised my hand to ring the bell before I noticed that the door was sealed. I did not loiter in getting down the stairs and out; but as so often, luck was on my side — the Gestapo was no longer keeping watch there.

The heavy pressure of work in the secretariat and the organisation, which made itself felt as the summer went on, meant that we were noticeably short of people with experience in illegal activities. Among the many skilful Home Front pioneers who had been obliged to transfer their services to Swedish soil, I thought particularly of Engen with his unusually strong nerves, and in September we succeeded in bringing him back to Oslo to resume his work of liaison with the Government. This was a great relief, as he fitted well into our milieu and conducted the 'foreign office' with a steady hand.*

Change in the editorship of the Bulletin

Around 1 May 1944 — right in the busy period of preparations for the action against the AT — Jansen's time in the Home Front was up. One of his colleagues at the University who had been arrested sent word from prison that he could not manage to withhold Jansen's name any longer, so he must reckon with a visit from the Gestapo at any moment. For almost four years he had been one of the pillars of the resistance, and those closest to him knew that he was also the link with the mysterious editors of the *Bulletin*, the illegal paper which seemed to be equally

*H.K. Engen (1912-66) became Norwegian Representative at the United Nations, 1952-8, and Ambassador in Washington, 1963-6.

well informed on the problems of the Home Front and on the course of the war in the outside world, and which since 1940 had served as a guide and direction-indicator for the conflict. Now, when he had to depart, he told me that he had edited the *Bulletin* alone ever since he came home from the summer holidays of 1942 to find that the previous editors had been arrested. I was dumbfounded because such a possibility had never dawned on me, although I had been his closest helper in the distribution of the *Bulletin* right from the start, and for four years his almost daily associate. On departing, Jansen merely said that Sigrid Steinnes saw to it that the manuscript reached the technical staff of the paper, and not until the last days of the war did I learn that this staff consisted of Bratsberg and herself and a third member of the KK secretariat.

As the only survivor of those who had been responsible for the *Bulletin* since 1940, I naturally agreed to Jansen's request to take over the editorship; it was clear, however, that in view of my all-absorbing role in the secretariat, I would need help. We agreed to ask the journalist Christensen, a veteran from the paper's earliest days, to write the feature article on the progress of the war; having been at liberty for some time, he at once accepted with characteristic willingness. Jansen proposed that I should also ask for the help of his colleague from the University's action committee, but as the latter was at the same time involved in editorial work for the press section of the secretariat, further reinforcement was required. Tore Sunde, an earlier companion of mine in resistance work, therefore joined us, and for most of the final year he carried the main burden as assistant editor. I myself was unable to do much more than write leaders and commentaries on the day-to-day struggle.

Illicit nation-wide conferences

After a 6-7 weeks' duel at the Channel bridgeheads, the Allied forces broke through — and their armour penetrated deeply into Hitler's Reich that had been supposed to last a thousand years. The reports we received from London were very optimistic, telling us in the late summer that the war would be over within a few weeks or months. This misled us into calling in the representatives from the districts to a two-day, nationwide conference, in order to discuss the intensification of the struggle against the occupying power and to divulge the various preparations which had been made with a view to the period of liberation. For security reasons this national conference was divided in two, with forty representatives each time, the first beginning on 19 August in a private home and continuing on the next day at the Home for the Deaf — both were in the Oslo suburbs — and the second being held on 4 and 5 September in a private house near the Home for the Deaf. Our own action group, armed to the teeth with newly-arrived guns and well camouflaged, was in position as security guards during the conferences. Each district sent up to three men, of whom one represented the illegal trade union organisation (FU). They were given various explanatory surveys, and the question of the attitude to be taken towards the Communists' agitation for a Freedom Council was discussed, the negative position adopted by the Home Front leadership being generally supported.

The meetings seem to have been specially important for the representatives from the workers' side. Their local contacts with the district leadership of the Home Front had certainly been defective at times — the Gestapo saw to that — but since the summer of 1942, when Jönsson became a member of the Co-ordination Committee and the Circle, arrangements for contact had been established in most districts and it had been possible to use our system of communications. In 1944, when the FU appointed a new member to the Co-ordination Committee, co-operation increased; and the national conferences may well be said to have strengthened the sense of unity and emphasised for the FU delegates who attended the importance of using, and if necessary extending, the means of contact available. Moreover, the big expansion of our secretariat during the summer of 1944 put it in a position to render fuller assistance to the illegal organisation of the workers.

The co-operation with Milorg was steadily widened in the course of the autumn. In September we agreed that our district leaderships, too, ought to be in touch with each other, and the SL also accepted a proposal from us that information should be given about Milorg's steadily growing acts of sabotage for use in the illegal press. For reasons of security the SL had long been reluctant to make these acts known, but the result of this was that the Communists had some success in making it appear that there were responsible for most acts of sabotage. When the SL at this time lost its advisers on industrial sabotage, we were able to supply them with new people.

Hard times for the Communists

It is difficult for outsiders to form a clear impression of internal conditions among the Communists in Norway during the war, for even then they were plagued by fractional disputes. Furubotn as party leader and Sunde as action leader — or partisan chief, as he sometimes called himself — did not get on well together, and their ways parted whenever they met. In the spring of 1944 Furubotn and his headquarters were at the summer dairies in the mountain district of North Etnedal at the pass over to Valdres, where he also had links with the local population; he was in the company of his co-workers, members of the family and a few guards, about twenty in all. Sunde spent the winter in the vicinity of Gjövik, where he was training saboteurs, having lost his closest associates in the previous year, when they were either captured by the Gestapo, died fighting or were executed. In the spring of 1944 he carried out a number of actions against small banks and secured considerable sums of money — on one occasion as much as 150,000 kroner — which did not go into the main party funds but were kept by him for his own organisation. The position, however, was unsafe; after some unsuccessful actions against members of the State Police at Gjövik at the end of March, the Gestapo caught some of his people, so Sunde found it necessary to move his headquarters to a lodging-house in the forest farther west, which had previously been used by Furubotn.

Just before the move, Sunde's group had been joined by a number of guards who had deserted Furubotn — who then moved to a summer farm nearer Valdres. The Gestapo had already obtained indications through arrests in the early spring that Furubotn was in the mountain area between Etnedal and Valdres, and at the end of May one of his former guards, now stationed at the lodging-house already mentioned, was caught nearby by a roving police patrol. Two actions quickly followed.

On the next day, substantial German forces, probably consisting of 200 men, attacked the lodging-house. After a sharp exchange of shots Sunde with six or seven others managed to break through and escape, but a number of his people were either killed or captured, and immediately afterwards two leading Communists were surprised and arrested farther south, in Hönefoss. Then in the middle of June German police troops, accompanied by a detachment of State Police, several hundred men in all, conducted a cleaning-up operation in the mountains between Etnedal and Valdres, in which one of the German groups came upon Furubotn and his party at a summer farm where they were quartered for the time being. They had placed outposts, however, so Furubotn, his wife, daughter and small grandchild escaped, as did six others of the party. But the Gestapo succeeded in arresting fourteen of his associates, and many of the Communists taken prisoner in both actions were later executed.

Furubotn did not manage to take away with him a comprehensive collection of documents, which fell into the hands of the Gestapo, thus giving them much important information about the illegal activities of the Party; further information was extracted from the arrested members by torture, and altogether the summer was disastrous for the Communists. Sunde's organisation, too, could not get properly on to its feet again after the attack on the lodging-house. But it was not until January 1945 that we knew much about this — or about the internal disputes of the Communist Party.

New attempts at co-operation

Despite its weakened condition, the NKP continued its efforts to get a Freedom Council established, and some places were interested in arranging to co-operate with the Communists. I discussed the question with Skjönsberg and Sanengen, and we agreed to try a co-operation limited to one region, which we could broaden if it went well. The region chosen for the first attempt was the county of Buskerud, with results which I recorded in a report to the Government in December 1944, countersigned by the Home Front committee for that region. One Communist had been included among the ten members of that committee, and had been given special responsibility for organisation. He nevertheless persisted in sending out directives which he had not submitted to his colleagues. When brought to book, he agreed that these ought not to have been issued as from the committee; but policies continued to differ, and out of four specific conditions which had been laid down for its work, the Communist representative had broken three.

In addition to the disputes detailed in the report, it was interesting to observe how the work went in Buskerud after the new committee had begun to operate, with Communists in charge of organisation. In the agitation for a Freedom Council we had constantly been told that the morale of the Home Front had sunk in 1943. An example which was commonly cited was the break-up of the businessmen's front; the next year we managed to weld it together again — but not in Buskerud. At the beginning of December 1944 the 'civic guard' was set up by the enemy in the town of Hönefoss after the exploding of an oil tank there, for which 350 men mustered, in spite of the plain directive to the people to refuse which had been in force from the beginning of the year. Only the teachers stayed away, and they reported the collapse of the front to us. When we asked those in charge of organisation about the missing effort, we received a report a week later, explaining that people had been taken by surprise because they had been instructed to assemble only two hours after the issuing of the summons; there had been many arrests in the town recently, and the atmosphere was nervous. The organisation leader therefore considered that, since calamity had already struck, an action to induce people to withdraw from the civic guard would hardly result in anything but the dislocation of the set-up in the town: all his own connections in Hönefoss were among those who had assembled. Thus the 'unified' leadership in Buskerud had not been able to mobilise much of the 'giant strength of the people' at Hönefoss; nor did it look as though the Communist thesis that the people would become more militant when exposed to the German terror had any validity when applied to that county.

Our district organisation for Bergen and Hordaland had not managed to recover from the weakening which had resulted from the discoveries of May 1943. The campaign against the national labour effort was not very vigorously conducted, and Bergen was one of the districts where the campaign against the registration of the three age-classes in May 1944 had failed; so we got in touch with the district leaders at the beginning of June to assist in a re-activisation. At the same time it became apparent that a forceful organisation had been set up in Hordaland called the Western Norway Freedom Council, which was certainly led by Communists but had support from other quarters as well. Bonnevie-Svendsen went to Bergen on the secretariat's behalf at the end of August and had discussions with our people and with representatives of the new Council, who were already in touch with our leaders in Bergen. The discussions resulted in the formation of a Home Front Western Council* and an agreement that the Western Norway Freedom Council, renamed the Council for the County of Hordaland, should be recognised as the civil resistance organisation for Hordaland, while the new Western Council should be responsible for Bergen. It was assumed by us that the Home Front Western Council would form an upper tier of leadership for the region and effect the contacts between ourselves and the Hordaland Council, and would obtain the money required for operation. The conditions were that their work should not affect Milorg's sphere of activity, and that all directives and guidelines from the Home Front leadership and the Government should be passed on further down the chain of command and loyally obeyed; if there was disagreement, we wanted to know of it, and the Hordaland Council must not agitate against decisions by the leadership through the press or the apparatus belonging to the organisation.

The Hordaland Council followed the directives given for civil resistance, and did a good job in influencing young people to stay away from AT and the labour mobilisation, finding them hiding-places and supplies. But it did not accept the guidelines agreed upon by the Government and the Circle for civil administration in the transition period, and in the autumn it launched a strong agitation against them. Moreover, those illegal newspapers which the Hordaland Council published, or with which it had connections, accused the Home Front leadership of opposing the re-assembly of the Storting and of preparing a *coup d'état*—in complete harmony with the agitation conducted at the same time in the Communist Party papers. A proposal from the leadership in Bergen for co-operation over press activities was rejected by the Hordaland Council, nor would it stop selling so-called freedom bonds, which from a security angle were a risky financial proposition, in spite of the offer of the money it needed through the Western Council in Bergen.

We could not agree that a district organisation should operate in the name of the Home Front leadership and make use of its authority, while at the same time working against it. The Western Council, in co-operation with our secretariat, drew up

*If West Norway had become isolated during military operations, this Council would have become the highest national authority for the region

a written proposal for guidelines and working arrangements, but the Communist representatives in the Hordaland Council rejected them at a meeting at the beginning of February 1945, and co-operation then ceased. The Hordaland Council was, however, split by this affair, inasmuch as most of its non-communist members joined our organisation in Bergen.

Impact on Norway of the attempt on Hitler's life

The contact with a group of anti-Nazi officers in the Wehrmacht, which Arvid Brodersen had maintained for four years, became an increasingly valuable channel of information for us as the war moved towards its end. The group's leader, Lieutenant-Colonel Steltzer, was connected with the group which carried out the unsuccessful attack on Hitler on 20 July 1944, and shortly beforehand he approached Brodersen with a request that we should influence the Allied leaders to be accommodating to the new German government which they were going to form when Hitler had been cleared out of the way. When the attack failed and its supporters were arrested and executed, Steltzer too was lured to Germany, arrested and sentenced to death; but he escaped execution owing to strong representations to Himmler from the Swedish side. After this, Brodersen had to depart to Sweden, but a lady of his acquaintance undertook to act as intermediary with Steltzer's successor in the group, Major F. Hammersen in the *Abwehr,* whose mother had Norwegian forebears. The intermediary was to link up with Hauge, since in Brodersen's opinion the situation in Norway was approaching a phase in which military operations would have most importance.

'Our secret weapon'

As the last phase of the war approached, the question arose of our ability to meet drastic actions by the occupying power with a united counter-action by the population, perhaps in the form of a general withdrawal of labour — a People's Strike. The population of Copenhagen had shown in July 1944 that such a strike could be kept going for some days,* but it was clear to us that if

*30 June-4/5 July; the strike began as a spontaneous protest against a curfew and other restrictions, on which the Germans were induced to make concessions; about 100 Danish lives were lost.

was not simply a matter of repeating what had been done there in Norway, where the occupying power was much stronger in proportion to the population, whom the Gestapo had held for a much longer period under an iron heel.

The Co-ordination Committee decided in September to nominate a People's Strike committee, in which those concerned with working life were strongly represented, to evaluate the matter and make recommendations. The engineer C.F. Mathiesen was asked to take charge, with Risting from the HLS as secretary; both of them were enthusiastic over the task, which they discharged with great energy. There was strong emphasis on linking up closely with the representatives of the trade union movement, both centrally and at the local level, but the workers in general had little desire for a big strike, as the memory of the State of Emergency of 1941 remained vivid in many minds. Nor was it easy to arouse the rural population to an appreciation of the strike weapon; some of our district leaderships doubted the possibility of a successful action, especially in the far north, where the German withdrawal was taking place and the whole life of the community was under military control.

A People's Strike would be met by drastic counter-measures from the German side, which would inflict great stress and suffering upon the population, particularly those in hospitals, homes for the aged and other institutions. The committee therefore examined carefully the assumptions supporting such a strike, and they concluded that the 'strike weapon' could only be used in an extreme situation, when we had no other weapon at our disposal to save us from national disgrace, or when the military situation demanded it. A People's Strike in reply to a German act of terror would have to be of short duration — up to three or four continuous days and nights — but in the last phase of the war it could be longer, for then it would be a case of risking all with a real chance of success. In addition to a nationwide, general People's Strike, consideration could also be given to actions limited to certain groups, particularly in the transport sector; or it might be limited to certain parts of the country. The committee considered furthermore that a People's Strike in answer to a German act of terror would have to be a spontaneous reaction, carried along by the individual citizen's personal disgust and indignation and a will to stop any repetition. On the other hand, the strike would need to be fully controlled by the responsible leadership of the Home Front, and one must be able to prevent ill-considered actions, all of which presupposed information and organisation on a big scale. Strike actions in connection with military operations must be the concern of the military authorities.

The views of the People's Strike committee were fully supported by the KK, which sent the district contacts a comprehensive account at the beginning of October, including practical advice and instructions. At the same time an enquiry was undertaken to see how good the contacts were at district level between the leadership and the various trade organisations, especially the local FU committees. Finally, information was requested as to the capacity of the district organisations to print and distribute directives, and the speed with which they could be distributed within the district. There was also an investigation to see how long messages from the secretariat over the normal system of communications took to reach district leaderships all over the country. Appreciating, too, that the strike would stand or fall by its development in the capital, the committee joined with the secretariat to set up a special plan for Greater Oslo. Thus energetic preparations were made in the autumn and winter of 1944-5, both in the secretariat of the Home Front leadership and in the apparatus of the district organisations.

The committee wrote a number of articles, which were taken into the illegal press and broadcast over the BBC under the slogan 'A People's Strike, our secret weapon'. Neither the Germans nor the NS could avoid observing the course the war was taking, but they comforted themselves at that time with the thought that the secret weapon being developed in the German armaments industry would soon turn back the ebbing tide of their fortunes. The articles in the illegal press had a double object: to prepare public opinion for the possibility of a People's Strike, and to deter the Nazis from actions which might provoke one. Our intelligence network was able to find several examples of the way that the strike preparations were actually affecting our opponents. One was the Gestapo's abstention, under Wehrmacht pressure, from its intended counter-measures against the workers at the two big Oslo shipyards after the major sabotage action under Communist leadership at the end of 1944, when six ships totalling 23,000 tons were sunk and important parts of the docks were destroyed.

In order to discuss the question of a People's Strike during an

Allied operation to liberate us, we got in touch with the military staff (SL): limited strikes, designed chiefly to hold up transport and communications, were most appropriate to such a situation. It was found that the dissemination of directives by radio was the only practical alternative, since it had been proved that messages from Oslo to the district leaderships by the ordinary system of communications took as much as a week and distribution inside the districts took equally long. In order to get the directives out to the districts as quickly as possible, the People's Strike committee worked with picked staff in the Telegraphs on a camouflaged system of telegrams; but even this proved impracticable for some points of contact, the operating arrangements being in many places too obvious. We therefore pressed for the procurement from London of small radio receivers to distribute throughout the country. We were given every possible help in this by Biering, Norum and Malm in Stockholm; dozens of the little 'sweetheart' radios arrived from London, and were sent out to the district organisations, the illegal newspapers and other necessary users. The longed-for small arms for self-defence likewise began to arrive, and spirits rose in our ranks as rapidly as did the numbers of our members.

Negotiations with the Government renewed

In the summer of 1943 the Government and the Circle had agreed on an interim arrangement for local government administration. In the course of 1944 a number of proposals or statements regarding civil preparations had been sent to the Government, partly by the Circle or committees which it had established, and partly by a committee on economic preparedness with which it had relations. It remained, however, to make an arrangement for the central administration in Oslo. The Circle had proposed, in a letter to the Prime Minister early in September 1943, that the Government should appoint a central administrative organ composed of people in Norway, which should take charge from the time of an armistice or German collapse until the Government and the King returned. After a long period of reflection, the Prime Minister stated in March 1944 that the proposal was unacceptable on constitutional and other grounds; instead, as soon as possible after a German collapse the Government would send a governing delegation to Norway with the Crown Prince at its head.

In June 1944 the invasion of France revived the question, which the Circle took up again in July. The next month, Oslo was visited by Norum, who had become a kind of travelling ambassador between the Home Front leadership and the Government; he was asked to take the matter up in London, and on his return to Stockholm he wrote an urgent appeal to the Foreign Minister, Trygve Lie. Just after this the Milorg leader, Hauge, returned from a visit to London, and at Skjönsberg's request gave an account of the military situation at a meeting of the Circle, which then learnt that the division presumed to be going to Norway to disarm the German forces had been sent to the continent, and that no substitute had been found. This made it still more likely that the governing delegation could not reach the country in time when the Germans collapsed.

On 1 September the Circle wrote to the Government again, proposing that the delegation should be supplemented by five members in Norway, who would be able to act on the Government's behalf if the other members did not arrive in time; they also forwarded a statement from the trade union committee (the FU), strongly supporting this proposal. At that time we were receiving reports that the Norwegian authorities in London expected the war to be finished in the course of the autumn, so it was incomprehensible to us at home that the Government took so long to make up its mind. At the beginning of October the Circle withdrew its proposal for supplementing the delegation, and again requested the Government to explain how the problem could be solved. This letter crossed with an answer from the Prime Minister, in which after expressing many reservations he accepted the proposal for a group of five.

In mid-October one of the representatives on the committee for economic preparations was arrested, which led to the immediate arrest of Gunnar Jahn of the Circle as well. At the same time the Gestapo sent a detachment of as many as twelve men to get their claws on Skjönsberg, but he had fortunately gone into hiding; there were also others in the two groups who were arrested or had to flee. Just before this an enquiry had arrived as to whether representatives of the Home Front leadership could meet the Foreign Minister, Trygve Lie, and the Minister of Justice, Terje Wold, in Stockholm. It was now decided that Skjönsberg and two others should attend from the Circle, as did Hauge, the Milorg chief, who in the course of 1944 had established an increasingly close relationship with Skjönsberg;

he had taken part, too, in the committee appointed by the Circle to prepare for the judicial settlement.

The discussions ranged mainly over transition questions of an administrative, judicial and economic nature, but no resolutions were adopted, as the two ministers made clear at the outset that they had not been prepared to meet the Home Front delegation. The latter was all the more astonished because the meeting took place in accordance with a request made by Schjelderup three weeks before. The exchange of information and opinions which took place was nevertheless useful, and the delegation put forward a proposal, launched by Skjönsberg a few weeks earlier, that the Home Front leadership should choose a special adviser for every Department, except those of Foreign Affairs, Defence and Shipping, for the purpose of assisting ministers in the period of transition. If the governing delegation did not arrive in time, these advisers would function in co-operation with the Home Front leadership as a provisional regime.

Mounting pressure by the Gestapo

It made a great difference to the result of the big struggle against the labour service and labour mobilisation in the spring and summer that, both at the centre and in the country at large, we had been able to work without overmuch disturbance from the Gestapo. In the autumn these idyllic conditions became a thing of the past, as the Gestapo during the last three months of the year directed one blow after another against the resistance organisations. We got our share and even more. Besides the action against the Cricle (already mentioned), it was a blow to the entire Home Front when the Gestapo's searchlight fell on Skjönsberg, who had long been the central figure, belonging to the Circle, the Co-ordination Committee and the Military Council, and conducting the daily struggle as a co-worker with us in the secretariat. It was intended that he should come back after the Stockholm meeting to work under cover, while Magnus Jensen, who in the course of the year had become increasingly active in both the KK and the Circle, would take his place in the contacts with the secretariat; Bonnevie-Svendsen also became more prominent in the daily management. But various circumstances, including a journey to London, delayed Skjönsberg's return until a few days before the liberation; so for the last six months of the war we had to manage without his decisiveness and readiness for action.

October was also the month when our district leaderships in Hamar, Arendal, Stavanger and Narvik were hit by arrests and discoveries. In Hamar this was the second disaster in the year, for there had been detections in July as the result of the shadowing of a Hamar youth in the British service, who had been recognised by a NS man on a visit to his native town. In Arendal, which had suffered severely in the autumn of 1943, the effect this time was to deprive the secretariat of all but sporadic contacts. In Stavanger there were 150 arrests, while in Narvik the chief doctor at the hospital was arrested at the beginning of the month; but nothing could be pinned on him, although he was in fact the local head of both Milorg and Sivorg and involved additionally in military intelligence.

These events were shortly followed by further trouble in Trondheim, where Rinnan had wrought such havoc before. One of the leaders, Tömmerås, was caught, so the others went into hiding, as did C.F. Mathiesen, the representative of the engineers in the KK, who had been in direct touch with the local leadership. Tömmeras endured nine days of torture before giving away any names, so that they might have time to escape; but the Gestapo spread a false report of his suicide in prison, whereupon most of those who had felt threatened by his detention came out of hiding. This was exactly what the Gestapo had hoped for: after a month they struck again, and this time a number of our people in Trondheim, and in Oslo Mathiesen and Sam Sunde, a prominent HLS member acting as the intermediary for couriers coming in from the districts, were arrested.

The Gestapo were now hot on the heels of the Co-ordination Committee and the secretariat, so for a while things looked dangerous. But none of the people under arrest knew anyone in the secretariat by name; moreover, they were in complete control of their difficult situation and disclosed nothing about the central leadership. Reports which came from them through our prison service enabled us to call off the alarm for that occasion. But the reconstruction of the district leadership in the five towns and the reorganisation of the contact arrangements for the couriers took much of our time and energies, when we already had our hands full with the preparation for the People's Strike and the developments in North Norway after the

German retreat on the northern front.

Our letters to friends in Stockholm at that period are strongly marked by the pressure of work from which we were suffering and by complaints over the scarcity of assistance and 'office'-room. The Gestapo — and not least the State Police — had increased their street controls to such an extent that we had to stop meeting in the street and obtain more space for our activities indoors. This was not easy, and we were highly pleased when we got hold of a couple of fifth-floor offices in a block in the centre of the town, where we camouflaged our activities behind an agency plate. We regarded it as an advantage that the SS had offices two floors below us; but one day when I was turning into the corridor towards our door, I had the unpleasant shock of seeing three or four men in green uniforms standing there, and quickly withdrew. This shock was certainly no smaller on the inside, where two of the staff just managed the fasten the cover on the secret space in the floor before the men in green stood in the doorway. However, it was not the Gestapo that time, only SS officers from the floors below, who also needed more room and were inspecting to see the possibilities of the fifth floor. We explained that it would be very damaging to our agency work if we had to give up the office without receiving equally good premises in exchange. The SS officers quite understood, and procured us another office!

The Communists' last round

At the end of 1944 some of the foremost Communists in charge of the work for setting up a Freedom Council in East Norway were arrested, and two of them 'split' completely. Hence the arrest of a number of people in the Oslo area, both inside and outside the ranks of the party, mainly artists and intellectuals, but also some from industry; most of them were released after a while. But the Gestapo extracted from the imprisoned Communist leaders a quantity of information about Party activities which, when coupled with what they had learned from the actions in the early summer, gave a complete picture of how the Communists were then organised. Fresh attempts to capture Furubotn failed, but in February the Gestapo got hold of the party leader for West Norway and a large number of members or 'fellow-travellers'. The leaders and many members of the Communist sabotage organisation in Bergen had been taken some months before, and the organisation in Oslo suffered the same fate at the start of 1945. The information reaching us through our police contacts regarding the interrogations of the imprisoned Communist leaders gave us the impression that their leadership set-up was compromised almost throughout, which prescribed extreme caution in our collaboration with them.

During the autumn and winter Furubotn's illegal newspapers published new accusations against the leadership of the Home Front, based on allegations that, together with the Government, it wished to hinder the summoning of the Storting after the liberation; black marks were likewise awarded to the illegal trade union management, the FU. At the same time Furubotn continued to demand that the Communists should be represented in the leadership. Both in their papers and in their private agitation, the Communists pretended that the laurels for all the sabotage performed at that time by Milorg and the Linge Company belonged to them whereas in reality the Communist share was little more than one-tenth — according to the most recent post-war study,* sixteen actions out of a total of 145. We eventually found this quite intolerable, so in February we replied in the *Bulletin* with the following article, entitled 'Distasteful agitation':

When the free Norwegian press saw the light of day in the summer of 1940, it had one great task: to open the people's eyes to the danger which a German victory implied for our freedom and our living conditions, and to plead for unity and devotion in the struggle against the oppressors and traitors. Later, when the radio sets were taken from us, a new task was added — to give the people a true picture of the course of the war.

Furthermore, the newspapers built upon the internal political truce which all good Norwegians made on 9 April, and which the Parties confirmed in the following summer. All party conflict was shelved. The papers which came out were organs of the Norwegian people, not of any political party. The summer and autumn of 1940 were an incredibly exciting time. Under the impression of German predominance there were many who wavered, and the free papers had to lay great stress upon pertinent and truthful writing. The first papers carried out their task. Thanks to the spirit they expressed, those small stencilled scraps have acquired an authority and goodwill which have meant an infinite amount for our struggle.

*T.A. Barstad, *Sabotasjen i Osloområdet 1944-45* (Oslo 1975).

There are not many of those first torches still burning. Most were extinguished by the stormy blast. New ones appeared. Most of them were conducted in the same spirit as their predecessors. But not all, unfortunately. Some papers of a special sort which first saw the light of day after 21 June 1941, have followed their own line. Admittedly they have also brought out news and appealed to people to campaign against the Nazis, but they have in addition made propaganda for a particular political outlook. It is a good indication of the firm basis the political truce has among our people that no other papers have felt impelled to abandon their line.

Party agitation has now got the upper hand in these organs to such an extent that they now contain little else. It is time to sound a warning. There must be a stop to the use for party purposes of the goodwill which the free press has built up. He who breaks down the authority of the free papers takes upon himself a heavy responsibility. There must also be a stop to the distasteful use made of the circumstance that today we cannot make public everything which is done — nor, above all, *who* does it.

It is a sign of weakness to be continually boasting of one's own efforts. To start making comparisons now only serves the enemy's object of sowing dissension. Let it be a task for later generations to write the history of the war in Norway in 1940-5.

More potatoes for the Germans!

The Communists' great concern on the civil front that autumn was to influence the farmers not to deliver their produce to the supply authorities or the Germans, but to see to it that the food reached the Norwegian people. The object was unimpeachable, but the Home Front leadership considered that it was still best to support the rationing system by the farmers making their deliveries to the Norwegian supply authorities as usual. It was in any case ridiculous *openly* to call for a strike against deliveries, as the Communists did in Vestfold at the end of September 1944. The course of events is related in the following report, which we sent to the Government a couple of weeks later.

THE ACTION IN VESTFOLD

In view of the existing situation as regards the food supply, it is of absolutely vital importance that the population should receive, to the greatest extent possible, the necessary quantities of potatoes. The question has been, and remains, very complicated, as one has had to reckon with extensive German requisitions. If there is to be the slightest prospect of a favourable result, one must act with low cunning. The solution must involve a minimum of fuss. The directive to the farmers indicated that they should make every effort to forward supplies to the Norwegian population, while at the same time having to deliver certain quantities to the Germans, so as to avert drastic steps by them which might make the Norwegian deliveries impossible. There was a good prospect that this procedure would work out in such a way that a good deal of the potato crop might be spread round among the consumers. The ability of the Germans to take what they wanted would thereby be greatly reduced. But then the Communists got to work. We forwarded last week a couple of directives addressed by them to the farmers, to the effect that all the deliveries to the Germans should be sabotaged. At the same time they resorted to open action in the form of destruction of packaging, removal of means of transport (vehicles), and finally on the night of 28-29 September they blew up a number of generator fuel factories in Vestfold and elsewhere. This at once called forth drastic counter-measures from the German side. German sentry posts were set up in the fields. In some places the harvesting itself was undertaken by German soldiers. The vehicles were confiscated, and every driver had a soldier to guard him wherever he went. The result of the action has been that the Germans get the potatoes they want, and the Norwegian population gets what is left over. The example gives one much to think about regarding the relative effectiveness of so-called active and passive sabotage.

The propaganda actions of the Communists on the supply question to a large extent cut across the line which the farm group in the HL had settled on in agreement with the heads of the Directorate of Rationing, who were completely patriotic. This line was to make sure on the quiet that civil requirements were met first, so that the Germans had to be content with what was left. Open sabotage of the deliveries to the authorities might also have led to the cessation of the German delivery of grain for Norwegian civil needs, our only compensation — or at least the most important one — for their plundering us of our fish and various farm products.

8

TOWARDS THE FINAL SETTLEMENT

Is the German retreat in the north to proceed unhampered?

On 25 October 1944 Soviet troops crossed the frontier in Finnmark, after the German troops had fled west to new positions in West Finnmark and northern Troms. The Germans practised 'scorched earth' tactics as completely as they could. In East Finnmark they achieved great destruction, but there they were unable to burn down everything or to drive out the entire population. In West Finnmark and North Troms, on the other hand, everything was burnt or blown up, and the population of 40,000 was compulsorily evacuated southwards.

We understood in Oslo that our compatriots in the north were exposed to great sufferings and strains, but we knew little of the details or scope of the horrors that were going on up there. Reports over our regular communications network normally took from one to two weeks, while we were now completely cut off from our district leaders in East Finnmark, and the scanty messages we received from other district leaders north of Bodö made us little wiser. A request was put forward in many quarters for a directive as to how the population should react to the compulsory evacuation, which we thought out in the first instance to be a matter for the Government and the military authorities in London, but no guidance for the population was forthcoming from them. In the middle of November we decided that we must send out a directive ourselves, not to the population in the zone of operations or to those compulsorily evacuated — this we still regarded as the Government's concern — but to the rest of the population in the north. The NS authorities had sent Jonas Lie north with the high-sounding title of 'Ruler over Finnmark', and NS auxiliary organisations were established; reports came that loyal Norwegians in several places found that they had to co-operate with them for the relief of evacuees. The situation was getting out of control.

Our evaluation took as its starting-point what we thought we knew, namely that conditions in the whole area were such as we had heard about from East Finnmark: news of what had really happened — the total destruction, the deportation of the people and the ruthless hunt for those who tried to evade it — came south only in driblets. As for the possibility of a People's Strike, in Southern Norway one of the most important conditions was lacking, namely an acute situation which produced spontaneous reactions, whereas in North Norway our representatives had recently declared that no such strike could be launched up there. Moreover, our own preparations for a People's Strike were not sufficiently advanced. Nevertheless, we had to reckon with the possibility that the Germans might continue the burning and deportations farther south, so we had to stop the NS from getting machinery for evacuation set up which might make it easier for the Germans to devastate other parts of the country as well. In other respects too, we had to see the matter in a wider context than a mere evaluation of what happened in the far north — we had to see it as an integral part in the whole national struggle.

The Co-ordination Committee had undoubtedly gone through a toughening process in the course of 1944: the successful results of the campaign against the attempted mobilisation were partly due to the use of stronger fighting methods than had been used previously in the Standfast struggle. A war of liberation was going on in Europe, which called for big sacrifices from the civilian population as well; the Committee saw the deportations as part of the German method of waging war and considered that we too must make big sacrifices for freedom. The Germans were engaged in transferring the bulk of their armies from the northern front to the fronts in Central Europe; the swifter and smoother the course of the compulsory evacuation, the smaller the obstacles to the troop transfers. Finally, the Germans had handed over the deportations to the NS authorities and organisations, and to reject co-operation with them was a cardinal feature of our struggle.

On the basis of these considerations the committee decided to issue a stern directive, which ended as follows:

> The forced evacuation is a military measure carried out with German brutality. The Germans make the land into a desert and drive out the population, so that it will not have the opportunity of supporting the Norwegian and Allied troops which take part in the liberation of our country. This is not evacuation but deportation.
>
> Our fellow-countrymen in the north have drawn their conclusions

Gamvik, a fishing centre in East Finnmark, devastated by the retreating Germans.

from this. Where there is any chance of getting away from the Germans and maintaining life until the liberators arrive, there they cling firmly to the spot. Neither must we support the Germans in their military plans. We must not make ourselves participants in the worst war crime which has yet been committed in our country. We must not help the Nazi authorities and the Nazi organisations with the deportation. That is and remains the Nazis' affair; they are answerable for the thousands of people in distress. We cannot involve ourselves in assistance activities which promote the realisation of the deportation. But the giving of individual help to people in distress is a duty for every good Norwegian.

Not many days passed before we realised that we had aimed too high. Criticism came from several quarters, and new information about the extent of the devastation and the lack of possibilities for the people to avoid compulsory evacuation in West Finnmark and North Troms caused the Committee, on 28 November, to make the following modification to its directive sent out ten days earlier:

Those who have been deported from North Norway are beginning now to come south. They have lost everything, and the sufferings they have gone through are indescribable. It is a matter of course that we do everything to relieve their needs. But it is equally a matter of course that we do not collaborate with the Nazi authorities and organisations which are jointly responsible for this war crime, and whose refusal to accept the Swedish offer* to give the deportees residence and maintenance in Sweden has set thousands of human lives in peril.

Help your fellow-countrymen! Help them with house-room, food, clothing, and later with employment! We must not risk the Germans getting a chance to use their labour power. But help them directly or through safe channels. Leave it to the NS to take care of its own.

December brought us a dressing-down both from our people in Stockholm and from the head of our district organisation in Tromsö for the hard line we had taken in the first directive. By then this had only academic interest: later reports from the north showed that our second directive was generally followed.

At the time when we were discussing the evacuation position, I received an application from contacts in the State Railways. The Germans had called for 220 railway staff to be moved north, evidently for use in German military transportation, but the railway people thought that an eventual refusal would merely hit Norwegian transport, as the Germans would know how to get hold of people. Instead it was recommended that actions should be undertaken to interrupt the Nordland railway. I sent the inquiry on to the military staff, who in turn dispatched it to London; but the answer was entirely negative, we were not to do anything to interfere with German railway transportation in Norway.

From our standpoint this decision was quite incomprehensible. Wondering what could be the reason, we concluded that the Government and the Defence Command (FO) were not aware of recent developments in public opinion in Norway; so the Co-ordination Committee sent a letter to the Government on 22 November, in which they wrote:

*Nothing came of a Swedish offer to the German authorities, but 2,220 refugees from North Norway made their way across the frontier in the period 1October 1944—31 March 1945 (O.K. Grimnes, *Et flyktningesamfunn vokser fram*, Oslo 1969, p.246). When Trygve Lie was in Stockholm at the end of October 1944 — the visit mentioned above, p.176 — he informed the Swedish Foreign Ministry that the people of North Norway would prefer not to evacuate, and that the Norwegian Government deprecated any Swedish action for the transfer of compulsorily evacuated persons from North to South Norway via Sweden.

The German withdrawal from North Norway and forced evacuation of the population are broadly speaking a military question; but the position which FO takes towards it also has a political aspect which deeply affects the Home Front's struggle. It is these considerations we would like to lay before the Government.

The Government will be aware that a striking evolution has taken place inside the Norwegian people in the course of the last half-year. We have all come to realise that the final settlement of the war will demand sacrifices which go much further than any we have made so far. It is our assured conviction that the Norwegian people as a whole are prepared to make these sacrifices, where it is clear that they will forward the cause of the Allies and our liberation. We can perhaps go further, and say that it will arouse strong criticism if everything which can be done is not done in that direction. It is this fighting spirit which the extreme forces in the resistance movement play upon, but we must all bear it clearly in mind that it is this fighting spirit, and this will for sacrifice, which are the mainspring in our resistance and that they demand to be used. As regards the retreat from North Norway, people are waiting for something to be done from the Norwegian side to delay or stop the German troop transports, even if it will lead to reprisals. They are thinking especially of sabotage actions against railways and roads. It is well known that the transport along the coast is in the best hands, but we can also say that we should have been disappointed if the Allies had not resorted to strong action there, in spite of the sacrifice this demands from the civil population.'*

We still heard nothing from the Government; it was New Year, when the question had lost its vital importance, before we received a reply, in which the Government gave general approval to our second directive regarding the evacuation. But there may be some connection between our application and a speech which Crown Prince Olav as Chief of Defence addressed to the evacuated population over the BBC on 30 November; however, this went further than our first directive, since it called upon them to hide away in safe places, put out the fires, and attack the Germans in the rear. This appeal was bitterly criticised in North Norway.

As Hauge was away at this time, we could not get to know the grounds for this attitude from the side of the FO and Milorg. It was only after the war that the matter became more

*The British blockade of shipping in the Leads was intensified after the closing of Swedish Baltic ports to German ships on 27 September 1944 (S.W. Roskill, *The War at Sea*, Vol.III, Part ii, London 1961, pp.141 and 162). This resulted in serious loss of life among the Norwegian coastal population.

comprehensible, when we learnt of the agreements made at meetings between the two parties. One such took place in Western Sweden in May 1943 when an earlier agreement, which had entitled Milorg in certain circumstances to undertake actions on its own account, was cancelled. From the turn of the year 1943-4 the Allied supreme command at SHAEF intervened still more directly in Milorg's strategy, and although parties from the Linge Company were sent to Norway to prepare railway sabotage, neither they nor Milorg could proceed to any action. The reason was the impending invasion of France: SHAEF did not wish its plans to be disturbed by having to spare forces for other theatres of war. These guidelines were accepted by the Military Council at meetings in Stockholm in the latter half of March 1944, but with the modification that Milorg should be able to carry out actions in support of the campaign against the AT and an eventual forced mobilisation; the concession in connection with the AT campaign may legitimately be interpreted as a result of the application from the KK. In addition, the organisation might prepare attacks against objectives of military importance.

After the invasion in June 1944, fresh instructions came from the Allied supreme command, giving heavy emphasis to the tasks of Milorg: to safeguard vital Norwegian interests from destruction by the Germans, and to maintain good order. Specially trained parties would, on orders from Britain, be able to carry out limited operations to impede an eventual German withdrawal from the whole of Norway, but not a withdrawal from North Norway alone. In the period of waiting, Milorg, now called the Home Forces, was permitted to attack the following objectives: ship traffic, stocks of oil and other sources of power, and select industrial concerns of special importance to the German war effort.

At the time of the German withdrawal from the extreme north of Norway, the order of June 1944 remained in force. But in December 1944, after the German forces succeeded in halting the Allies by the Ardennes offensive, SHAEF had to change its attitude, and in that month Milorg and the Linge Company received orders for attacking the north-south railways in Norway. But by then the compulsory evacuation in North Norway was virtually completed, and the new order had little significance for the problems confronting the Home Front leadership in that connection.

The Home Front leadership (HL) reorganised

The letter which the Co-ordination Committee had sent to the Government on 22 November 1944 had been addressed by Magnus Jensen 'To the Government from the Co-ordination Committee (HL* for what concerns civilian *campaigns*)'. This was done because he supposed that the Government would be aware of the weakening which the Circle had suffered through arrests and the departure to Sweden of so many of its most prominent members. But the explanatory parenthesis was questioned by Skjönsberg in Stockholm, and when Hauge came back from there he got in touch with Magnus Jensen, the central organising figure among the remaining members of the Circle; they were already well acquainted, and Hauge knew that Jensen was also in the Co-ordination Committee. Hauge demanded in strong terms that the committee should be put in its place and told that it had no right to send out directives or announcements in the name of the HL, which only the Circle was entitled to do. The assertion that the idea of a Home Front leadership had been misused seemed to us to be as meaningless as it was unjust: it was first and foremost through the campaign against AT and 'the mobilisation of labour', a campaign which the KK had initiated and conducted, that the HL's authority had become a reality for the people and for the resistance organisations. It did not improve matters that the assertion came from someone who had not been in either the Circle or the KK.

The disagreement was on the point of developing into a crisis of confidence between the two organs, and we were afraid that, if certain new brooms appointed to the Circle were to have their way, the result would be a dangerous weakening of the leadership and organisation of civil resistance. We therefore agreed that Jensen should make it clear to Hauge that a spirit of co-operation would induce us to try hard to find a solution, but if the Circle attempted to be dictatorial, it would receive notice that it was in no position to dictate to the Co-ordination Committee.

**Hjemmefrontens Ledelse*. A book under this title by O.K. Grimnes, published in 1977, devotes more than 500 pages to the phenomenon of the 'Home Front Leadership', seen to be at variance with the strictly democratic practices established during 126 years of uninterrupted peace; the enemy occupation being unforeseen and complete, HL could have only a *de facto* authority, accepted by an indeterminate but increasing proportion of the population.

Hauge had further conversations with Jensen, in which he to some extent modified his remarks about the KK's role and claimed that Jensen had misunderstood him on several points. Hauge maintained strongly, in conversations with me among others, that the leadership needed to be consolidated out of regard for the chain of responsibility and the co-operation with the Government; it had to be clear who it was that represented the leadership. Nevertheless, there had never before been any dispute between the Circle and the KK about their respective spheres of competence — they had worked together completely without friction — and the KK had always regarded discussion with the Government on the civil administration and other measures affecting the transition period as the business of the Circle. Yet, with liberation as close as we believed it to be, there might be a case for a closer correlation between civil and military preparations. And the difficulties which had arisen about the letter from the KK to the Government gave Hauge's arguments at least a show of justification.

Discussions held at Christmas and just after New Year resulted in agreement on a new, formal leadership of the Home Front, an arrangement which Norum helped to bring about on his arrival in Oslo from Stockholm just at this juncture. The new HL was to consist of twelve members with Paal Berg as chairman, and was constructed from the remnants of the Circle, two additional members from the Co-ordination Committee (making its total representation four), and one apiece from Milorg, the Police Organisation, and the groups in charge of economic and judicial preparations, and finally one from the farmers. This committee being too big to take charge of day-to-day business, an executive of four was chosen (Magnus Jensen, J.C. Hauge, Arnfinn Vik and H.O. Christophersen), and Jensen notified me that I should attend the executive — for which contact with the apparatus for organisation was clearly indispensable. In the last months of the war, Paal Berg moved back to Oslo and was often present at the meetings.

This reconstruction was more than a consolidation; the new Home Front leadership was also based on a more formal representation of elements in the community and of illegal organisations. Yet in my view it did not bring about any substantial change in the distribution of responsibility. The KK worked as before at campaign questions on the civil front; the new HL, like the Circle before it, was chiefly engaged in preparing for the period of the liberation; and the executive was the joint operational command centre, which however could not carry out its decisions without someone being present from the HL secretariat, even if this representative had no formal seat in the Leadership. Milorg remained under the FO in London, but as the war was drawing to an end, the main weight of its activities shifted from the operational side to that of contingent preparations — duties of protecting installations, business concerns and lines of communication which were important to the community, and of joining with the police organisation to maintain peace and order — so that the military work was more and more closely interconnected with the civil. The new system undoubtedly facilitated the requisite co-ordination and functioned efficiently. It was, however, more vulnerable to exposure, and its success was attributable, not only to the closeness of the day of liberation, but also (as we shall shortly see) to a good deal of luck.

The start of 1945 — Norway's sixth year of war

The German counter-offensive in the Ardennes, which began in mid-December and threatened Antwerp, one of the principal supply ports for the Allied forces, suddenly put a damper on our hopes that the war would end in 1944. Our enemies were encouraged, alike by the counter-offensive and by their development of the V2 rocket, to start new terror actions in the early months of the New Year. The collapse of the Ardennes offensive after a month or so did not appear to discourage the Gestapo or the State Police in Norway. The Home Forces, as Milorg was now called, increased their sabotage activities during the autumn and winter, especially against the enemy's stocks of motor fuel and repair shops. The Nazi authorities replied with a propaganda crusade against 'banditry', immediate death sentences on captured saboteurs, and comprehensive mobilisation of the civic guard. The Home Front issued a new, strongly worded directive against attending; in Oslo many did not turn up, and the Nazi police had to go round at night and fetch by force those who had been called up.

When there was a heavy ring on the door bell at my cover address in a West Oslo street one midnight at the close of January 1945, I supposed that it was a 'collection' for civic guard which was going on, and did not open the door. Immediately the lock was picked; I moved towards the door, and the next moment received a pistol in the stomach and a number of blows on my head and other vital parts from three State Police troopers who stormed in. I stood there fully dressed and had no good explanation of why I had not opened the door when they rang. I had recently moved to the cover place and had not yet obtained the necessary false papers. The jacket with my correct identification card and the address of my apartment about a mile away, which was still our main place of work, was hanging in the wardrobe. So there was no hiding the fact that at this late hour of the night I was in a different place from where I ought to be. I explained that after the closing of the University I did not like to sleep at home and had received permission from the landlord, who had moved into the country, to use an apartment in the house. It was a very thin explanation, and the policemen obviously did not believe it.

For security I had for a long time been shifting my sleeping quarters from one cover place to another. How they had come upon me so quickly after I had moved into this one was a puzzle, but in the situation as it was there was no point in speculating about it. Even if it was chance, and they did not know my central position in the Home Front, I could not let them keep hold of me. After the activities of more than four years, I knew the correct names of far too many people — not only among the civil resistance leaders, but also in Milorg and the intelligence service. The mere fact that I was in detention might injure large sections of the organisations in the important closing phases of the war. I had therefore only one thought in my head: I must at all costs get away.

These policemen were fully aware that there was something mysterious about me, and I was put through it for half an hour inside the room, partly with blows and kicks to the head, groin and back — for this a poker they found in the fireplace came in useful — and with continually repeated demands to tell the truth. Finally I was made to lie face-down on the floor, with a pistol at my neck and a warning that they were going to pull the trigger, if I did not tell what they wanted to know before they had counted to twenty. I almost smiled as I lay there, knowing for certain that, as long as I did not tell what they wanted to know, they would refrain from shooting, and let them count out. They were indeed bluffing, and so came the next round in the interrogation, which I could recognise from many prison reports: I must be straightforward and put my cards on the table, and then no mischief would befall me. When that too failed to loosen my tongue, the leader gave up for the time being and went off to a telephone, situated just by the door out into the hall, evidently to call up reinforcements. The other two stood in such a way that the one who continually waved a pistol about could not fire it without endangering his colleagues. I spotted a chance. At the moment when the leader, having drawn a chair under him, put his finger on the dial, I made a tremendous leap, and before the police knew what was happening I tore open the door, slipped out into the hall, and was away on to the staircase. I was three or four yards ahead down the stairs. All three shot as best they could; I felt the whiplash of a bullet on my shoulder and thought 'That was a close one', while I rushed round each turn in the staircase as fast as I could; and at each floor I passed. I came back into sight and got another salvo after me. It was then the regular routine, when arrests were made in blocks of flats, for the police to set one man on watch with a machine-pistol down at the main entrance — to which I dashed as there was no other way out. Fortunately they had neglected this, and there was no one standing there. The next second I was outside in the street with the bright light of a full moon all around. A small police car stood close by — that too was empty.

I now felt my shoulder beginning to smart and the arm stiffening: I had after all been hit, but there was no time to think about that. In the course of the interrogation the fellows from the State Police had found the identity card in my jacket and therefore knew the address of my proper apartment, where important papers lay in three secret spaces in the floor. I recalled the appalling difficulties Skjönsberg and I had had to face the previous year in rescuing the archives of the Circle after the Gestapo had tried to arrest Boyesen; I must endeavour to avoid a similar crisis. The other apartment was a mile or so away; although the policemen had a car, there was a chance that I might forestall them if I was quick. After a detour to a nearby stream to destroy the scent for possible police tracker dogs, I ran at top speed to the block — no police cars there yet — and woke up my helpful neighbour, the caretaker. He rapidly emptied the papers from their places of concealment into a bag, while I waited outside for some tense minutes, squeezed into a doorway on the opposite side of the street. When he came out, I seized the bag and continued at a steady trot to a good friend in the same neighbourhood, with whom I left the bag.

Then I telephoned to Bratsberg, who was soon on the spot and started to warn people. It was most urgent to find Sanengen, who was in hiding at an address unknown to me; he usually ate dinner with me at the place where I had been arrested, and might drop in there at any time. Then I telephoned the girl who prepared our food there, and told her to go into hiding at once. After that I set off to a doctor — one of the pioneers in R-group, who had been arrested earlier on and had now been at liberty for some time. On the way I crossed the road only about 200 yards from my apartment, and in the clear moonlight could see a large gathering of police outside it. The doctor took my noctural visit as the most natural thing in the world, examined and treated the bullet-wound in my shoulder, and instructed me to stay in bed until the fever from the wound had abated.

From my sick bed in my good friend's home, to which I returned, I started a major operation in the early morning to prevent any of my colleagues from falling into a trap either at the cover address or at our place of work. I was particularly anxious about Sanengen, whom Bratsberg had not yet found, and I began to fear that he was already taken; but Bratsberg got hold of him in the course of the morning. All our offices were abandoned for a day or two, while we tried to discover the reason for the police visit to my cover apartment; we could not find any leakage, so work was resumed in the usual way. (It was not until after the war that I got the explanation of the visit from the State Police: it was not me but my landlord whom they were after. The occurrence caused him to be sent immediately over the frontier.)

My freedom of movement was now considerably reduced. There were a couple of men in the State Police in Oslo who came from the district where I had lived as a child and who knew me by sight, so for some weeks I tried to move about only at night, except for the most necessary meetings. Henceforth nearly all the daily management of the secretariat was taken over by Sanengen, and when Risting, who was in hospital at the time, heard what had happened, he refused to stay in bed any longer and reported for service again.

Next it was Bonnevie-Svendsen's turn to get into difficulties. One of those arrested during the discoveries in Stavanger admitted that he had been present at the illegal national conference which had been held at the Oslo Home for the Deaf; it had been conducted by 'a man who looked like a clergyman'. We were warned of the leakage at the beginning of February. Bonnevie-Svendsen was one of the front-line pioneers, as resourceful in practical affairs as he was unyielding in conflict, so it was much against our wishes that we gave our clerical friend marching orders for Sweden.

The Allied armies were continuing their breakthrough on the Western front, and crossed the Rhine at the same time as the Red Army was advancing on Berlin: Hitler's thousand-year Reich was drawing near its end. But in Norway the Germans were still strong. Reports came from various intelligence sources that the Gestapo intended to annihilate the captives in prisons and concentration camps, who numbered thousands — friends and fellow-workers from the earlier phases of the struggle. There was also talk of further deportations of prisoners to Germany. We must do what we could to prevent such threats from being carried out.

Preparation for the People's Strike was speeded up. The Home Forces and the Workshop Organisation (a secret organ, formed partly for silent sabotage and partly for safeguarding the larger industrial concerns)* became directly involved and joined the strike committee. In Oslo our secretariat co-operated with the FU trade unionists in a thorough examination of the printing capacity of the organisations and the illegal press, and of their ability to disseminate directives quickly among the population. A special distribution corps, founded on the action group of the secretariat, was set up to break through the controls which the Germans might be expected to establish in the event of a People's Strike. The discussions of the strike committee favoured supporting Allied military operations for our liberation by crippling important parts of the transport system — especially railways and ports — through strikes at selected points by key personnel. These were prepared in elaborate detail with reliable people at the head of the services and among the functionaries, while the district organisations were instructed to prepare for a transport strike. But for countering Nazi terror actions against the population or the prisoners, a general

*'Silent sabotage' included go-slow actions: A.S. Milward's *The Fascist Economy in Norway* (Oxford 1972) notes the decline of productivity during the war years. The 'safeguarding' was to prevent the destruction of plant by German orders, such as had already occurred in North Norway.

People's Strike was still regarded as the best weapon.

Because such a strike might possibly be linked with military operations for the liberation, in mid-February the HL sent a full statement on the question to the Government. In discussing the matter with Skjönsberg, who was on a visit to London at the beginning of March, the Prime Minister expressed strong reservations but said that the Home Front could do as it liked, 'though I think it is horrible'. Immediately afterwards the Government sent the HL a letter, in which it gave its approval to the proposal for using a people's strike as an instrument of war. At home too, there were many who had doubts, particularly in the trade union organisation, but also in some of our district leaderships. At the end of March the concept of the strike was examined at a meeting in Gothenburg between representatives of the FU and their trade union colleagues who had been exiled to Sweden or Britain; it was resolved that a People's Strike could only be recommended if found necessary in connection with the final settlement and as an integral part of a military action.

A civil warfare general meets his fate

A meeting of the HL executive about the end of January received reports — based partly on telephone monitoring — which showed that the head of the State Police, 'General' Marthinsen, was planning to seize complete control over the fighting organisations of the NS party in order to put them into the battle against the Home Forces in the closing phase of the war. He already commanded both the *Hird* and the State Police, and wanted to take over the Police Department as well. Even if reprisals must be taken into account which would cost many lives, much bigger losses might be incurred if this desperate, ruthless and forceful man were given the chance to realise his plans. The HL therefore approved a proposal that he should be liquidated, and on 8 February he was shot in his car on the way to his office in Oslo. Quisling and Terboven replied by announcing the execution of thirty-two prisoners (five were not actually carried out) and of five hostages, the latter having been taken in their homes early in the morning. It was perhaps more than individuals among us had reckoned with, and for some hours we considered whether to respond by proclaiming a People's Strike, but after a rapid sounding of opinion among our organisations we found that we must give it up. Under the conditions governing our warfare, we could not count on the population giving sufficiently full support to a directive for striking, in a situation where we had taken the first step by liquidating the chief of police. It was not our object to provoke a People's Strike by our action, which had a purely defensive purpose.

We chose instead to intensify a propaganda action which we had already started against the members of the NS to deter them from further outrages in the closing phase of the war. Leaflets were spread about with warnings that every aggressive action against a fellow-countryman would be carefully recorded by our intelligence sections. As a step in the preparations for the judicial settlement we had just sent the district organisations a request to register all members of the NS, the *Hird* and other NS fighting organisations, people in the State Police, and those who took part in informing, the selection of hostages, or other outrages against compatriots. This request, which was also repeated in the illegal press, helped to emphasise the seriousness of our reminder that the day of retribution was not far off. But so far the party hierarchy and the NS fighting organisations had not lost courage — much less Terboven and his Gestapo. More propaganda was churned out; it was now more than ever a duty 'to save Europe from the peril in the east'. NS county leaders were everywhere trying to draw prominent figures in the community to meetings for the condemnation of sabotage, 'bolshevism' and 'the emigré government'. The summons to Labour Service and Youth Service went out again, and the demand for subscriptions to the NS-controlled associations continued. We were accordingly obliged to go on with the Standfast struggle, even when the organising machinery was more and more heavily burdened with preparations for the period of liberation, which could not be far off.

At the beginning of January 1945 the Home Front leadership was formally notified by the Government that it approved the proposal for special advisers to be introduced into the central administration. Candidates for the posts had been under consideration since the previous autumn and must now be picked out, while gaps in local government administration, many of them due to the machinations of the Gestapo, had likewise to be filled. Credentials, ordinances and other documentation from the Government, needed by the new authorities for the various alternative courses which the struggle for liberation might take, had to be passed on to the districts. Preparations for purging public life and important services of NS members were being pressed forward. Much work had been done both from outside the country and by the organs of the Home Front to safeguard working life in the period of transition. The solidarity between social classes which had been developed under the occupation made it possible for agreement to be reached quickly by representatives of employers and employees. A special problem was that of the large number of workers in the German concerns, which were already being wound up, and the Home Front leadership sent out appeals to employers to take on more people in order to combat unemployment. However, many businesses were short of coal, oil and raw materials, and it was difficult enough for them to keep the wheels turning. Forest owners and farmers were likewise urged to take on more people.

The economic committee, which assisted the Government in arranging to supply the country after its liberation, had been reconstructed after the detections in the autumn of 1944 and was now working under high pressure. After five years' occupation the country was completely stripped, and its equipment was worn out. Thousands of lists of essential equipment, fuels and raw materials for industry, handicrafts and transport, as well as of seed corn and fertiliser for agriculture, were sent to the Norwegian authorities in London and Stockholm.

In the course of the autumn and winter the civil and military leaders of the Home Front had discussed certain aspects of the Allied armistice terms for the Germans with the authorities in London. The scarcity of Allied troops for the task of liberation, in contrast to the huge German forces stationed in Norway, caused the Home Front leadership to press hard for the German military authorities to be required to disarm German and Norwegian Nazi forces and to arrest key persons in the German and Norwegian Nazi administration. The HL also succeeded in obtaining changes in an earlier decision of the Allied supreme command that after the capitulation the *Wehrmacht* should keep watch over prisoner-of-war camps, prisons, frontiers, and other important places — tasks which it was natural to allot to the Norwegian Home Forces and the police.

The Home Forces had been greatly developed in the last winter of the war through good co-operation between the central military staff (SL), the districts, and the British and

Railway administration building in Oslo after being blown up by the 'Oslo Gang', March 1945.

Norwegian military authorities in London. After the invasion of the continent, the Home Forces received strict orders to lie low, no support being available for any revolt by Norwegian forces whose primary function was to protect the country from destruction by the Germans as they retreated or were evacuated from the country — they should first of all guard power stations, lines of communication, habours, etc. If the German forces should flee the country, the Home Forces were to preserve order along with the civil organs in readiness for the take-over by legitimate authorities. But sabotage could be continued against German shipping, stocks of oil and fuels, and selected industrial concerns.

The Allies were by now increasingly able to supply the secret resistance movements in Europe with significant quantities of weapons, mainly from the air. While the struggles in the occupied lands of Western Europe were still at their height, the Norwegian Home Forces received little; but in the late autumn of 1944, and still more in the following winter, Allied aircraft dropped considerable quantities of arms and equipment in the

Norwegian mountains and forests. Out of some 700 successful air operations for this purpose more than 200 date from 1944 and 470 from the first four months of 1945. The Home Forces now became an armed body, which they had previously been to only a modest extent. But it was still almost entirely a matter of small arms up to the size of machine guns, with nothing to overpower German tanks and fortifications and no anti-aircraft artillery. And even though recruitment to the Home Forces increased greatly during the winter and spring, the German forces in Norway still outnumbered them ten to one.

The leaders of the Home Forces were fully aware of the relative situation and did not let themselves be tempted into any military adventures; the 'directive for protection' of June 1944 was consistently obeyed, and the organisation extended surely and steadily to provide forces in readiness on a nation-wide basis, North Norway being gradually included. The district communications system was strengthened with new radio transmitters, and the Norwegian defence command in London (FO) could have direct contact with the district leaderships. The Workshop Organisation was likewise expanded. In the event of an Allied invasion the power of command, even over the districts, rested solely with FO in London, but in the meantime authority over administration and organisation belonged to the SL in Oslo. Milorg's great activity in the forests, which also involved a big increase in the road transport of weapons and a general escalation of Home Force movements, could not escape the notice of the Germans. In the winter of 1944-5 the Gestapo's attention was accordingly directed chiefly towards Milorg, which was made to suffer many hard blows without their leading to detection on the same scale as in 1942-3.

Under the impact of the German offensive in the Ardennes in December 1944, the scope for actions by the Home Forces was widened to comprise sabotage of the north-south railway network in Norway, so as to prevent the transfer of German troops to the continent — a plain reversal of the policy implied in the negative answer of a few weeks before to the KK's proposal to sabotage the Nordland railway. The military staff in charge of planning decided upon a united attack against the railways leading to the ports of shipment between Halden on the Swedish border and Kristiansand. It was launched in the middle of March, when the lines were broken in nearly 1,000 places and the State Railways office, used as headquarters for the German railway administration in Oslo, was simultaneously reduced to rubble. This could almost be considered as a general rehearsal for an operation in support of an Allied invasion; the fighting spirit of the Home Forces was boosted by the action, which inspired respect both in the Germans and in our Allies.

The German reaction was to sentence to death and execute fourteen young men who had been arrested for taking part in sabotage, to which the HL replied with a stern warning to the Germans that further acts of terror against prisoners or other groups of the population would be met with new methods and forms of resistance, while the people were urged to be ready for resistance to be intensified. The reference was to the People's Strike, now fully organised, and the appeal was followed by a communication to the Government, stating that the HL would carry out a short People's Strike if the Germans carried out their threats of further deportations of prisoners. But they were now restraining themselves — this was the last round of executions. The collapse in Germany was impending, and the thought of the day of reckoning could no longer be pushed aside. It is true enough that to the very last day of the war we received warnings of German plans to annihilate prisoners whose testimony could be dangerous for them; but we for our part were so situated that we did not wish to provoke a development which might throw away the chance of an orderly military capitulation. So it stayed at threats.

Preparing for the final test

At the same time as the preparations we were able to make on the Home Front to safeguard the transfer of the country to Norwegian rule, we were making our organisation ready for many possibilities. While we might hope for a peaceful alternative, we had to allow for the worst, namely that the Germans would try to hold Norway for as long as possible and would have to be overpowered.

Even in the last year of the war, the civil resistance movement was fated to suffer severe blows in several districts. The Gestapo contrived again to penetrate the organisations in Rogaland and on the south coast, and round Sognefjord. The reason there, and in other places, was the involvement of our people in the constantly increasing military preparations within their districts.

The need to restrict oneself to a single form of illegal activity could not be respected in all parts of our thinly populated land, if the tasks were to be carried out.

At the beginning of 1945, the Gestapo's steadily intensified pursuit of the resistance movement caused us to strengthen our security organisation. Brunsvig, as the contact with the free press, had made effective safety arrangements there, and he also had good connections in the police; so we took him out of the press section and had him take over the security work for the whole of the civil resistance organisation. His functions with the press were transferred to M. Skodvin,* who had been working on the preparation of press material. In the autumn of 1944, when reports from London forecast a German capitulation before the end of the year, we presumptuously arranged a 'press conference' with the editors of the illegal newspapers. We had been promised masks for this large assembly by our friends in SL, but there was a hitch and no masks were forthcoming. However, we were never short of good ideas in those days, and we hurriedly got hold of 10-kilo paper flour bags, in which we cut the needful holes for eyes, nose and mouth. The paper masks were not exactly made to measure, and when several participants stuck their pipes through the nose- or eye-holes it was somewhat hard to preserve the seriousness which the situation otherwise required. At this press conference, and at a second one nearer the end of the war, there were individuals on both sides of the table who called on HL to exert a stricter control over the press, whose representatives notwithstanding made it clear that, except for loyalty to directives for the struggle and the decisions of the Government, the editors had complete freedom in their choice of materials and commentaries.

At the end of October 1944 the head of the civil 'export' organisation was arrested in the frontier area after a journey to Stockholm, and for a while the whole 'export' system was in danger. But its new head, who had worked up the route from Sandefjord into our most important route for refugees, considerably increased the over-all capacity, especially as he was able to bring in big quantities of materials with the help of sand sloops which plied along the west coast of Sweden.

In the New Year we felt that the need for propaganda

*Magne Skodvin (b.1915), since 1960 a professor at Oslo University, where he has specialised in the history of the occupation and following years.

material from Sweden was no longer pressing, whereas we wanted more arms, both for ourselves and still more for the Home Forces; but the several offices in the Legation, through working for many years under difficult conditions, had been obliged to place special tasks in an order of priority, and the rearrangement we desired proceeded rather slowly. My encounter with the State Police had left me with a strong urge to undertake more training in the use of arms — I had no wish to meet the Nazi police a second time unarmed. So at the end of February I went across to Sweden, and spent the first fortnight in Stockholm, speeding up the change-over from propaganda to weapons on our import routes and in other transactions at the Legation. I fixed an arrangement for the conveyance of weapons with a colonel from FO who was then in Stockholm: they were to be brought from Britain to Gothenburg in submarines, and thence to Norway in sand sloops, but for reasons unknown to me the weapons never reached Gothenburg. The other fortnight of my visit I spent at a camp in the West, where officers in the Norwegian Home Forces were secretly given five or six weeks of special training. After a concentrated course there in pistol shooting, I felt almost like a new man on my return to Norway just before Easter.

I found the organisation extremely busy, but Sanengen had everything under control; so as far as that went, I need not have come back. But my most essential task in these last weeks of the war was to attend the HL executive and look after relations with our secretariat and the other civil resistance organisations.

We had decided in every possible eventuality to remain in Oslo to the last, and had chosen as our campaign quarters an unfinished cellar space under a block of flats a little way from the town centre, where an underground connection with the next building would enable us to get out into the town if the adjoining streets should be closed. We had contacted the district leadership of the Home Forces for Oslo through the SL, and had agreed on setting up a system of communications between our staffs. We established reserve posts at three places outside the city for contact with the district organisations, in case Oslo should be cut off, and from our campaign quarters we could also join ourselves on to the underground telephone cables. In the event of fighting in Oslo, we reckoned on having only two of the most suitable members of the Home Front leadership in these quarters below ground. The others, we

Underground headquarters prepared for Home Front Secretariat, May 1945.

thought, should transfer their activities together with a minor part of the secretariat to an area in the vicinity of the city, outside the iron ring which we supposed the Germans would place around it.

The Gestapo's last efforts

The conditions for illegal activity steadily worsened, as controls on roads and streets were intensified and extended. One day Magnus Jensen was on his way to a meeting of the executive, when he was stopped for examination by a State Police patrol. His attaché-case contained a letter from the Prime Minister, some reports and a draft for a proclamation from the Home Front leadership. Fortunately these papers all lay in a secret pocket in the case, which the policemen did not discover, but it is not too much to say that our friend's heart was in his mouth while he was being examined. We who sat waiting for him likewise had a bit of a shock when he arrived and told of his experience; he could be somewhat *distrait* at times, and if he had not been so careful on that occasion, the State Police would have made a considerable haul. In the last year of the war it was almost indefensible for anyone to have illegal papers on him in

Oslo: just after my return from Sweden at Easter, I was stopped for examination four times in a single day. In that situation the girls on our staff made a fearless and effective contribution by conveying important documents to and from our meeting-places, concealed inside bras and girdles.

The public spirit and sense of national solidarity among wives and mothers had from the outset of the struggle been one of the fundamental conditions for resistance activities. Furthermore, the direct participation of the women had by degrees attained to heights of which neither we — nor, fortunately, the Gestapo either — had ever dreamed. But the Gestapo began to have its suspicions, and it was one of our great anxieties in the final weeks that they would also start to make personal searches of women during the checks on the streets. Luckily for us it did not go beyond sporadic sampling without results. But one considerable female haul was made by the Gestapo before the war ended. For years a woman postal official in Oslo had put aside, opened and 'censored' the Gestapo's letters, and was one of the most important sources of information for the Home Front's security group. In March 1945 the Gestapo got hold of a clue, and she was arrested and badly ill-treated. This business was one in which the postal deputy Lid, the key man in our internal communications network, also had a finger, so he was forced — after almost five years of illegal activity — to go into hiding. But then there were only two weeks left before the liberation.

A little earlier, we had had two nerve-racking experiences. One day in April Sanengen was walking in one of the main streets and discussing a common concern with one of the two deputy heads of the SL, when they were suddenly surrounded by two of the State Police street patrols. His companion was allowed to go, but Sanengen was found to have two identification papers — one for Oslo and one for the frontier zone in Östfold — so he was arrested and taken to the State Police headquarters. Being warned by SL a couple of hours later, I had an anxious and busy time until Sanengen reappeared in triumph. The police had released him after five hours, as it had been established that his papers — including the frontier pass — were in order, as his place of residence was Fredrikstad. What had worried him most had been the many keys that were in his pockets, all of which were for our illegal offices; these he had smuggled away inside his hat, which lay on a table throughout the interrogation. At about the same period the head of Milorg,

J.C. Hauge, and the other second-in-command were arrested in a car check just outside Oslo. This came as a thunderbolt. Hauge held all the threads inside Milorg, so SL was almost paralysed, and there was almost equal consternation in the Home Front leadership, where during the early months of the year Hauge had achieved a central position. The importance of Milorg was of course steadily increasing as the final round drew near, and no substitute had been provided for Hauge. The HL executive considered the situation so serious that Milorg ought to make an attempt to lift the two arrested leaders from the State Police headquarters where they still were; but SL hesitated, so on the day after the arrest I arranged to meet one of its leaders in a park to discuss the possibility of an action. It was with indescribable relief — and pleasure — that I met Hauge himself there, unshaven and pleased as Punch! The police had not found sufficient grounds for holding either of them. On that occasion too we escaped with a fright.

The Home Front then had two sources reporting from the Gestapo headquarters, from whom we received repeated statements made by leading Gestapo people to the effect that they knew every member of the Home Front leadership and were only waiting for a suitable moment to strike. That this was mere boastfulness — or fantasy — is shown by the fact that in the last four months of the war they had hold of five of the most important men in the civil and military side of the organisation without knowing anything whatever about their roles. But the events just described also show how hard it was in the long run to keep out of the Gestapo's clutches, even in a town as big as Oslo, when one was heavily engaged in illegal work.

But the last days of the war and occupation had more to offer than alarms. Some of our former colleagues, whom we would have been sorry to be without when difficult decisions were to be taken, came back and rejoined the inner ring. To our mutal pleasure Jansen returned a couple of weeks before the liberation, and Skjönsberg and Norum at the beginning of May.

*'Norway shall be held!'**

Work in the Home Front leadership continued at high pressure: we hoped for a peaceful handing-over of power, but everything was still uncertain, so we had to continue working on the basis

**Deutsche Zeitung in Norwegen*, 21 April 1945.

of many alternatives. In Norway the Germans remained strong, and the question which gnawed at us day and night was this: would they capitulate when the German forces on the continent were beaten — or would they fight on? Was our land to become a theatre of war again? We had seen what that meant in Troms and Finnmark. The reports from our contact in the German general staff, now stationed at Lillehammer, told of mounting support inside the German military command, for a peaceful solution, but Terboven and the strongest among the senior officers remained inflexible. A German party meeting in Oslo on 20 April, Hitler's birthday, attended by the Reichskommissars of Norway and Denmark, sent a greeting to the Führer: 'Norway shall be held!' Our contact was also able to tell us of the German plans for destroying Norwegian communications, power plants and industry in the event of fighting.

On the Norwegian side the attitude was clear. We must do nothing to imperil a quick and peaceful settlement, and there could be no question of going into action otherwise than in a link-up with an Allied invasion. But the Allies for the time being had no troops to spare, and the possibility of getting Sweden to intervene and if need be overpower the German forces in Norway was discussed by the respective Governments. The proposal did not appeal to us, but the HL was ready to support it; however, events in the last days of the war made the question unrealistic.

It was a situation in which we had little chance of influencing the attitude of the Germans, but we were better placed as regards the NS. Its leaders, indeed, took a strong line for as long as they could. In January 1945 the so-called 'emergency units' of the *Hird*, numbering 3,000, had received arms from the Germans, and it was intended by a compulsory call-up to form *Hird* battalions of 12,000 men in all. One of the most ruthless NS leaders, Henrik Rogstad, became head of the State Police after the death of Marthinsen. The *Hird*'s Factory Corps, in spite of its name, was one of the most aggressive NS organisations at this time, and in March we had reports that it was engaged in weapon-training along with other *Hird* formations. At the end of April, when Quisling sent out a secret mobilisation order to all *Hird*-men between eighteen and forty-five, we replied by sending out sharp warnings to the *Hird*-men's parents: 'You have a son in the *Hird*. Take care that you do not, in a few weeks time, have a son in the churchyard.' Likewise to the *Hird*-men: '*The penalty of death* will be applied to all those who bear arms against any Norwegian man or woman ... ' And a sharp new directive was addressed to the sheriffs: 'Under no circumstances must you undertake any action which can harm Norwegian Home Front people or Norwegian or Allied forces ...' Sensible party members went against the proposed resort to arms, while the aggressive NS people also lost courage, and the final days were full of clandestine approaches with offers of co-operation. The response to the new NS mobilisation effort was not large; many went into hiding.

At the end of April we received a great encouragement — but one which created a somewhat alarming situation. The news of Himmler's offer to capitulate to the Western Powers* spread like a bushfire through Oslo and other towns and brought people out on to the streets, cheering and demonstrating. This was to anticipate victory, for the Allies would only accept a capitulation which was complete and unconditional and we still knew little of how the Germans in Norway would react. We held a crisis meeting, at which we put forward the slogan 'Dignity — quiet — discipline' (originally formulated by the Rector of the University for students during the State of Emergency in 1941), and the Home Front leadership then sent out its Instruction No.1 to the population; this conveyed a warning against gathering in crowds, demonstrations, rumours and false reports. The instruction was broadcast over the BBC, and about 100,000 copies were distributed in Oslo alone through the network which had been elaborated in preparation for a People's Strike. In addition, the HL helped to ease the situation by the practical step of instructing the state liquor monopoly to close its shops.

Preparedness reached its peak. Instructions to the nominated *fylkesmenn* had often to be sent by courier in order to arrive in time, which caused confusion in some places where the courier tried to make use of military intermediaries. At the end of March all key personnel in the Home Forces were ordered to go into hiding; during the following month the forces were issued with arm-bands, and an increasing number were mobilised and lay in wait in the forest. But if there was to be an orderly

*Transmitted on 23 April through Count Folke Bernadotte, the head of the Swedish Red Cross, who had already negotiated the evacuation from Germany of some 20,000 Norwegian and Danish prisoners.

German capitulation, it was of the utmost importance that clashes between the Home Forces and German detachments should be avoided, and in mid-April sabotage was discontinued. The HL aimed throughout to avoid bloodshed, and as late as 30 April it received a report from Stockholm (where the Norwegians were in touch with Count Folke Bernadotte) to the effect that Himmler would end the occupation peaceably if the Norwegians refrained from hostilities. After Himmler's offer of a capitulation, the Home Forces likewise received their first Instruction, which gave a warning against actions or other displays of aggressiveness against the enemy and demanded discipline and quiet from officers and other ranks alike. There were two places where clashes nevertheless occurred. At the head of a valley in Buskerud there was a fight lasting for one day in the forest between the Home Forces and German and NS detachments; and in the mountains north of Bergen Norwegian forces were attacked by German mountain troops and had to withdraw and scatter after a longer engagement, in which the Germans suffered considerable losses. In both places FO ordered the Norwegians to stop fighting.

In the final days of the war the spokesmen for the daily papers of Oslo and some other towns came to an agreement with the Home Front for an interim press arrangement in Oslo. One object was to give the papers which the Nazis had suppressed a better chance to get started again and to assert themselves in competition with those which had appeared under the control of the occupying power; another was to make sure that the news would be presented responsibly in the critical period of transition. It was agreed that HL should be the publisher of a paper without party colour, *The Oslo Press*, edited by a committee representing all the older papers, with Christensen as its natural chairman. In co-operation with the Government complete preparations were also made for taking over the Norwegian State Broadcasting.

It was on 30 April that Hitler nominated Grand-Admiral Doenitz as his successor and head of the German armed forces, before taking his own life in the beleaguered bunker in Berlin. On 3 and 4 May the German civil and military leaders in Norway and Denmark were summoned to Doenitz and received their orders. We heard of the meeting at once, but it was not clear what decisions had been taken; it was rumoured that the forces in Norway were to be used as a bargaining-counter to secure the best possible terms of capitulation for Germany. Then on the 4th and 5th the German forces capitulated on the northern continental front. While we rejoiced at the news that Denmark had recovered its freedom, we all asked each other 'What about Norway?'*

The reports which came through our contact were grave, telling of much disagreement among the leading German officers and that there was no strong personality among those in favour of surrender. On the evening of the 5th the command of the Home Forces received a telegram from Eisenhower, instructing them to inform the German commander-in-chief in Norway of the wavelengths, frequencies and call signals for making contact with SHAEF. These were delivered to the German military chiefs in Oslo by two young Home Front women who went boldly through the sentry posts with their important message, which was passed on to the German general staff at Lillehammer by courier. On the same day (5 May) the Government telegraphed credentials to the Home Front leadership which, in the event of the Germans in Norway capitulating, empowered it to do what was necessary to maintain good order pending the arrival of Government representatives; the nominated departmental advisers and *fylkesmenn* would at the same time take up their new responsibilities. The powers for HL went further than was contemplated in the earlier agreement between the parties, and was received with all the more enthusiasm because it suggested that the capitulation could be expected at any moment.

The committee members of the Home Front leadership assembled now in an apartment in the west end of Oslo, but we of the secretariat still found the situation too precarious and kept to our old quarters as much as possible, though I went to the flat now and then to follow developments. As we monitored the radio continuously, we were utterly astonished to be informed from the flat on the 6th that the Germans in Norway had capitulated. We sent back a rather sharp reply that we knew of no such capitulation, and after a while the misunderstanding was cleared up: a member of the committee had heard that Böhme (the German commander-in-chief in Norway) had capitulated, but the reference was to the surrender of the

*The armistice came into force in Denmark at 8 a.m. on 5 May — more than 3½ days earlier than in Norway.

German forces in *Böhmen* (Bohemia). On the morning of the 7th the picture was still unchanged, so we began to be somewhat sceptical about the chances of a speedy capitulation. We had slackened-off a little in our preparations for the alternative of war. Now we went ahead with them again, warning our district organisations to be in constant readiness and hurrying on with equipping our underground wartime quarters.

On the afternoon of 7 May I had been on business in the outskirts of the town and was cycling back to my cover address, when I met a procession of children with flags and singing. Flags were likewise draped over the balconies, and I realised that the moment of release had come. I could not restrain my tears: the tyranny was finally broken and Norway was free again. Several of my colleagues arriving at the cover flat were able to confirm it: the BBC had announced that the German forces had surrendered unconditionally on all fronts, the capitulation having been signed by the new Supreme Command in the early hours of the same morning. Yet we did not feel safe enough until early the next day to stop the gang who were making war preparations in our quarters.

It was still not peace or even an armistice; the latter would only come into force more than twenty-four hours in the future, at midnight on the 8th-9th. I went on to the HL committee, which was seething with activity. A victory proclamation had already been composed, which should naturally adorn the front page of the next day's *Oslo Press* and be broadcast as well by the State Radio in Oslo; but it was not yet known when the capitulation was to take place or when the Allied military mission would arrive. Still more important, when could our Home Forces and the civil administration come forward? But our secret contact in the German general staff was again of great service, for through him negotiations were taken up with the German commander-in-chief.

At first he was altogether unwilling to allow the Norwegian Home Forces or authorities to make any appearance before the arrival of the Allied military mission. But Hauge as fellow-negotiator succeeded in convincing him that this would be to the advantage of the Germans, and arranged that the Home Forces could emerge, so long as their arms were not directed against the German Troops, and that the *Oslo Press* could be published next morning. But the German commander-in-chief did not accept a sentence in HL's victory proclamation, referring to the prospective disarming of the enemy 'by Norwegian and Allied forces'. The first edition of the *Oslo Press* had already been printed with the original version, so it had to be cancelled and a new version printed with no reference to disarming by Norwegian forces. The Germans were still in power in Norway. Nor were they willing to relinquish control over the State Radio building in Oslo: when Jan Jansen went up on behalf of the HL on the morning of the 8th to have an announcement broadcast, he was turned away by the German guards.

The Home Forces were given orders for 'routine mobilisation' on 7 May, and in Oslo the first units could begin to take up their positions discreetly in the course of the evening; but the majority first moved forward the following day, and some places could not be occupied until after the armistice came into force at midnight.

The new leadership in the police took over the deserted central police station on the evening of the 7th, and the Palace in Oslo and most government offices were likewise occupied in the course of the night. In the late evening there were rumours that NS police were going to attack the police station, so it was a great relief when Sönsteby, the leader of the 'Oslo gang', turned up with his men in full uniform and fully armed. No attack came; the NS collapsed by itself. The Police Minister and the head of the State Police (Jonas Lie and Rogstad) had ensconced themselves at a farm in Bærum, where they put an end to their lives, while Quisling surrendered with the remains of his Government at the Oslo police station on the morning of the 9th. The previous day, an offer of internment pending trial had been made to him by a representative of the Home Forces, who were now engaged along with the uniformed Norwegian police in arresting NS people and others who had aided the occupying power in all parts of the country.

But we continued to feel insecure with the fully-armed Germans still at their posts, at least until the arrival of the Allied military mission on the afternoon of 8 May. It consisted of only a handful of British and Norwegian officers, but their bearing was authoritative and determined; they were quickly in control of the situation, and the disarming of the German forces began. Next morning the interim civil administration began to function, both in Oslo and in the provinces. The transfer of power went like a dream: instead of shots and cannon fire, we

Home Forces emerging from the forest after the German capitulation, May 1945.

heard church bells all over the country ringing in the peace. Both the German forces and our own behaved with exemplary discipline; and so did the huge crowds in Oslo and the population everywhere. None of us had expected such a painless liberation, but it was not handed to us on a plate. It was due to the careful preparations initiated by the Norwegian authorities in London in close collaboration with the Allies and with us at home, and not least to responsible military leadership and strong discipline on the German side. But first and foremost it was a result of the Germans being defeated on other fronts, at enormous cost in blood and treasure, by the Soviet Union and our Western Allies. As is acknowledged in a plaque in our Home Front Museum, our freedom was won in the skies over London, in the ruins of Stalingrad, in the African desert, on the watery battlefields of the Atlantic, and in the factories of America.

On 13 May — in sparkling spring sunshine — the Chief of Defence, Crown Prince Olav, came to Oslo at the head of a government delegation. He was welcomed at the Quay of Honour by the entire population of the city, headed by the leader of the Home Front, Chief Justice Paal Berg. The wheel had turned full circle, the struggle was over. At a meeting in the Palace the next day, the Home Front leadership was able to hand over power and responsibility to the lawful Norwegian authorities. Its swan-song underlined what the struggle had been about: 'Never have we had more at stake. Our very existence as a people was threatened — legal security, intellectual freedom and the dignity of man, our entire cultural inheritance, everything that makes life worth living.'

INDEX

(*compiled by the Translator*)

Note

Names of persons participating in the Resistance are provided with a note of their then occupation or military rank. Page numbers in italics refer to the illustrations.